In Pursuit of Liberty

ALSO BY EMMY E. WERNER

Passages to America:
Oral Histories of Child Immigrants from Ellis Island and Angel Island

In Pursuit of Liberty

*Coming of Age in
the American Revolution*

Emmy E. Werner

Potomac Books, Inc.
Washington D.C.

Library of Congress Cataloging-in-Publication Data
Werner, Emmy E.
 In pursuit of liberty : coming of age in the American Revolution / Emmy E. Werner. — Paperback ed.
   p. cm.
 Originally published in hardcover by Praeger Publishers, 2007.
 Includes bibliographical references and index.
 ISBN 978-1-59797-268-0 (pbk. : acid-free paper)
 1. United States—History—Revolution, 1775–1783—Children. 2. United States—History—Revolution, 1775–1783—Participation, Juvenile. 3. United States—History—Revolution, 1775–1783—Personal narratives. 4. Children—United States—History—18th century. 5. Youth—United States—History—18th century. 6. Child soldiers—United States—History—18th century. 7. Children's writings, American. I. Title.
 E209.W47 2009
 973.3083—dc22

                              2008047621

Printed in the United States of America on acid-free paper that meets the American National Standards Institute Z39-48 Standard.

Potomac Books, Inc.
22841 Quicksilver Drive
Dulles, Virginia 20166

10 9 8 7 6 5 4 3 2 1

For Nick Anastasiow and Stanley Jacobson—with love

Contents

Acknowledgments

I gratefully acknowledge the assistance of the following individuals and institutions for granting permission to quote excerpts from letters and diaries in their archives and for the use of pictorial material in their collections:

  Kim Nuscow, Massachusetts Historical Society, Boston, Massachusetts;
  John C. Dunn, Clements Library, University of Michigan, Ann Arbor, Michigan;
  Kerry McLaughlin, The Historical Society of Pennsylvania, Philadelphia, Pennsylvania;
  Peter Harrington, Brown Military Collection, Brown University, Providence, Rhode Island;
  Steve Massengill, North Carolina State Archives, Raleigh, North Carolina;
  Marilyn Ibach, Prints and Photograph Division, Library of Congress, Washington, D.C.;
  Amy Burton, United States Senate Commission on Art, Washington, D.C.;
  Jennifer Robertson, Smithsonian National Portrait Gallery, Washington, D.C.;
  The staff of the Still Pictures Department, National Archives, College Park, Maryland;
  The archivists of the city of Frankfurt and the state of Hessen in Kassel, Germany.

For help with photographs I am indebted to Paul Victor Ghysels, Berkeley, California, and to Simon Menard, Sorel-Tracey, Quebec. The University of California's Washington Center provided financial support for my travel and research in the nation's capital. My husband, Stanley Jacobsen, used his superb research skills in locating children's diaries and letters, and Elizabeth Demers, an editor without peer, gave generously of her time and counsel. I thank them both for their steadfast emotional support. Thanks also to the staff of Apex Publishing for all their help along the way.

Prologue

On a fine spring day in the year I became an American citizen, I visited the towns of Lexington and Concord, where the first shots were fired in the Revolutionary War. At the Concord bridge I saw a marker on the grave of two British soldiers who had died there on April 19, 1775. They were buried by the Americans where they fell. It read,

> They came three thousand miles and died to keep the past upon its throne.
> Unheard, beyond the ocean tide, their English mothers made their moan.

I thought of a young boy from Hessen, where I was born. He and I share the same family name. He was a soldier in the British "auxiliary" troops—indentured by his sovereign to fight a war that was not his cause. On Christmas Day 1776 he was captured in the battle of Trenton. Like many of his compatriots, he was only in his teens—a German farm boy fighting American boys who were sons of farmers as well. Among his adversaries was Joseph P. Martin, born in November 1760, who wrote a narrative of his adventures in the Continental Army that historians today view as one of the most detailed and important accounts of the War for Independence. Chiseled into the granite stone on his grave in the Sandy Point cemetery, near the Penobscot River in Maine, is a simple description that he would have been proud of: "A Soldier of the Revolution."

America was a young country then—the first census taken after the Revolutionary War (in 1790) shows that half of the population were children and youths up to the age of 16.[1] Though literacy was not universal, there were many youngsters who had learned to read and write in the public schools of New England, or in schools sponsored by religious groups, such as the Quakers and the Moravians, or in independent, private academies. In the South, wealthy planters hired their own tutors. Both boys and girls kept diaries and journals and wrote letters and memoirs that reported about the events surrounding the birth of a new nation. Their voices have been rarely heard in the historical accounts of the American Revolution.[2] This book tells their story.

It is based on the eyewitness accounts of 100 boys and girls who were between the ages of 5 and 16 at the time of the Revolutionary War. Their letters and diaries can be found in the historical societies of the 13 original colonies—especially in New England and the Mid-Atlantic states—and in the Library of Congress in Washington, D.C. The book also contains excerpts from the Revolutionary War veteran pension applications located in the National Archives. The youngest soldier in this group had enlisted when he was eight years old, and nearly one out of four were below the age of 16 when they began their service.[3] I include reports from black as well as white boy soldiers, from teenagers imprisoned on land and on prison ships, from slave children and children held hostage by Indians, and from the children of loyalists or pacifists who opposed the war for political or religious reasons. A third of the eyewitness accounts are from girls, most of whom lived in cities; the remaining two-thirds are from boys, most of whom lived in rural areas.

I also present the "enemy view," recorded in the diaries of Hessian teenagers who fought in the American Revolutionary War.[4] Literacy rates in their home state at the time were comparable to those in New England. The original manuscripts can be found in the Stadtsarchiv (city archives) in Frankfurt, in the library of the University of Kassel, and in the Hessian state archives in Marburg. They are written in a unique German script (Sütterling) that I was taught as a child. I have translated the excerpts used in this book directly from the original diaries.

Chapter 1 tells of the events leading up to the Revolutionary War from eyewitness accounts of children and teenagers in the city of Boston. Among them was one of the first casualties of the American Revolution, a German boy, 11-year-old Christopher Seider, who was killed on February 23, 1770, in a rally against a Boston tea importer, Theophilius Lillie. Angry Bostonians, who disliked the British tax on tea, were boycotting Lillie's store when Christopher was struck by a rifle shot. The outpouring of grief over the boy's death was overwhelming. Hundreds of schoolchildren attended his funeral.

Two weeks later, on March 5, 1770, five Bostonians died in the Boston Massacre, a skirmish between teenage boys, including the wigmaker's apprentice Edward Gerrish, and British soldiers, who were pelted by snowballs and stones from the unruly mob. In the ensuing trial the British captain and his men were exonerated by the skillful defense of

John Adams. His legal papers provide ample testimony for the fairness with which the Boston lawyer pursued his case.

The troubles in Boston culminated with the Boston Tea Party on December 16, 1773, in which a score of teenage apprentices, disguised as Indians, participated. Peter Edes, the son of the organizer, later wrote an eyewitness account of the events. Local disorders over the drinking of tea even reached the hallowed halls of Harvard and were dutifully recorded in the *Faculty Records* on March 1, 1775.

Chapter 2 describes the battles of Lexington and Concord on April 19, 1775, from the vantage point of several teenagers who participated in the skirmish. Among them were the drummer William Diamond and the fifer Jonathan Harrington Jr., both age 16. Among the young girls who witnessed the events was 12-year-old Elizabeth Clarke, who took care of the wounded and helped bury the dead. Her letter to her niece is a poignant account of that fateful day.

The Battle of Breeds Hill on June 17, 1775, was witnessed by several children, including eight-year-old John Quincy Adams, who later wrote about it in a letter to an English Quaker. Fifteen-year-old John Greenwood and the teenage drummer boy Robert Steele gave eyewitness accounts of their exploits under British fire.

The siege and evacuation of Boston by the British (on March 17, 1776) was recorded by several youngsters who had joined the militia, among them Israel Trask, age 10, John Greenwood, age 15, and Nathaniel Goddard, age 9. It was also noted in the letters of anxious mothers, including Abigail Adams, and in the diary of Dorothy Dudley. Anxiety turned to joy in their accounts of the celebration of the Declaration of Independence.

Chapter 3 records the first major battle between the American and British forces on Long Island (August 27, 1776). One of the casualties in the battle was a boy named Will Sands from Annapolis, Maryland. His letter to his parents, written on the march from Philadelphia, arrived home a few days after his death. Private Joseph P. Martin, who enlisted at age 15, gives an account of his battlefield experience, as does the Hessian Grenadier Johannes Reuber, who joined his infantry regiment at age 16 and kept a diary throughout his American "tour of duty."

There are also eyewitness accounts of the British invasion of Manhattan and the Battle of Harlem Heights by two American teenagers, Joseph Martin and David How. Private Martin and the Hessian grenadier Johannes Reuber report on the Battle of White Plains (October 28, 1776), and Johannes Reuber chronicles the capture of Fort Washington in November 1776.

December 1776 brought both misery and joy to the combatants. Marauding British troops in New Jersey frightened anxious mothers—as witnessed in the journals of Margaret Morris from Burlington, New Jersey, and Mary Titus Post. Thirteen-year-old Abigail Palmer and15-year-old Elisabeth Cain were raped by British soldiers. Their testimony can be found in the 1777 papers of the Continental Congress.

As Christmas drew closer, Polly Wharton of Trenton, New Jersey, wrote a hopeful letter to her cousin, putting her faith and the fate of the struggling nation in the hands of God. On December 26, 1776, George Washington's army scored a surprise victory: They captured a regiment of Hessians in their winter quarters in Trenton. The account of that decisive event is given by two teenagers on opposing sides of the conflict: John Greenwood, an American, and the Hessian Grenadier Johannes Reuber.

Chapter 4 describes the journey of the Hessian and British POWs to Philadelphia, where they arrived on January 1, 1777, and the reaction of the civilian population to their presence in the local barracks. Two weeks later, the prisoners were moved to Lancaster County. In the beginning of summer the Hessian prisoners had the opportunity to work for local farmers, who guaranteed their safety and well-being and paid them with food and (worthless) Continental paper money. As British forces drew closer, the prisoners were removed from Pennsylvania and marched to Winchester, Virginia, where they were billeted in private homes and worked on the surrounding farms.

On July 5, 1777, John Adams, a delegate to the Continental Congress, wrote a letter to his 12-year-old daughter, Abigail, in which he describes the celebrations of the first anniversary of the Declaration of Independence. The joy surrounding that event was short-lived. Congress soon had to evacuate Philadelphia. The British entered the city on September 26, 1777. Among the teenage diarists who recorded the daily life under British occupation were several Quakers, among them 16-year-old Robert Morton and 15-year-old Sally Wister. Sally's friends, a Quaker girl named Deborah Logan and a Jewish girl named Rebecca Franks, kept up a steady stream of correspondence when the Wister family left town.

In the fall the Americans were able to score a decisive victory in the battle of Saratoga in upstate New York. A large contingent of British and Brunswick troops were forced to surrender on October 17, 1777. The story of that event is told by two American teenagers: Robert Morton and Hugh McDonald. The enemy view comes from the pen of a remarkable woman: the young wife of the German commander, Baroness von Riedesel, who had traveled with her three small daughters, ages six, three, and one, from Germany to North America to be at her husband's side.

Chapter 5 relates the sufferings of Washington's soldiers at their camp in Valley Forge in the winter of 1777–1778. The voices are those of two American teenagers, John P. Martin and Hugh McDonald, who tell of the hunger and cold they endured. The memoirs of 17-year-old

Pierre Du Ponceau, the French interpreter of Baron von Steuben, add some humor to their stories.

The spirits of the American troops lifted when the British evacuated Philadelphia on June 18, 1778. Ten days later, the Americans fought them to a draw in the Battle at Monmouth Courthouse in New Jersey. Private Joseph P. Martin wrote an eyewitness account of that event. But in July 1778, in the Wyoming Valley, fortune turned against the Americans. In what has been called "the surpassing horror of the Revolution," the defenseless farm settlements at the Connecticut–Pennsylvania border were put to the torch by Tory Rangers and their Indian allies. Many of the inhabitants, old men, women, and children, died. But there were also acts of decency amid the horror: Some Indians saved the orphaned children and raised them as their own. Frances Slocum, who was nine years old at the time, survived to tell her tale.

The city of Savannah fell into British hands in the last days of 1778. The events are described from two perspectives: in the diary of the Hessian Grenadier Johannes Reuber (whose regiment had been exchanged for American prisoners of war) and in the journal of 15-year-old Elizabeth Johnston Lichtenstein, a loyalist.

Chapter 6 tells the story of the British efforts to occupy the southern colonies in 1779 and 1780. On March 20, 1780, British and Hessian troops began the siege of Charleston, South Carolina. The city fell to the British on May 12. Samuel Baldwin, a schoolteacher, kept a diary of the siege, and Elizabeth Wilkinson, a young widow who lived on a plantation nearby, wrote letters about the social life in the city under British occupation. The Hessian perspective is related in the diaries of Johannes Reuber and Velentin Asteroth, who taught in a school for Hessian children located on the premises of a Quaker church in Charleston. A few months after the capture of Charleston, two battles in South Carolina turned the tide of the war in favor of the Americans: the Battle of King's Mountain on October 7, 1780, and the Battle of Cowpens on January 17, 1781. James P. Collins and Thomas Young, age 16, who participated in both battles, tell of their successful skirmishes with the British.

Chapter 7 introduces Isaac Jefferson, one of Thomas Jefferson's slaves, who was captured by the British when they made a foray into Virginia. The boy was five years old at that time and was brought to Yorktown, where he witnessed the decisive battle of the Revolutionary War. In the summer of 1781 a 16-year-old girl, Emily Geiger, daughter of a German planter, rode a hundred miles through British-held territory in South Carolina to convey a message from the Quaker General Nathanael Greene to General Thomas Sumter. She was captured by the British on the second day of her ride, but they found no incriminating evidence on her and let her go.

The story of how she eluded her captors is told by the daughter of the woman who was asked to search Emily when she was detained in a farmhouse as a suspected spy.

The ultimate showdown between the British and the American forces began on September 26, 1781, at Yorktown, Virginia, and ended on October 19, 1781, with the surrender of the British and Hessian troops. The story is told in a number of eyewitness accounts by American teenagers. The youngest soldier among them was John Hudson, age 13. The enemy view is dutifully reported in the diary of the Hessian soldier Johann Döhla. The civilian perspective is recorded in the letters of 16-year-old Mildred Smith, who remained in Yorktown during the siege.

Elizabeth Drinker and Anna Rawle, two Quaker maidens, noted in their diaries that the people of Philadelphia celebrated the victory on October 25, 1781, by lighting candles in the windows of their homes. The houses of the loyalists were left in darkness. Their windows were shattered by breaking glass from stones thrown by an unruly mob.

Chapter 8 tells the story of American boys who fought the Revolutionary War at sea. Some, like Israel Trask and Ebenezer Fox, were only 12 years old when they went to war. Most served on privately owned, armed ships that preyed on British merchant ships in the Atlantic, the Caribbean, and between Ireland and England. Among the young privateers was 15-year-old James Forten, a free black American from Philadelphia, who had been educated by the Quakers. He served as powder boy on the privateer *Royal Louis* and was captured by the British.

Some teenagers served on the frigates and gunboats of the Continental Navy. Among the young sailors were 15-year-old John Blatchford and Andrew Sherburne, who was 14 years old when he enlisted. Others patrolled the coast in whaling boats.

When captured by the enemy, American sailors were usually confined to prison ships. These were abandoned vessels, moored in the harbors of Halifax, New York, and Charleston , where thousands died of disease and malnutrition. Christopher Hawkins, who became a privateer when he was only 13, and Andrew Sherburne, age 14, described the misery they saw aboard the infamous *HMS Jersey*.

Chapters 9 and 10 are based on the eyewitness accounts of two remarkable transatlantic travelers who chronicled the American Revolution from two different perspectives: the wife of a German general who traveled with her young daughters from upstate New York through New England and the Mid-Atlantic states to Virginia; and the perspective of John Quincy Adams, who traveled with his father to Europe when he was only 10 years old. They include excerpts from the journal and letters of Baroness von Riedesel, from the Adams Family Correspondence, and from John Quincy's diary, which he began in 1779 when he was 12 years old.

In April 1783, eight years after the first shots of the Revolutionary War were fired at Lexington and Concord, the Continental Congress announced the cessation of hostilities between the United States and Great Britain. Chapter 11 recounts the joy of children in New England and New York who were let out of school to celebrate the good news. There were bonfires and parties everywhere. In Frederick, Maryland, where a large contingent of POWs was housed in the local barracks, Hessian soldiers provided the fireworks and the music for the festivities. The officers of the captive regiments were invited to join the local dignitaries in a joyful celebration of the end of the long war.

On September 4, 16-year-old John Quincy Adams wrote his mother from Paris that the definitive peace treaty had been signed by his father on behalf of the United States the day before. The last Hessian units departed for Germany from New York and Sandy Hooks on November 25, 1783. Their diaries tell of their long and stormy journey back to the "fatherland." With them sailed a contingent of "black Hessians," former slaves from the southern colonies who had served as musicians and order-lies in German regiments and pursued their liberty overseas.

Some 80,000 loyalists left as well. They had lost their property and their welcome in the land where they were born. They sailed to Canada, the Caribbean Islands, and to England to begin a new life under the British crown. Eleven-year-old Hannah Ingraham from New York was among them, and so was the teenage bride Elizabeth Lichtenstein Johnston from Savannah. Hannah wrote about her journey to exile in Nova Scotia, Elizabeth about her travels to England. Despite their initial hardships, they and their descendants would survive and thrive.

The last chapter examines some of the social forces that shaped the postwar lives of the young people who came of age during the American Revolution. Many veterans moved to the western frontier to work and own their land. Others turned a special skill into a lucrative trade or business, and still others followed a profession. Two young lawyers, John Quincy Adams and Andrew Jackson, both born in 1767, the year the British imposed a tax on tea in the American colonies, would eventually hold the highest office of an independent nation—the Presidency of the United States of America.

Middle- and upper-class women of their generation gained more access to educational opportunities and established more egalitarian marital relationships than their mothers. Their resourcefulness, hardiness, and optimism about the future of their country would become the enduring legacies of the children of the American Revolution. So would the yet incomplete promise of liberty and justice for all.[5]

"July 4, 1776," from *Good Things of Life* (New York: White, Stokes, and Allen, 1887), p. 20. *Courtesy Library of Congress.*

PART I
Witnessing the Revolution

CHAPTER 1

Troubles in Boston

On February 23, 1770, a shot rang out from an upstairs window next to the establishment of Theophilus Lillie, a tea importer in Boston's North End neighborhood. Eleven-year-old Christopher Seider, who had been milling about in the crowd outside Lillie's shop, was killed by the discharge. He would be among the first casualties of the American Revolution.

Lillie had been suspected of importing tea on which tax had been levied by the British Parliament—a tax that had led to a great deal of resentment and the boycott of British goods in the American colonies. A shouting crowd of Boston schoolboys and apprentices had erected a post outside Lillie's shop, upon which was a carved head and underneath it, a hand pointing toward the door. It alerted people that the merchant was violating the anti-import resolutions of the colonies. Ebenezer Richardson, who lived next door to the tea merchant and who had a reputation as a customs informer, tried to take the sign down.

When Richardson was pelted by snowballs thrown by some of the boys, he retreated into his house. The crowd began throwing stones and broke several windows. Richardson emerged with a shotgun and pulled the trigger. When Christopher Seider was mortally wounded, some of the onlookers turned sober, but others were enraged. Richardson might have been tarred and feathered on the spot had not one of the Whig leaders hustled him to jail.

Christopher Seider's funeral was attended by some 500 schoolchildren who marched two by two behind the coffin, followed by hundreds of carriages, along the main street of Boston. Six of his schoolfellows

"The Exasperated Merchant," from Benson J. Lossing, *History,* vol. 3 (Funk and Wagnalls, New York, 1877), p. 680. *Courtesy Library of Congress.*

were pallbearers. John Adams recorded in his diary that he had never seen such a large funeral. "It was the largest perhaps ever known in America," according to the royal governor of Massachusetts, Thomas Hutchinson.[1]

Tensions had been growing in the colonies ever since the British had been trying to recover some of the expenses of their seven-year French and Indian War by taxing a variety of goods. The Stamp Act, Parliament's first direct tax on the American colonies, issued in 1765, had taxed newspapers, almanacs, pamphlets, broadsides, legal documents, dice, and playing cards. The stamps were affixed to documents or packages to show that the tax had been paid. The British further angered the American colonists with the Quartering Act, which required the colonies to provide barracks and supplies to British troops.

The American colonists had responded to these acts with organized protests and a refusal to use imported British goods. In 1766 the Stamp Act was repealed, but in 1767 the Parliament passed the Townshend Acts to help pay the expenses involved in governing the American colonies. This time, taxes were levied on imported glass, lead, paint, and tea.

Broadside depicting the murder of Christopher Seider in February 1770. *Courtesy Historical Society of Pennsylvania.*

The colonies continued to discourage the purchase of British imports. Because of the reduced profits resulting from that boycott, Parliament finally withdrew all of the Townshend Acts in 1770—except for the tax on tea. The troubles in Boston did not subside.

By the time of Christopher Seider's funeral, his hometown was practically under siege. British troops had been stationed in Boston since 1768; British soldiers patrolled the streets; British warships were anchored in the harbor. On March 5, 1770, in the evening, the tensions between the townspeople and the soldiers erupted in the Boston Massacre. British troops, who were being harassed and taunted by a mob of "saucy boys," opened fire, killing five Americans.

According to his testimony at the trial of the Redcoats, it all began with a remark made by Edward Gerrish, a wigmaker's apprentice, who was standing on King Street at eight o'clock in the evening on March 5 when Captain John Goldfinsh walked by. Edward told his fellow apprentices, "There goes the fellow who hath not paid my Master for dressing his hair!"[2]

Captain Goldfinsh later testified that he "walked on without taking notice of what the boy said." He had paid his bill that very afternoon and had his receipt in his pocket. "I found that any Man wearing the King's Commission was lyable to be insulted at any Hour of the Night," he said.[3] The sentry on guard at the customs house on King Street had overheard the boy's remark as well and told him, "The Captain is a gentleman and if he owes you anything, he will pay."[4]

"There are no gentlemen in this Regiment," Edward retorted. Angered, the sentinel struck the boy's ear with his musket. Edward cried and ran away, but his fellow apprentices walked up to the red-coated British soldier and called him "Bloody Lobsterback." Then they threw snowballs at him. At the nearby main guard station Captain Thomas Preston watched as the crowd grew and tempers rose. He decided to march to the sentinel's assistance with a force of six privates and one corporal. Once they arrived near the sentry box, they found themselves surrounded by an angry mob that hurled snowballs, ice, oyster shells, and stones at them. Preston ordered his men to load their muskets.

Suddenly, a piece of ice hit one of the British soldiers, who slipped and fell to the ground. When he regained his footing, he fired his musket into the crowd. The other soldiers did the same. Three men died instantly; another succumbed a few hours afterward; and a fifth man died several days later from his wounds. One of them was Chrispus Attucks, an African American freeman; the others were all workingmen. Two apprentices—Patrick Carr and Samuel Maverick—were still in their teens.

John Greenwood, who was nine years old at the time, remembered the event: "One of those [killed] was my father's apprentice, a lad seventeen years of age, named Samuel Maverick. I was his bedfellow, and after his death I used to go to bed in the dark on purpose to see his spirit, for I was so fond of him and he of me that I was sure it would not hurt me."[5]

The funeral of the slain men took place on March 8, 1770. An overwhelming majority of the people of Boston clamored for a guilty verdict and a sentence of death for the Redcoats. Because of his reputation for fairness and integrity, John Adams was asked to defend the soldiers and their captain in court. The first trial, *The King vs. Captain Preston on an Indictment for Murder,* took place in late October. The evidence was in favor of the accused: Even those eyewitnesses who stood closest to Preston when the shooting began testified that the captain never gave the order to fire. The jury took only three hours to bring in a verdict of "not guilty."

The second trial of the six soldiers did not conclude until the first week of December. Self-defense became the keystone of Adams's argument in favor of the Redcoats. "Facts are stubborn things," he told the jury, "and whatever may be our wishes, our inclinations, and the dictum of our passions, they cannot alter the state of facts and evidence."[6]

John Adams's closing argument on December 4 ultimately secured the freedom of the accused soldiers: "I am for the prisoners at bar," he began. Close study of the facts had convinced him of their innocence. He continued,

> We have entertained a great variety of phrases to avoid calling this sort of people [who attacked the soldiers] a mob. The plain English is, gentlemen [it was] most probably a motley rabble of saucy boys. And why we should scruple to call such a people a mob, I can't conceive unless the name is too respectable for them.... Soldiers quartered in a populous town will always occasion two mobs where they prevent one. They are wretched conservators of peace.... If an assault was made to endanger their lives, the law is clear they had a right to kill in their own defense; if it was not so severe as to endanger their lives, yet if they were assaulted at all, struck and abused by blows of any sort, by snow-balls, oyster-shells, cinders, clubs, or sticks of any kind, this was provocation, for which the law reduces the offence of killing down to manslaughter, in consideration of those passions in our nature which cannot be eradicated. To your candor and justice I submit the prisoners and their cause.[7]

Nine months after the Boston Massacre, on December 5, 1770, after two and a half hours of deliberation, the jury announced the verdict. Of the eight soldiers, six were acquitted, and two were found guilty of manslaughter, for which they were branded on their thumbs. There were angry reactions to the decisions, but there were no more riots in Boston that year.

The tax on tea was retained indefinitely because King George III believed "there must always be one tax" to maintain the right of parliamentary taxation of the colonies. The Americans thought otherwise. Three hundred women of Boston from families with the highest standing in the city signed an agreement not to drink any tea until that tax was repealed. Their daughters followed the example of their mothers and pledged "to deny ourselves the drinking of foreign tea, in hopes to frustrate a plan that tends to deprive a whole community of all that is valuable."[8]

Dried leaves of the raspberry plant, thyme, and smuggled tea from Holland became cheap substitutes for British imports. Some 17 million pounds of tea began to accumulate in the East India Company's warehouses in London. Without access to the American market, much of it rotted away. In desperation the company asked permission from Parliament to export tea, without first paying taxes when it landed the tea in Britain, and to charge only an "exportation tariff" of three pennies a pound when it landed the shipment in America. Their tea would now be cheaper than the smuggled tea. But the colonists would not give up their boycott.

Most American ship captains refused to ship East India tea on their vessels. Those who did were compelled by the merchants of New York and Philadelphia to turn about and head back to London. In Charleston the tea was landed but locked up in a warehouse and never sold. In Boston the governor of Massachusetts, Thomas Hutchinson, finally intervened. When the *Dartmouth* arrived in Boston harbor with a cargo of tea, followed by the *Eleanor* and the *Beaver,* he ordered the closure of the harbor mouth so that no ship could return to London. On the evening of December 16, 1773, a band of Bostonians took matters into their own hands.

Among the three troops of "Mohawks"—painted or soot-smeared men—who raced down to Griffith's Wharf were a number of teenage apprentices. Among the observers of the spectacle that would go down in history as the Boston Tea Party were young schoolboys who later told of what they saw that night.

Peter, the son of the printer Benjamin Edes, was a teenager at the time. "I recollect perfectly well," he wrote, "that in the afternoon preceding the evening of the destruction of the tea, a number of gentlemen met in the parlor of my father's house.... I was not admitted in their presence; my station was in another room to make punch for them.... They remained in the house till dark—I suppose to disguise themselves like Indians—when they left and proceeded to the wharf where the vessels lay.... I thought I would...walk to the wharves as a spectator where was collected...as many as two thousand persons..."[9]

Benjamin Russell, a schoolboy at the time, saw his father and a neighbor smearing each other's faces with soot and red ochre on the night of the tea party. Peter Slater, a 14-year-old rope maker's apprentice, overheard the excitement on the street and jumped out of his bedroom window. At a nearby blacksmith's shop a disguised man told him to put charcoal on his face, tie a handkerchief around his shirt, and follow him.

Sixteen-year-old Joshua Wyeth was a journeyman blacksmith in the employ of Tory masters. He later gave a detailed account of how the Boston Tea Party was executed:

> I had but a few hours warning of what was intended to be done.... To prevent discovery we agreed to wear ragged clothes and disfigure ourselves, dressing to resemble Indians.... Our most intimate friends among the spectators had not the least knowledge of us.... At the appointed hour, we met in an old building at...the wharf, and fell in one after another, as if by accident, as not to excite suspicion. We placed a sentry at the head of the wharf, another in the middle, and one on the bow of each ship as we took

possession. We boarded the ship moored by the wharf, and ordered ... the captain and crew to open the hatchways, and hand us the hoisting tackle and ropes, assuring them that no harm was intended them .... Some of our numbers then jumped into the hold, and passed the chests to the tackle. As they were hauled on deck others knocked them open with axes, and others raised them to the railings and discharged their contents overboard. All who were not needed on this ship went on board the others ... where the same ceremonies were repeated. We were merry, in an undertone, at the idea of making so large a cup of tea for the fishes ... but we used no more words than absolutely necessary.... I never worked harder in my life. While we were unloading, the people collected in great numbers about the wharf to see what was going on. They crowded around us.... Our sentries were not armed, and could not stop any who insisted on passing.[10]

There were some exceptions. William Tudor, a law student in the office of John Adams and acquainted with some of the members of the Tea Party, remembered an incident he witnessed: "Two of the persons [who wore a kind of Indian disguise] in passing over Fort Hill to the scene of operations, met a British officer, who, on observing them naturally enough drew his sword. As they approached, one of the Indians drew a pistol; and said to the officer: 'The path is wide enough for us all; we have nothing to do with you, and intend you no harm; if you keep your own way peaceably, we shall keep ours.'"[11]

John Adams, returning to Boston the following day, saw at once that the Tea Party marked a major turning point in the relationship between

"Destruction of Tea in Boston Harbor." *Courtesy Library of Congress.*

Britain and the American colonies. "This destruction of tea is so bold, so daring," he wrote in his diary, "it must have so important consequences, and so lasting, that I cannot but consider it as an epoch in history."[12]

King George was enraged: "We must master [the colonists] or totally leave them to themselves and treat them as aliens," he declared.[13]

In 1774, in response to the Boston Tea Party, the British Parliament passed several "coercive acts" to punish the people of Massachusetts. The Boston Port Bill banned the loading or unloading of any ships in the Boston harbor. The Administration of Justice Act offered protection to royal officials in Massachusetts, allowing them to transfer to England all court cases against them involving riot suppression or revenue collection. The Massachusetts Government Act put the election of most government officials under the control of the crown. Lastly, the Quartering Act (first passed by Parliament in 1765) was broadened so that British troops from now on could be quartered in any occupied building.

The colonies promptly organized a protest and named delegates to the First Continental Congress to meet in Philadelphia on September 5, 1774, to discuss their united resistance against the British. Twelve of the 13 colonies, with the exception of Georgia, sent a total of 56 delegates to Philadelphia. Among them were John Adams and his cousin, Samuel Adams, from Massachusetts. The First Continental Congress urged all colonists to avoid using British goods and to form committees to enforce this ban. When British troops began to fortify Boston and seized ammunition belonging to the colony, Massachusetts convened a Provincial Congress and created a special Committee of Safety to decide when its local militia (the minutemen) should be called into action.

By the spring of 1775, the Boston garrison stood at 4,000 men. Such a military force had a visible negative impact on the 16,000 townspeople. Tensions between them and the Redcoats were rising. A few well-meaning academics tried to create an oasis of peace at nearby Harvard College. The *Records of the College Faculty* contain the following resolution passed at a meeting of the President, Professors, and Tutors on March 1, 1775[14]:

> Since the carrying [of] India Teas into the Hall is found to be a source of uneasiness and grief to many of the students, and as the use of it is disagreeable to the people of this country in general; and as those who have carried Tea into the hall declare that the drinking of it in the Hall is a matter of trifling consequence with them; that they be advised not to carry it in for the future, and in this way that they, as well the other students in all ways, discover a disposition to promote harmony, mutual affection, and confidence, so well becoming members of the same society; that so peace and happiness may be preserved within the walls of the college whatever convulsions may unhappily distract the State abroad.

Meanwhile, both sides, the colonists and the British, were preparing for war. On April 14, 1775, the military governor of Massachusetts, Lieutenant General Thomas Gage, received his "get tough" orders from his superiors to subdue the "most daring spirit of resistance and disobedience" that existed in the colonies. Force was to be quickly applied to crush the rebellion before it spread. The leaders of the Provincial Congress were to be arrested, and the arsenal of arms that the Committee of Safety had stored at Concord was to be seized. Gage realized that most leaders of the Provincial Congress were already on the way to Philadelphia, where the Second Continental Congress was due to convene in early May. But he could seize the store of arms at Concord! He collected his best troops—the grenadier and light infantry companies—and placed them on standby orders.

CHAPTER 2

୭

From Lexington to Cambridge

In the early morning of April 19, 1775, some 700 British grenadiers and light infantry, on the way from Boston to Concord to "seize and destroy" a store of arms hidden by the patriots, heard the sounds of church bells pealing in every village through which they passed. Nearing Lexington, just as the sun rose, they could also hear the muffled sounds of a drum. It belonged to 16-year-old William Diamond.[1]

The boy had been directed by Captain John Parker, the commanding officer of the Lexington minutemen, to go across the Common and beat the call to arms. He did so with great enthusiasm, and as he rolled out the call to the villagers, the War of the American Revolution was about to begin. In response to his drumbeat, some 70 men assembled near the Common—12 were in their teens. Working alongside the drummer boy was another 16-year-old, the fifer Jonathan Harrington Jr.

His mother had woken him at three o'clock in the morning, calling, "Jonathan! Jonathan! Get up. The reg'lars are coming and something must be done." "I dressed quickly," he remembered. "Slung my light gun over my shoulder, took my fife from a chair, and hurried to the parade near the meeting house…. We did not wait long, wondering whether reg'lars were really coming, for a man darted up to Captain Parker and told him that they were close by. The captain ordered [us] to beat the drum, and I fifed with all my might. Alarm guns were fired to call distant minutemen to duty. Lights were now seen moving in all the houses. Daylight came at half past four o'clock. Just then the reg'lars who had heard the drum beat rushed toward us."[2]

At daybreak the Lexington militia watched a long line of Redcoats march into their town. The British officers called for the militia to put down their muskets. Captain Parker told his company to disperse. The minutemen who heard his order started to break ranks, but no one followed the British order to lay down their arms.

Suddenly, a shot rang out. Who fired it or why remains a mystery, but in the ensuing melee, 8 Americans were killed and 10 wounded. Four minutemen were killed on the Common, including two of Jonathan Harrington's cousins. One crawled across the Green and died on the doorstep of his house, at the feet of his wife and eight-year-old son. The rest of the American dead were killed after they had left the Commons.

Later, on the morning of April 19, after the British had marched on to Concord, Captain Parker reassembled his Lexington minutemen. William Diamond beat his drum again. The company marched off toward Concord, with some of the wounded, now bandaged, struggling along. The beat of the drum and the music of the fife echoed after them, the sun high in the sky. The thermometer had risen to 85 degrees, and the little fifer saw that "the door yards were all bright with dandelions."[3]

Back in Lexington, the doors of the houses opened, and the women and children came out to help the wounded and to count the dead. Parents evacuated their children from all the houses lining the main road from Concord to Boston through the town and hid the family silver and the communion service. They knew the British would have to come back through their town.

Among the 12 children in Jonas Clarke's house that fateful day was 12-year-old Elizabeth Clarke. Years later, she wrote a letter to her niece, Lucy Allen, evoking her memories of April 19, 1775:

> I can now see from this window as here I sit writing, in my mind, just as plain, all the British troops marching off the Common to Concord, and the whole scene: Aunt Hancock and Miss Dolly Quincy, with their cloaks and bonnets on, Aunt crying and wringing her hands and helping Mother dress the children, Dolly going around with Father to hide money, watches and anything [valuable] down in the potatoes and up the garret, and then Grandfather Clarke sent down men with carts, took your Mother and all the children but Jonas and me and Sally, a Babe six months old. Father sent Jonas down to Grandfather Cook's to see who was killed and what their condition was and, in the afternoon, Father and Mother with me and the Baby went to the Meeting House, there was the eight men that was killed, seven of them my Father's parishioners... all in Boxes made of four large Boards Nailed up and, after Pa had prayed, they were put into two horse carts and took into the grave yard where Grandfather and some of the Neighbors had made a large trench, as near the Woods as possible and there we followed the bodies of those first slain, Father, Mother, I and the Baby,

there I stood and there I saw them let down into the ground, it was a little rainy but we waited to see them Covered up with the Clods and then for fear the British should find them, my Father thought some of the Men had best cut some pine or oak bows and spread them on their place of burial so that it looked like a heap of Brush....[4]

Two days before the Redcoats arrived in Concord, the Committee of Safety had ordered the dispersal of the military supplies into the neighboring towns. The troops who made a house-to-house search on April 19 found only remnants of the original store, among them 500 pounds of bullets that they sent splashing into the millpond and a few gun carriages that they set on fire. The smoke was seen by the militia companies from the neighboring towns and villages that had marched in the defense of Concord and were stationed on a ridge overlooking North Bridge.

Lucy Hosmer's diary entry from April 19, 1775, tells what happened next:

They marched in double file toward the North Bridge to the fife strains of "The White Cockade" with Captain Isaac Davis' company in front of the lines.... Our men marched nearer and nearer to the bridge to the beat of Abner Hosmer's drum. The British fired warning shots into the air. Our men were marching forward. Suddenly the Redcoats fired a volley and Abner Hosmer and his Captain, Isaac Davis, fell dead.... Joseph [my husband] carried Abner Hosmer's body and that of Captain Davis to Major Butrick's farm nearby.... About noon today, the Redcoats began their retreat to Boston, going back the way they came, but without the glory of their fife and drum with which they arrived in our village. Waiting for them behind a ridge which runs beside the road were the Minutemen.... As the British came into sight... our men opened fire on them Indian fashion.... A great many Redcoats soon lay dead and the rest [was] demoralized. Near Fish Hill in Lexington, they broke ranks and fled. Many of our Minutemen, including Joseph and his brother Benjamin, pursued the Redcoats all the way back to Boston.... My dear husband is safe at home now and our family secure. Thank God. The house is very still and all but me are asleep.[5]

News of the fighting had spread swiftly across the countryside. Throughout the afternoon of April 19, militiamen converged in the thousands on the Concord-to-Boston road. From fields and wooded groves, and behind stone walls, the colonists took aim at the Redcoats. The return of the British soldiers to Boston looked like a headlong flight.

In a determined attempt to stop the concealed fighters the British infantry inspected every house along the road to Cambridge. When they came to the house of Deacon Joseph Adams, they found only his wife with her 18-day-old infant in bed and nine-year-old Joel and his twin brother Amos under a bed. Their father had run across the field to hide in the hayloft of his neighbor's barn. Joel and Amos followed the soldiers around the house, warning them not to take any church silver, and used their father's home-brewed beer to extinguish a small fire that the British set when they left.[6]

All afternoon and into the night, the Massachusetts militiamen shot at the Redcoats. In the evening, as the British crossed the narrow Neck into Charlestown, 14-year-old Edward Barber, son of a retired sea captain, peeked out of the window of his house. One of the soldiers, thinking he was another sniper, shot him dead. He was the youngest person to die that day.[7]

Not until midnight did the last British soldier reach the city of Boston. The casualties of the day included 73 Redcoats and 49 colonials dead and hundreds wounded or missing. News of the battle spread rapidly through the colonies. Within three days, thousands of armed patriots poured into Cambridge and Roxbury. They wanted to make sure the British remained bottled up within the confines of Boston.

During the next two months a steady stream of New England men flowed into Cambridge and nearby towns to form a besieging force, holding the troops in Boston at bay. Unable to forage in the countryside, the British became dependent on a supply line 3,000 miles long. One of Gage's officers wrote home to England: "However we block up their port, the rebels certainly block up our town, and have cut off our good beef and mutton."[8]

Dorothy Dudley of Cambridge wrote in her diary about the deteriorating situation in Boston:

April 24th: Boston is in great distress...deprived of its supplies from the surrounding country. We cannot realize how hard a life its poor besieged inhabitants must lead.

April 25th: Good news for Boston sufferers! General Gage has proposed a treaty, as much for his own safety and that of his troops, as from any kindlier motives, and agrees "that all such inhabitants as are inclined may depart from the town, with their families and effects, and those who remain may depend on his protection...." He asks "that those persons in the country who might incline to move into Boston with their effects might have liberty to do so without molestation."

April 29th: The road to Roxbury is a busy scene, covered as it is, with an ever lengthening procession of voluntary exiles from Boston, and crowded with loyal subjects of the King, anxious to hide themselves under the protecting care of his Majesty's troops.[9]

Among the weary travelers was 15-year-old John Greenwood. He had left his uncle's home at Falmouth (Portland) at the beginning of May and walked some 100 miles to see his family in Boston. "My reason for going was I wished to see my parents," he wrote, "who I was afraid would all be killed by the British, for...nothing was talked of but murder and war."[10]

It took him four and a half days to reach Charlestown, opposite of Boston. Armed with his fife and sword, he stopped along the way at taverns where there was a muster and played a tune or two for his supper. "When I told them I was going to fight for my country," he recalled, "they were astonished such a little boy, and alone, should have such courage."[11]

When John Greenwood reached Charlestown, he was told by the guards there that he needed a pass from General Ward at Cambridge to cross over on the ferry. He set off to Cambridge and got his pass, but after he traveled back to the Charlestown ferry, he was not allowed to cross over. "Here I stood alone, without a friend or house to shelter me for the night," he wrote, "surrounded by women and children.... Boston people who were flocking out of town over the ferry, in crowds, with what little ... they were permitted to take with them.... At the ferry stairs [they had searched] their trunks and little bundles and taken from the women and children their pins, needles and scissors."[12]

The boy returned to Charlestown, generally deserted by its inhabitants, entered a large tavern, and, seeing his fife sticking out in front of his coat, was asked by some of the militiamen in the crowd to play a few tunes. They promptly persuaded him to enlist as a fifer in their company. He joined for a period of eight months after being told that he would receive eight dollars a month and provisions.

He was quartered in Cambridge in the deserted house of a loyalist, an Episcopal minister who had gone to Boston. "We had to sleep in our clothing on the bare floor," he wrote later. "I do not recollect that I even had a blanket, but I remember well the stone which I had to lay my head upon."[13]

On June 14, 1775, the Second Continental Congress assumed responsibility for "the American Continental Army." The following day, Congress selected George Washington, who had shown up in Philadelphia in his blue Virginia militia uniform, to serve as "General and Commander-in-Chief of the Army of the United Colonies, and the forces now raised and to be raised in defense of American Liberty."

General Gage had received reinforcements from Britain that raised his troop size to some 6,500 men. Gage was about to conduct a limited offensive action against the colonists. Before he could act, the Americans dispatched a force of some 1,000 men onto the Charlestown peninsula, just north of Boston, on the night of June 16. Dorothy Dudley saw the men parade on the Common before they left Cambridge.

> The men are all farmers, and have no uniforms, and no arms except fowling pieces without bayonets, and carry in horns and pouches their small supply of powder and bullets.... At nine o'clock they marched, two sergeants carrying

dark lanterns in front, and in the rear the tools for throwing up entrenchments. The soldiers are ignorant of the object of their march and will not be
told till they reach its end. Now they have gone and we are left in suspense.[14]

Ordered to fortify Bunker Hill, the commanding officer, Colonel
William Prescott, chose to bypass it and moved forward to Breed's Hill,
which could be more easily held. There his 1,000 men worked through
the night to construct a defensive position. At dawn on June 17, a British
Marine sentry, staring through the dissolving mist, saw in disbelief that the
Yankees had erected a fortification six feet high and one foot thick, about
50 yards in length, commanding a view of the city of Boston. At high tide,
around three o'clock in the afternoon, the British launched their attack.

Ships in the harbor and batteries on Copp's Hill in Boston showered
Charlestown with red-hot balls and iron balls pierced with holes and filled
with pitch. Within moments the town was on fire. Street by street, houses
collapsed against each other in walls of flames, and the high steeples of
the churches burned like torches. Dorothy Dudley, in nearby Cambridge,
jotted hastily in her diary, "We can hear the booming of the cannons and
see the smoke arising from Charlestown which the British have set on fire.
It is a terrific battle."[15]

And so it was. Some 2,200 Redcoats under the command of General
Howe tried to storm the American positions. The British twice moved
forward against the American entrenchments, only to be decimated by
the accurate musketry of the Americans. Young John Greenwood, whose
company was stationed with two field pieces on the road in sight of the
battle, remembered, "The road was filled with chairs and wagons, bearing the wounded and dead .... Never having beheld such a sight before,
I felt very much frightened, and would have given the world if I had not
enlisted as a soldier. I could positively feel my hair stand on end."[16]

But he was cheered by a Negro soldier, who, wounded in the back of
his neck, passed by him. The boy asked him if the wound hurt him much.
He said no, he was only going to get a plaster put on it and meant to
return. "You cannot conceive what encouragement this immediately gave
me," John Greenwood wrote in his memoirs. "I began to feel brave and
like a soldier from that moment, and fear never troubled me afterward
during the whole war."[17]

Meanwhile, the American marksmen on the hill transformed the tight
formation of Redcoats that approached them into packs of stunned and
stricken men. The British soldiers spun and toppled forward or staggered
away, streaming blood. But a quarter hour later, they attacked again.

About midway in the American entrenchment was Robert Steele, a
drummer boy, who had come up with his regiment from Cambridge in
the morning, beating "Yankee Doodle" all the way. Years later, Robert
told a friend, "The second battle was harder and longer than the first,

but being but a lad and this the first engagement I was ever in, I cannot remember much more ... than great noise and confusion."[18]

He did, however, distinctly remember one incident: "About the time the British retreated the second time, I was standing by the side of Benjamin Ballard, a Boston boy about my age, who had a gun in his hands, when one of our sergeants came up and said, 'You are young and spry, run ... to some of the stores and bring some rum. Major Moore is badly wounded. Go as quick as possible.'"[19]

The boys ran as fast as they could into Charlestown and went into a store, where they found the owner hiding in the cellar. They told him what they wanted and asked him why he stayed down in the cellar. He answered, "To keep out of the way of the shot," and then said, "If you want anything in the store, take what you please." Robert seized a pitcher and filled it with rum. Ben took a pail and filled it with water. Then they ran back to the entrenchments on the hill. The British were advancing a third time. "Our rum and water went very quick," Robert remembered.[20]

The Americans were running out of ammunition and lacked bayonets to defend their redoubts. Still they fought on, bare-handed or with clubbed muskets. But more and more Redcoats with bayonets were pouring over the walls, and the Americans began a retreat, still fighting from one fence or wall to another, until their force had managed to get across Charlestown Neck onto the mainland.

The thunder of the British cannons could be heard at a distance in Braintree, where Abigail Adams and her children lived. Intent to see for herself, Abigail had taken her oldest son, little Johnny, by the hand and hurried up the road to nearby Penn's Hill. From the summit they could see the smoke of battle 10 miles up the bay. "How many have fallen we know not," she wrote that night to her absent husband. "The constant roar of cannons is so distressing that we cannot eat, drink, or sleep."[21]

The sight of burning Charlestown and the roar of the battle left an indelible impression on John Quincy Adams. Years later, he gave his own recollections of the events in a letter to Joseph Sturge:

1775 was the eighth year of my age. Among the first fruits of the war was the expulsion of my father's family from their peaceful abode in Boston to take refuge in his native town of Braintree .... My father was separated from his family on the way to attend the Continental Congress, and there my mother lived in unintermitted danger of being consumed with them all in a conflagration kindled by the torch in the same hands which on the 17th of June lighted the fires in Charlestown. I saw with my own eyes those fires, and heard Brittania's thunders in the Battle of Bunker Hill and witnessed the tears of my mother.[22]

"Viewing the Battle of Bunker's Hill," *Harper's Magazine, 1901.*

Although victorious in the end, the British suffered staggering losses. On June 18, 1775, Dorothy Dudley wrote in her diary, "Our enemies rejoice at *our* loss, but *their* victory is a dear one to them.... Eleven hundred of their choicest men, including a great many officers, is no small loss, when they receive in exchange only a little hill overlooking Boston. One hundred and forty-five killed ... among our soldiers. It really is wonderful how a small body of undisciplined farmers could stand so long against an army of English regulars."[23]

Washington arrived in Cambridge on July 3 and took command of the Continental Army. In her diary Dorothy Dudley ventured a guess that "he will find his task a hard one, that of making an army out of the rude material gathered from all parts of our Colonies" and that his generals "will surely find their hands full of work in putting this body of men into readiness for war, there is so much confusion in the camp, so little discipline, and such terrible want of supplies of any kind."[24]

Washington was faced with the unique problem of forming and training an army on the battlefield while attempting to replace it with more permanent troops. Most of the existing militia had short-term enlistments, usually for six months. He had to accept the fact that the army he was trying to fashion in the summer of 1775 would melt away by the end of the year, before he could raise another. Constant recruitment was necessary.

Military recruiters for the Continental Army took any able-bodied fellow they could get and rarely asked for proof of age. With roughly 50 percent of the population under 16, teenagers constituted a disproportionate share of available males. The army sought them out for they were the easiest to train. For poor boys and teenagers, many of whom were in some form of indentured service or apprenticeship, serving in the fledgling Continental Army offered the prospect of greater freedom. Boys with little property, no marital ties, and visions of military glory were considered "very proper for service."[25]

One of those boys was Israel Trask, who volunteered at age 10 and served two tours in the Massachusetts line, from summer 1775 through December and from January 1776 until the next summer. He served as mess boy and messenger and was excited by army life.

Among his most endearing memories were those of a snowball fight between a rifle corps from Virginia and a group of soldiers from Massachusetts that took place in the winter of 1775–1776, when his regiment was quartered in Cambridge on the campus of Harvard College. A rifle corps had come into camp, made up of recruits from the backwoods and mountains of Virginia, in a uniform totally different from that of the New Englanders. Their white linen frocks, ruffled and fringed, attracted the curiosity of the Marblehead regiment, whose soldiers were clad in short jackets and fishermen's trousers. They looked with scorn at the Virginians' rustic uniforms and confronted them on the campus when they arrived:

> Their first manifestations were ridicule and derision...with resort being made to snow, which then covered the ground. These soft missives were interchanged but a few minutes, before a fierce struggle commenced [between both parties], with biting and gouging on the one part, and knockdown on the other part, with as much fury as the most deadly enmity could create.... In less than five minutes more than a thousand combatants were on the field, struggling for mastery.
>
> At this juncture General Washington made his appearance.... He leaped from his saddle, threw the reins of his bridle into the hands of his servant, and rushed into the thickest of the melee, with an iron grip seized two tall,

brawny, savage-looking riflemen by the throat, keeping them at arm's length, alternately shaking and talking to them.... Its effect on the belligerents was an instantaneous flight at the top of their speed in all directions from the scene of the conflict.... Bloodshed, imprisonment, trials by court-martial were happily prevented, and hostile feelings between the different corps of the army extinguished.[26]

The siege of Boston lasted from the summer of 1775 to the spring of 1776. Young John Greenwood wrote,

The English were so penned up in Boston that they could get no fresh provisions except what they stole from the poor unprotected inhabitants near the seashore.... They were in such want as to be obliged to risk their lives ... to steal some cows that were grazing at Lechmere's Point, about half a mile from the encampment of our regiment.... We ran and just got down to get a shot at them before they pushed off. They did not take anything with them ... only stabbed two or three cows with their bayonets.[27]

At night, the British bombarded the American camp relentlessly. On one occasion, a bomb dropped directly opposite the door of the guard-house. A teenage sentry in Greenwood's company ran out, knocked the fuse from the shell, and took the powder out of it so that it could be used by his comrades in their muskets. "We became so accustomed to this bombardment," observed Greenwood, "that we thought nothing of it. For a half pint of aniseed water one soldier who was a little timid could get another to stand for him as sentry in the most perilous place."[28]

In October 1775 General Gage was replaced by General Howe, who presided in Boston through a cold and difficult winter, waiting for new ships and supplies. "During the entire winter we were amused [by nightly bombardments]," wrote John Greenwood, "[but] nothing material was happening."[29]On February 27, 1776, Dorothy Dudley noted in her diary that

there has been a good deal of card playing and gambling of various kinds. The enforced quiet of the soldiers has been irksome, and they enliven the monotony in any way they can devise. Many have had the opportunity to work at their trades of shoemaking, tailoring and the like, or to add to their income by selling such things as nuts, apples, and cider, which make a little variety in the daily rations.... These short winter days, candles are quite a necessary article and are given every week to the soldiers.[30]

A week later, Washington took the initiative. During the night of March 4 his troops constructed fortifications on Dorchester Heights, just south of Boston. Nine-year-old Nathaniel Goddard remembered, "My father had men employed in cutting and making fascines [long bundles of sticks of wood bound together] to carry onto the Hill and in getting the teams ready to transport all the stores for the troops…. When all was ready and the time fixed they started in profound silence, not a word to be spoken even to the cattle, and all went on in deathlike silence toward Dorchester Heights."[31]

By daybreak, on the sixth anniversary of the Boston Massacre, a long line of earthworks and batteries overlooked Boston. "When the British perceived that it would be impossible to drive us from Dorchester Heights…they concluded to quit the town," wrote John Greenwood. "The first thing they did was to march from Bunker Hill in the night, leaving the cannon in the fort and two wooden men to stand sentry with guns upon their shoulders."[32] Twelve days later, on March 17, the British embarked on their ships and were off to Halifax.

They left behind a city in which hunger and filth had heightened the population's vulnerability to smallpox. Its first ominous signs had shown up in Boston and outlying towns in the early months of 1775. During the siege and evacuation of Boston, anyone even suspected of carrying the disease had to be kept from the American troops until the danger of infection had passed. Two days after the British evacuation, Dorothy Dudley wrote from Cambridge, "General Washington will not allow any person to enter Boston without a pass, owing to the prevalence of smallpox, and has issued orders that as soon as the selectmen report the town to be cleansed from infection, liberty will be given to those who have business there to go."[33]

To diminish the risk of infection, Washington sent a vanguard of 1,000 immune troops to clean Boston and to quarantine those afflicted with the disease in the "most westerly part, where the infection may be contained." On March 23 Dorothy Dudley noted in her diary that "the town is [now] open for all who wish to go in, and yesterday an immense concourse of people from the surrounding country crowded the streets…. It was very touching to witness the tearful meeting of mothers with their children, of sisters and brothers whom the terrors and sufferings of the past months have kept ignorant of one another's condition."[34]

But Abigail Adams was still anxious about the smallpox. As spring turned into summer, no end of the disease was in sight. So Abigail had herself and her four children—Nabby, age 11, Johnny, age nine, Charles, age six, and little Thomas, age three—inoculated. They came to Boston to undergo the treatment and drove a cow all the way down from their farm in Braintree to supply the children with fresh milk. "The little folks are very sick and puke every morning," Abigail wrote to her husband. "But after that they are comfortable."[35]

Patriot Bostonians continued to return to their homes on horseback and on foot. But John Greenwood, whose first term of enlistment had

Pulling down the statue of George III, Bowling Green, New York City. Published by Joseph Laing (ca. 1875). *Courtesy Library of Congress.*

expired during the siege of the city and who had reenlisted for one more year, did not have a chance to be reunited with his parents. His regiment left for New York before the British left town. Israel Trask *did* march into Boston "about the dawning of the day when the last of the enemy were leaving it."[36]

While in Boston, the boy witnessed a mutiny in the army. It was promptly quelled and the ringleaders seized, tried, and convicted by a court-martial, two of them to be shot. When Issac visited the men in prison, "the tears of penitence coming down their rough cheeks" made an indelible impression on him. To his relief, Washington granted the condemned men an unexpected pardon.

On July 2, 1776, 11 weeks after George Washington's first military victory in the war, Congress voted in favor of independence, and on July 4 the Declaration of Independence was approved. Four days later—on July 8—it was published, and copies were sent throughout the colonies to be read publicly. It would take another 10 days until the momentous news reached Boston and Cambridge. Dorothy Dudley, writing in her diary on July 19, tells of the excitement shared by the eager crowds:

> Independence is declared at last! The glorious document which proclaims our Colonies to be free and independent, has been read

from the balcony of the State House and in Faneuil Hall, and greeted with cheers of welcome from thousands of patriotic throats.... The bell ringer of the State House stood at his post in the steeple from the early morning that he might be prompt to announce to the people that their independence was formally declared. His little boy was stationed where he could get the earliest news of the event, and at last, as the old man grew impatient at the long delay, the boyish voice rung through the air: "Ring! Ring, Father! Ring" And then the bells sent forth a triumphant peal which was answered by shouts of joy from the excited multitude.... [37]

The people of Boston tore the royal coat of arms from the state house. The residents of Savannah burned King George III in effigy.

Reading the Declaration of Independence to Washington's troops, July 1776. *Courtesy Dover Pictorial Archives.*

In New York, some "saucy boys" pulled down his statue with ropes at the Bowling Green. Crowds of men, women, and children—and barking dogs as well—watched as the royal rider on horseback tumbled from his pedestal. His statue would supply plenty of lead for the next American campaign. Patriots from Connecticut melted it down for bullets.

PART II
Fighting the War of Independence

CHAPTER 3

ᕷᕷ

From New York to Trenton

On August 22, 1776, British troops and their Hessian auxiliaries began landing on Long Island. Britain had never before assembled such an armada: An army of some 34,000 superbly armed and well-trained soldiers were about to confront some 23,000 ragged, ill-equipped, and poorly trained Americans in the Battle for New York. Among the adversaries were two farm boys in their teens—Joseph Plumb Martin from Medford, Connecticut, and Johannes Reuber from the German principality of Hessen-Kassel. Both boys left us narratives of their adventures during the eight long years of the Revolutionary War.

Joseph Plumb Martin had enlisted in the Continental Army at age 15. "I was as warm a patriot as the best of them," he wrote later. "It would not do to put the hand to the plow and look back, I felt more anxious than ever to be called a defender of my country." He had sailed with several others of his company from New London to New York and joined the rest of his regiment for three months of basic training. In the latter part of August his regiment was ordered to Long Island, "the British having landed in force there."[1]

Johannes Reuber, his adversary, was among the German troops that had been hired by the British for the American war. His sovereign, the Landgrave of Hessen-Kassel, had offered the services of his regiments to King George III for an annual payment of $500,000. Britain had also agreed to pay all expenses of the Hessian soldiers as well as $35.00 to their prince for each soldier killed and $12.00 for each one wounded. In return, the British were getting troops considered "as good in all respects, as any in Europe." They were well disciplined and had a low desertion rate.

Some 30,000 German soldiers would eventually fight with the British in the Revolutionary War. Only half returned home at the end. Seven thousand died; the others remained in North America and settled in Canada and the United States. Most of the Hessians were sons of artisans and farmers who observed at least the outward signs of their Protestant faith. They married the women who accompanied them to America. Their children were baptized and confirmed and given instruction in reading and religion in the schools that were set up for them in their garrisons from New York to Charleston.[2]

Johannes Reuber, at age 16, took the oath of a grenadier (foot soldier) in the Rall Regiment. His troopship left Bremen on April 16, 1776, reaching Portsmouth 10 days later. It sailed for America on May 6, carrying a detachment of British guards as well as Hessians. Their voyage was dismal and prolonged. They encountered severe storms in May and heavy fog in June. They had to endure the last part of their voyage without taking on fresh water and provisions. By the end of July, the biscuits were rotting, the water was foul, and many men had scurvy and swollen legs.

On August 14 Reuber recorded their arrival in New York harbor in his journal: "Our command ship fired a *feu de joie* with 32 cannon shots.... The English also took part because of the Hessians' safe arrival in America.... We sailed, both fleets mixed together, into the harbor near

"Conscription of German Soldiers for Service in America." *Courtesy Library of Congress.*

Staten Island, and thereby our voyage ended happily.... Praise the name of the Lord...who has sheltered us from all harm and misfortune up to this time. God will continue to protect us on the solid ground when we march against our enemies."[3]

Landing did not ease the sickness problems. Once ashore, some 700 to 800 men came down with fevers and diarrhea. There was little time for the Hessians to get used to the unaccustomed summer heat. Only a week after arrival, Reuber's regiment lined up near Flatbush, "moving forward towards the woods in which the rebels were hiding."

On the opposing side was Private Joseph Plumb Martin and his Connecticut regiment, sent by General Washington across the East River as reinforcement for the American lines. "We soon landed at Brooklyn, upon the Island," remembered Martin, "and marched up from the ferry to the heights. We began to meet the wounded men, a sight I was unacquainted with, some with broken arms, some with broken legs, and some with broken heads. The sight of these daunted me a little, and made me think of home."

Martin's regiment headed for a millpond where a large party of Americans and British were engaged. "By the time we arrived," reported Martin, "the enemy had driven our men into the creek where such as could swim got across. Those that could not swim and could not procure anything to buoy them up, sunk.... Some of us went into the water after the fall of the tide, and took out a number of corpses, and a great many arms."[4]

On August 27 the Americans were caught between the British and the Hessian lines. Grenadier Johannes Reuber noted in his diary, "We could see a rebel corps...with flags flying.... Colonel Rall ordered the regiment to fire at the Americans. When they saw what was in store they surrendered and dropped their rifles...and laid down all their weapons.... A noncommissioned officer of our regiment seized the rebel flag."[5]

The Battle of Brooklyn was the first battle ever fought by the United States as an independent nation. The Americans were soundly defeated. Washington lost about 970 men killed, wounded, or missing and 1,079 taken captive—almost half of the troops engaged. The others, including Private Martin, were ferried across the East River to New York during the foggy night of August 29. They landed safely in Manhattan about three o'clock in the morning on August 30, grateful to be alive.

The retreat was covered by some 400 troops from Maryland and Delaware. They held their own against an overwhelming British force until Washington's army had escaped. When the battle ended, 256 of the 400 Maryland and Delaware men lay dead. One of them was Will Sands, a young boy from Annapolis who had written to his parents two weeks earlier: "We are ordered to hold our Selves in Readyness.... We have Lost a Great many of our troops.... We expect Please God to Winter at home, those that Live of us." The letter that Will wrote did not reach Annapolis until September 5. On the back, someone had written "Killed on Long Island, August 27, 1776."[6]

The campaign in New York continued over the next three months: On September 15, 1776, the British army invaded Manhattan Island, landing at an open field on the East River, just south of where the United Nations building sits today. When the British descended on Kip's Bay during the night, only raw recruits, like Private Martin, were sent to defend its shores. "We had a chain of sentinels quite up the river, for four or five miles in length," he remembered. "At an interval of every half-hour, they passed the watchword to each other, 'All is well.'"

A little before 11 o'clock on the morning of the 15th, the British landing crafts drew near. "All of a sudden there came such a peal of thunder from the British ships that I thought my head would go with the sound," Martin recalled. "I made a frog's leap for the ditch and lay as still as I possibly could and began to consider which part of my carcass was to go first." The British and Hessians started coming ashore unopposed. "We kept the lines until they were almost leveled upon us, when our officers, seeing we could make no resistance ... and that we must soon be entirely exposed to ... their guns, gave the order to leave the lines."

Private Martin and a neighbor from home, whom he met on the retreat, struggled to keep up with a body of men who were heading in their direction. They turned out to be Hessians, and the two boys from Connecticut quickly changed course. "The enemy's party was small, but ... the demons of fear and disorder seemed to take full possession of all and everything that day.... The ground was literally covered with arms, knapsacks, staves, coats, hats and old oil flasks," he remembered. Eventually, he and his comrade rejoined their regiment at Harlem Heights on northern Manhattan Island. "We were the last who came up, all the others who were missing were either killed or taken prisoners."

Martin and his regiment remained at Harlem Heights, expecting another attack by the British. "The next day, in the forenoon, the enemy ... followed us ... and were advancing through a level field.... We arrived on the ground just as the enemy were entering a thick wood.... We soon came to action with them. The troops engaged ... and kept them until they found shelter under the cannon of some of their shipping lying in the North River."

The Battle of Harlem Heights on September 16 gave a tremendous boost to American morale. The same soldiers who had narrowly escaped from Brooklyn to Manhattan, and then had fled the British invasion at Kip's Bay, saw that they could have a "smart fight with the enemy in Harlem Woods." "Our Army Drove them And Killed a Grate many," wrote David How, age 17, in his diary that day.

"We remained at the battleground till nearly sunset," continued Martin, "expecting the enemy to attack again, but they showed no such inclination.... The men were very much fatigued and faint having had nothing to eat for forty-eight hours.... One of the men complained of being hungry. Our colonel, putting his hand into his coat pocket, took out a piece of burnt Indian corn. 'Here, ' he said to the man complaining, 'eat this and learn to be a soldier.' "[7]

A few days after the Battle of Harlem Heights, British warships successfully ran the batteries at Fort Washington and Fort Lee along the Hudson River. Washington decided to move north to the mainland into Westchester County to avoid being completely encircled by enemy forces. It was a nightmare march. His hungry troops, still dressed in summer outfits, shivered in the autumn cold. Private Martin remembered the chilly nights: "I have often ... lain on one side until the upper side smarted with cold, then turned that side down to the place warmed by my body, and let the other side take its turn at smarting.... In the morning the ground was white as snow with hoar frost."[8]

His regiment arrived at White Plains at dawn on the 22nd of October. Washington's troops had by then taken a defensive position on high ground. Their lines extended from the steep and wooded Chatterton's Hill above the Bronx River (on the right) to a nearby lake on the left. "When we arrived at the camp," Martin wrote, "we found that the British were advancing upon us." Green-coated Hessian troops soon appeared in front of them on the slope of an apple orchard. Their bayonets glittered in the sunlight, their high miters making them seem like giants.

Grenadier Johannes Reuber reported in his diary that

All the English and Hessian troops broke camp and marched against the Americans in a line on a hill at White Plains. Then both sides commenced firing at one another with cannons. The Lossberg Regiment had to advance toward a stream, the Bronx Creek, which lay in a valley. However, it suffered great losses of wounded and had to pull back.... As the Americans were before us, our Colonel Rall ordered his regiment to immediately ascend the hill.... We could see above the hill that the rebels were advancing and also meant to occupy this hill. We were able to move in the back of the American lines, and our army obtained an advantage. We captured a powder wagon ... but soon night was upon us. It was so dark that no one could see. The order was given that each man should make a fire and should run back and forth, making a noise, so that the enemy would believe that we were being reinforced on the hill. Colonel von Donop ... also made plans to deceive the Americans during the night by driving the cannons and horses back and forth, and with the rattling of chains and the swearing of the drivers to make them think that additional heavy artillery had arrived. At daybreak the American army had withdrawn.[9]

But the rebel troops had fought bravely and had inflicted more than 200 casualties in the fight for Chatterton's Hill. After the heat of the battle, the hardships of camp life reasserted themselves. "During the night we remained in our new-made trenches," wrote Private Martin, "the ground of which was in many parts springy. In that part where I happened to be stationed, the water before morning was nearly over the shoes, which caused many of us to take violent colds by being exposed upon the wet ground after a profuse perspiration."[10]

When the British were finally ready to renew their advance against the rebels on October 31, 1776, nature interceded once more on the side of the Americans: A heavy rainstorm lasting 24 hours canceled the enemy's plans. The next day, they found that Washington had moved his line back into North Castle Heights, where the hilly terrain made it too difficult to pursue his troops. The Continental Army had been saved again.

The British soon after left White Plains, and Washington, with part of his army, crossed the Hudson River into New Jersey. Private Martin was sent off with a number of sick soldiers to Norwalk, Connecticut, to restore his health and then was discharged on Christmas Day, having completed his six-month enlistment in the Continental Army.

By mid-November, only Harlem Heights and Fort Washington remained to be captured for the British to possess all of Manhattan and to dominate the entire length of the Hudson River. On November 15 a party of British officers approached the 230-foot-high fort with a white flag and a drummer to demand the surrender of its garrison. The American commander refused.

Early the next morning, on November 16, Hessian troops launched the main attack against the fort. Wrote Johannes Reuber in his diary, "At daybreak, the Americans became aware of us, but it was too late. Suddenly the two warships on either side [of the Hudson and Harlem Rivers] opened fire against Fort Washington. At the same time the land attack began with cannon fire…. All the regiment…marched forward to clamber up the hills and stone cliffs. One fell down, still alive, the next one was shot dead. We had to pull ourselves up by grasping the wild box tree bushes and could not stand upright until we arrived on top of the height."

When Colonel Rall shouted to his men, "All who are my grenadiers, forward march!" the drummers beat their march, the oboists played their mournful tunes, and the Germans swept forward, shouting, "Hurrah!" "Everyone was at once mixed together," observed Reuber. "Americans and Hessians were as one. No more shots were fired, everyone ran toward the defenses…but we stopped them…. Two hours later the rebels surrendered Fort Washington, and all ammunition and provisions in and outside the fort were turned over to the Hessian General von Knyphausen."[11]

The Hessians lost 326 killed or wounded; the American losses were 59 killed, 96 wounded, and nearly 3,000 soldiers held captive, many of them "lads under fifteen." The successful retreat in the campaign for New York had ended in a disaster. "Yet we are by no means to despair," wrote Governor Trumbull of Connecticut to General Washington that day. "We are in this way to be prepared for help and deliverance."

During November and December 1776, when the Continental Army moved south from New Jersey into Pennsylvania, a number of teenage girls living in British occupied areas were subjected to repeated rapes by the Redcoats. Depositions collected by the Continental Congress give a vivid account of the experiences of four New Jersey women in late 1776: 13-year-old Abigail Palmer; her aunt, Mary Phillips; her friend, Sarah Cain; and Sarah's 15-year-old sister, Elisabeth.[12]

One December day, a number of British soldiers from a nearby camp came to the home of Edmund Palmer, an elderly farmer. One of them dragged Palmer's 13-year-old granddaughter Abigail into a bedroom. According to her testimony, she "scream'd and beged of him to let her alone," but to no avail. Abigail was raped three times. She testified that for three days successively, "divers soldiers wou'd come to the house and treat her in the same manner."

On one of those days her aunt, Mary, and her friend, Sarah Cain, were also assaulted. On the eve of the third day, two soldiers demanded that Abigail and Sarah's younger sister, Elisabeth, age 15, accompany them to their camp. The two teenage girls were then forced into another room. Elisabeth recalled that "the said Soldiers Ravished them both and then took them away to their Camp where they was both Treated by Some other of the Soldiers in the same cruel manner" until they were rescued by an officer.

In all occupied areas, women often had to quarter troops in their homes. The journal of Lydia Mintern Post, a patriotic Long Island housewife, reveals that most threatening to her was the relationship between the homesick Hessians and her children. The soldiers taught her son German and made baskets for her daughters, telling them of their little ones at home. "The children are fond of them," she noted, but "I fear lest they contract evil." Margaret Morris, of Burlington, New Jersey, was more accommodating. On December 21 she wrote in her journal, "Before we retired to bed this evening, an attempt was made to teach the children to pronounce '*vegates*' [*Wie geht's?* (How are you?)] like a Dutchman. Our good neighbors are concerned to think that there is not one in the

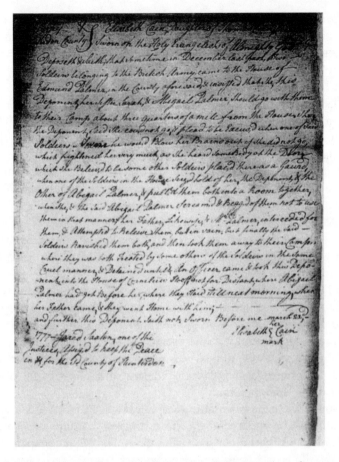

Deposition by Elizabeth Cain regarding the rape of two
teenage girls by British soldiers. *Congressional Record, March
1777.*

neighborhood that will be able to interpret for us when the Hessians are
quartered on us."[13]

Two weeks earlier, the last of Washington's main army had crossed the
Delaware from New Jersey into Pennsylvania. Washington had ordered
that all boats on the river from Trenton northward and southward be
secured by his troops. In temporary safety across the Delaware, with all
boats under guard, Washington placed his most experienced battalions
along the river north of Yardly, Pennsylvania. Opposite Trenton and
north of Yardly, there is a rise of 60 feet within a mile of the riverbank
where the Americans could watch the arrival of the Hessian troops.

On December 18, Johannes Reuber, whose regiment had occupied
Trenton, wrote in his diary, "It was quiet for us at Trenton and we posted

our watches, commands, and pickets as usual. It also began to freeze which was our desire as we then would be able to cross the river and capture Philadelphia." By December 20, the ice on the Delaware had begun to freeze but was not yet solid enough to cross on foot.

Warned by some of the inhabitants of Trenton that the American army planned to attack, Colonel Rall took a detachment from his brigade and a cannon and marched to the river (to a point opposite New Frankford) in order to determine if Washington's troops were making preparations for a surprise attack. Nothing was seen or noticed. So the Hessians marched back to Trenton.

Reuber's diary entry on December 21 reads, "Everything was quiet and peaceful. Nevertheless, it was ordered that every evening a company was to remain in the 'alert house' with the rifles provided for that post stacked ... before the house door. The soldiers were to remain dressed as if on watch and the officers were to enforce strict compliance."

The 1,600 Hessians in Rall's three regiments had been quartered in the houses along Warren and Broad streets between State and Hanover streets. Every day, for 24 hours, from four o'clock each afternoon, one regiment, the "du jour" regiment, was fully dressed and quartered in the "alert houses," ready to turn out in five minutes. This duty once every three days, in addition to the many patrols that responded to the harassment by the American militia, kept the Hessian units often without sleep for two days at a time.

On December 22 a small contingent of Americans crossed the river near a Hessian detachment at the Delaware, set some houses on fire, and then retreated back across the river. The next day, the inhabitants of Trenton intensified their warnings of a rebel attack. "On Christmas Eve, in the afternoon, there were suddenly alarm shots at our outposts," reported Reuber. "Colonel Rall took two companies and one cannon and marched through the woods in order to reconnoiter around the outposts, but nothing happened and he returned. After his return ... everyone had to enter the 'alert houses' and occupy our positions."[14]

On December 25, 1776, while Washington and his army waited on the icy slopes of the river Delaware, preparing their attack on the Hessian troops in Trenton, young Polly Wharton, in a nearby house, wrote a letter to her cousin:

> Dearest Mary, This Christmas Day is cold and bleak. It snowed yesterday and the fields are deep in drifts. There are many soldiers about in the woods and fields near the river, and some officers stopped by yesterday to ask for food. Father gave them a basket of eggs. One of the officers was very handsome despite his ragged appearance and he smiled at me. I have stayed indoors and passed my time in sewing and reading.... I read first from the Bible.... I also read from Mr. Janways' *A Token for Children*. He teaches us

that…good children must rise early and be useful before going to school, and do their chores at evening. He tells us to love the Lord and serve our elders. I confess that I often feel an unwillingness to do good duties, and I often avoid doing my chores…. I confess I find wickedness more attractive than virtue. Though I am well in body, I question whether I grow in grace. Do write to me…. Father says that letters are the messengers of the mind and bring friends closer together. As ever, Your dearest Polly[15]

As the daylight of December 25 began to fade, the American troops began to move toward McKonkey's Ferry. Here were gathered the boats that Washington had secured. The main attack on the Hessians with 2,400 men would be led by Nathanael Greene, accompanied by Washington. The American sign and countersign that day was "Victory," "Or Death." The soldiers silently huddled by the ferry landing. It began to snow. "In the night we crossed the River Dullerway with a large body of men and field pieces," wrote the teenager David How in his diary.

Sixteen-year-old John Greenwood remembers, "Over the river we went in a flat-bottomed scow, and as I was with the first that crossed, we had to wait for the rest and so began to pull down fences and make fires to warm ourselves, for the storm was increasing rapidly. After a while it hailed, snowed, and froze, and at the same time blew a perfect hurricane." Washington had hoped to have his troops on the New Jersey shore by midnight, but it was nearly 4:00 A.M. before the crossing was completed.

"The noise of the soldiers coming over and clearing the ice, the rattling of the cannon wheels on the frozen ground, and the cheerfulness of my fellow comrades encouraged me," wrote John Greenwood. "After our men had all crossed we began to march, not advancing faster than a child ten years old could walk…. I recollect very well that…when we halted on the road, I sat down on the stump of a tree and was so benumbed with cold that I wanted to go to sleep, but my sergeant came, and rousing me up, made me walk about. We then began to march again until the dawn of day, about half past seven in the morning."[16]

With daylight they flushed the Hessian pickets, who shouted, "*Der Feind! Heraus! Heraus!*" (The enemy! Out! Out!). This was the second day of Christmas for the Hessians, who had had little time to feast and drink. The rank and file soldiers had been on constant duty in the alert houses. Young John Greenwood, eyewitness to the ensuing battle, sets the record straight:

I have heard that we surprised the enemy…but any who would even suppose such a thing must indeed be ignorant, when it is well known that our whole country was filled with informers of all descriptions, and our march so slow that it was impossible but they should be apprised of it.

It was likewise asserted...that the enemy were all drunk.... I can swear that we were *all* sober to a man...and I am willing to go upon oath that I did not see even a solitary drunken soldier belonging to the enemy. As we advanced, it being dark and stormy so that we could not see very far ahead, we got within 200 yards of about 300 to 400 Hessians who were paraded, two deep, in a straight line with Colonel Rall, their commander, on horseback, to the right of them. They made a full fire at us, but I did not see that they killed any one.... As we had been in the storm all night we were not only wet through and through ourselves, but our guns and powder were wet also.... When we were all ready, we advanced and, although there was not more than one bayonet to five men, orders were given to "Charge bayonets and rush on!" and rush on we did. Within pistol shot they again fired...we dodged and they did not hit a man. Before they had time to reload we were within three feet of them, when they broke in an instant...and ran into town...we after them pell-mell.[17]

Grenadier Johannes Reuber of the Rall Regiment gave his perspective of the battle in his diary:

On [the second] Christmas morning, at daybreak, the Americans marched against our 100-man picket and at the same time the Americans fired on our outposts. At the first salvo, we turned out from our alert houses and went to the alert areas to form and prepare our battle formations. Now the rebels pressed in on us.... The Americans charged Colonel Rall's quarters, overran it, and took the [two] cannons from the regiment. Then Colonel Rall charged with his grenadiers. Although we went against enemy cannons...Colonel Rall commanded, "All those who are my grenadiers, charge!" The rebels, in three lines, marched around us, and as we tried to retreat, they brought seven cannons into the main street. We had to go past them, but things went badly for us before we could accomplish this purpose. If the colonel had not been so seriously wounded, they would not have taken us alive.[18]

With Colonel Rall mortally wounded the German soldiers were unable to organize themselves. As the Americans moved into the city, they rounded up many confused prisoners.

John Greenwood picks up the story:

After passing a number of dead and wounded Hessians we reached the other side of town and on our right beheld about 500 or 600 of the enemy paraded, two deep, in a field.... They had been taken prisoners by another party and we marched between them and their guns which they had laid down. A few minutes afterward a number of wagons came behind us, into which the guns were placed.... Our regiment was then ordered to conduct them down to the ferry and transport them over to the other side.... The Hessian prisoners, who were all grenadiers, numbered about 900.... The scow which was used in transporting them over the ferry was half a leg deep with rain and snow, and some of the poor fellows were so cold that their underjaws quivered like an Aspen leaf. On the march down the boat, seeing some of our men were much pleased with the brass caps which they had taken from the dead Hessians, our prisoners, who were besides exceedingly frightened, pulled off those that they were wearing, and giving them away, put on the hats which they carried tied behind their packs. With these brass caps on, it was laughable to see how our soldiers would strut—fellows with their elbows out and some without a collar to their half-a-shirt and no shoes. [19]

Almost 900 Hessians were captured with all guns and equipment. Six hundred had escaped. Another 100 lay dead or wounded in the streets of Trenton. The American victory was complete. There were only two casualties among the Continental Army. Washington began his return to the ferries almost immediately after the battle, but escorting the prisoners across the Delaware required all night. Some of the American troops did not reach their huts until three o'clock in the afternoon on December

Surrender of Hessian flags after the Battle of Trenton. *Courtesy Library of Congress.*

27—after a 48-hour round trip of 40 miles in a severe snowstorm—without food. Half of the army was reported unfit for duty on December 28.

That day, Grenadier Johannes Reuber wrote in his diary, "We were confined in a rotten prison: [in New Frankford], consisting of a high wall on each of four corners, under the open sky.... They poured sea biscuits in a basket through a hole, and we collected it in the snow. It was very cold."

On the last day of 1776 the captured Germans were paraded through the streets of Philadelphia before an ecstatic crowd. "As we entered the city," noted Johannes Reuber, "all the people... old and young, assembled to see what kind of men we were.... The old women screamed and wanted to strangle us because we had come to America to steal their freedom. Others... brought brandy and bread and wanted to give it to us.... Because the people were so angry and threatening toward us, our American guard said to us: 'Dear Hessians, I want to make sure you are safe! ' He marched us directly into the barracks."[20]

"The next day," wrote the Hessian lad, "General Washington posted broadsides all over town and in the countryside stating that we were innocent and had not entered this war voluntarily, but had been forced to do so. We should not be regarded as enemies, but should be accepted and treated as friends.... Because General Washington had given his word of honor, conditions improved for us." So did the spirit of the American troops!

CHAPTER 4

ᔫ

From Philadelphia to Valley Forge

At the end of the first week of January 1777, as Washington's exhausted men set up winter quarters in Morristown, New Jersey, the prisoners of war they had captured at Trenton were moved out of Philadelphia to Lancaster, Pennsylvania. "We arrived at noon, and entered the barracks," wrote Johannes Reuber on January 12, 1777. "We Hessians were in the middle wing; the 900 English prisoners were in the side wings, for security, and were watched by an American guard force, and everything was peaceful and quiet for us. Daily we received one pound of bread, and as much meat and wood as necessary for cooking and heating, and everything which we needed."[1]

As spring came, the Americans offered the Hessian POWs a chance to work on the nearby farms. Johannes Reuber described the hiring process in his diary: "An American farmer ... must first register with the city commandant as one who wishes to obtain a Hessian to work on his land. Next, he must present a signed declaration that he will honestly return him ... or if he has taken him to the English army or allowed him to desert, he must pay a fine of 200 pounds to the city commandant. Also, the farmer shall provide food and drink and pay a wage of 15 *pfennings* daily."[2]

In April, as the weather warmed, the Hessian prisoners left their barracks to work on the farms in Lancaster County. That same month, Joseph Plumb Martin, now a seasoned veteran of 16, reenlisted in the Continental Army "for the duration of the war." Like many boys his age, he was willing to substitute for a more "opulent" draftee who was unwilling to serve. He remembered,

The inhabitants of the town were about this time put into what were called squads, according to their ratable property.... Each of these squads were to furnish a man for the army, either by hiring or by sending one of their own number.... One of the ... squads , wanting to procure a man ... attacked me, front, rear and flank. I thought, as I must go, I might as well endeavor to get as much for my skin as I could. Accordingly, I told them that I would go for them and fixed upon a day when I would meet them and clinch the bargain.

The day which was a muster day for the militia of the town arrived. I went to the parade where all was liveliness, as it generally is upon such occasions; but poor I felt miserably; my execution day was come. I kept wandering about till the afternoon, among the crowd, when I saw the lieutenant who went with me into a house where the men of the squad were, and there I put my name to enlisting indentures....The men gave me what they agreed to, I forget the sum, perhaps to keep the blood circulating during the short space of time which I tarried at home after I had enlisted. They were now freed from any further trouble, at least for the present, and I had become the scapegoat for them.[3]

One of the first procedures Martin had to endure in his second tour of duty was vaccination against the smallpox, which had become a significant obstacle to the enlistment of new soldiers in the Continental Army. "The small pox has made such Head in every quarter that I find it impossible to keep it from spreading thro' the whole Army in the natural way," wrote Washington to the President of the Continental Congress, John Hancock. "I have therefore determined, not only to innoculate all the Troops now here, that have not had it, but shall order Doc Shippen to innoculate the Recruits as fast as they come."[4]

In May 1777 Private Joseph Plumb Martin went through the procedure with some 400 other Connecticut soldiers. Housed in an old set of barracks, and attended by a guard of previously immunized troops from Massachusetts, the men came through variolation unharmed. "I had the small pox favorably as did the rest," observed Martin. "We lost none."

In June Martin was ordered to join a detachment of troops that guarded the Hudson River Highlands against a possible invasion by the British from Canada or New York. He recalled,

No one who has never been upon such duty as those advance parties have to perform can form any adequate idea of the trouble, fatigue and dangers which they have to encounter. Their whole time is spent in marches, especially night marches, watching, starving, and, in cold weather, freezing and sickness. If they get any chance to rest, it must be in the woods or fields, under the side of a fence, in an orchard or in any other place but a comfortable one, lying down on the cold and often wet ground, and, perhaps, before the eyes can be closed with a moment's sleep, alarmed and compelled to stand under arms ... an hour or two, or to receive an attack from the enemy.[5]

After six weeks, Martin's troops marched south to join the main army in Pennsylvania. In Philadelphia it was time to celebrate the first anniversary of the Declaration of Independence. On July 5, 1777, John Adams, a member of the Continental Congress, convening in that city at the time, wrote a letter to his 12-year-old daughter, Abigail (nicknamed "Nabby"):

> My dear Daughter, Yesterday, being the anniversary of American Independence, was celebrated here with a festivity and ceremony becoming the occasion.... In the morning the *Delaware* frigate, several large gallies, and other continental armed vessels ... were all hauled off in the river, and several of them beautifully dressed in the colors of all nations, displayed about upon the masts, yards, and rigging. At one o'clock the ships were all manned, that is the men were all ordered aloft, and arranged upon the tops, yards, and shrouds, making a striking appearance—of companies of men drawn up in order, in the air. Then I went on board the *Delaware* with the President and several gentlemen of the Marine Committee, soon after which we were saluted with a discharge of thirteen guns, which was followed by thirteen others, from each other armed vessel in the river; then the gallies followed the fire, and after them the guard boats. Then the President and company returned in the barge to the shore, and were saluted with three cheers from every ship, galley, and boat in the river. The wharves and shores were lined with a vast concourse of people, all shouting and huzzaing, in a manner which gave great joy to every friend to this country, and the utmost terror and dismay to every lurking Tory. At three we went to dinner, and were very agreeably entertained with excellent company, good cheer, fine music from the band of Hessians taken at Trenton. and continual volleys between every toast, from a company of soldiers drawn up ... before the city tavern where we dined.... After this, two troops of light horses, raised in Maryland, here on their way to camp, were paraded through Second Street, after them a train of artillery, and then about a thousand infantry, now in this city on their march to camp, from North Carolina. All these marched into the commons where they went through their firings and maneuvers ...
>
> In the evening, I was walking about the streets for a little fresh air and exercise, and was surprised to find the whole city lighting up their candles at the windows. I walked most of the evening, and I think it was the most splendid illumination I ever saw.... I was amazed at the universal joy and alacrity ... and at the brilliancy and splendor of every part of this joyful exhibition. I had forgot the ringing of the bells all day and evening, and the bonfires in the street, and the fireworks played off.... I am your affectionate father, John Adams[6]

Among the infantry men from North Carolina who paraded through the streets of Philadelphia on July 4, 1777, was Hugh McDonald, who had enlisted at age 14. He wrote in his journal,

The order of the day was that every man should wash himself and put on his best apparel, powder his hair, black his boots, and be ready to fall in ranks at 8 o'clock which was done. We ... marched to and fro in the streets until about 11 o'clock when we ... commenced firing with our muskets and were succeeded by the artillery, both by land and water, who fired 13 times for every State in the Union. The artillery jarred the houses to such a degree that the glass was jingling on the pavements below, and at every round ... three cheers were given: "Huzza! Liberty or Death!"

After the firing was over, we marched back to the commons and formed into a line, when the Members of Congress marched out of Philadelphia, dressed in drab-colored clothing, with their hair creped and powdered, and, beginning at the right wing, marched in front of the army with their hats off, until they passed the left wing, when they left us and we marched back to camp.[7]

Things were not going so well in the barracks of Lancaster, Pennsylvania, where the English prisoners of war were celebrating the birthday of King George III. Observed Johannes Reuber,

In midsummer the English prisoners of war ... got together and made a bonfire in the barracks' courtyard from their wood supply. This displeased the American guards. Because the English were so drunk and created such a noise, fifteen men of those who were on guard wanted to stop this stupid action. However, the English prisoners refused to desist ... and attacked the American guards, took their rifles, broke them into pieces, and threw them into the fire. The guard withdrew without further action. But ... it was not long until an entire regiment with two cannons marched into the barracks' courtyard, swung toward the first wing and delivered fire against the English. Some were ... killed, and some wounded, and the others crept behind the brick walls. We Hessians were not involved, and we did nothing to get mixed up in this affair. Therefore the English ... bore a grudge because we Hessians thereafter received better treatment than the English.[8]

The next entry in Johannes Reuber's diary reads, "Now that we were prospering in the land, the English fleet suddenly approached ... and landed on the Elk River on August 23 in the province of Maryland.... Many POWs who were in the neighborhood of Philadelphia were recaptured and returned to the English army."

A month earlier, on July 23, the British had left New York with an armada of warships, carrying some 18,000 soldiers, innumerable horses, artillery, and a vast supply of provisions. The sea voyage from Sandy Hooks to the Chesapeake Bay had caused much sickness among men and beasts, especially the horses, which suffered horribly. When they landed at the head of the Elk River, the Redcoats were struck by two days of unrelenting and violent storms, full of thunder and lightning. On August 26, 1777, three days after the Maryland landing, General William Howe's army began marching toward Philadelphia. Hoping to intercept them was George Washington's force, with about 12,000 men fit for duty. On September 11 the two armies collided at Brandywine Creek in Pennsylvania.

The British troops had been marching for more than 10 hours on a sweltering hot day. Washington's troops were positioned opposite Osborne's Hill. The British began climbing the hill in a silent mass, with the Hessians in the lead. With loud cries they fell upon the Americans, who fought fiercely. "The engagement began a little after sunrise and continued all day till sunset," remembered Hugh McDonald, the teen-age infantryman from North Carolina. "It went on incessantly, with the muskets and artillery. The enemy made an attempt seven or eight times to charge upon us with bayonets ... but our acute marksmen ... stained the pure stream of Brandywine crimson."[9]

About dark, Washington ordered a retreat. It had been a fierce fight, and although the British were victorious, the Americans showed a tenacity and discipline that surprised their enemies. George Washington had saved his army once more, but in nearby Philadelphia, fleeing congressmen dug their spurs into the hides of their horses, which carried them from the threatened capital to the safety of York, Pennsylvania.

One of the young eyewitnesses of their flight was 16-year-old Robert Morton, who kept a diary of the British occupation of Philadelphia. He was a Quaker, a member of one of the pacifist communities that opposed the Revolutionary War on religious grounds. A number of prominent members of the Society of Friends, including his stepfather and two of his brothers, had been subjected to oppressive measures by order of the Continental Congress and the Supreme Executive Council of Pennsylvania and had been sent to exile in Winchester, Virginia.

The boy wrote, on September 19, 1777,

> This morning ... an Express arrived to Congress, giving an account of the British Army having got to the Swedes Ford on the other side of the Schuylkill which so alarmed the Gnt'n of the Congress, the military officers and other Friends to the general cause of American Freedom and Independence, that they decamped with the utmost precipitation and in the greatest confusion, insomuch that one of the Delegates, by name of Fulsom was obliged in a very *fulsome* manner to ride off without a saddle. Thus we have seen the men from whom we have received, and from whom we still expected protection, leave us to fall in the hands of (by their accounts) a barbarian, cruel, and unrelenting enemy.[10]

A few days later, 15-year-old Sally Wister began a journal addressed to her friend Deborah Norris, daughter of a Quaker merchant, whose home was just two doors down from the State House where the Declaration of Independence had been announced to the public in July 1776.

Shortly after the Battle of Brandywine, when it became evident that the British would occupy Philadelphia, Sally's father had removed his family to Montgomery County, Pennsylvania. Sally was writing to her dearest friend, who had remained behind in the city:

> Though I have not the least shadow of an opportunity to send a letter, if I do write, I will keep a sort of a journal of the time that may expire before I see thee.... Yesterday... the 24th of September, two Virginia officers called at our house and informed us that the British army had crossed the Schuylkill.... Well, thee may be sure we were sufficiently scared.... About seven o'clock [in the evening] we heard a great noise—to the door we all went. A large number of wagons, with about three hundred of the Philadelphia militia, begged for drink, and several pushed into the house. One of those that entered was a little tipsy, and had a mind to be saucy. I then thought it time for me to retreat...running in at one door, and out at another, all in a shake with fear; but after a little, seeing the officers appear gentlemanly and the soldiers civil, I called reason to my aid. My fears were in some measure dispelled, tho' my teeth rattled and my hand shook like an aspen leaf. They did not offer to take their quarters with us; so, with many blessings, and as many adieus, they marched off.[11]

On September 26, the day the British entered Philadelphia, Sally wrote in her journal, "About 12 o'clock, cousin Jesse heard that General Howe's army had moved down towards Philadelphia. Then, my dear, our hopes and fears were engaged for you. However, my advice is, summon all your resolution, call Fortitude to your aid, don't suffer for your spirits to sink, my dear; there is nothing like courage; 'tis what I stand in need of myself, but unfortunately have but little of it in my composition. .... The uncertainty of our position engrosses me quite, perhaps to be in the midst of war, and ruin, and the clang of arms. But we must hope for the best...."

Back in Philadelphia, Robert Morton recorded the arrival of the British troops:

> About 11 o'clock A.M. Lord Cornwallis with his division of the British and Auxiliary Troops, amounting to about 3000, marched into this city...to the great relief of the inhabitants who have too long suffered the yoke of arbitrary power.... We had some conversations with the officers, who appeared well disposed towards the peaceable inhabitants, but most bitter against, and determined to pursue to the last extremity the army of the U.S. The British army in this city... already begins to show the great destruction of the fences and other things, the dreadful consequences of an army, however friendly.[12]

The Hessian POWs had been removed from nearby Lancaster County. Wrote Johannes Reuber in his diary, "We were transported fifteen miles farther to Newton where a church belonging to the Herrnhuters was used as an assembly place. We lay in the church until September 26 when the general commandant ordered 300 Hessian prisoners and 300 of the English to march to the wild borders of Virginia. We were put under escort and marched the same day."[13]

In the days to come, 16-year-old Robert Morton's diary reflected a growing change of sentiment toward the British occupation of Philadelphia—a change which seems to have resulted from the conduct of the army toward the civilian population and their property[14]:

September 28th—About 10 o'clock this morning some of the British Light Dragoons stationed near [our] Plantation broke open the house, 2 desks, 1 Book Case and 1 closet besides several drawers and other things, and ransacked them all. I applied to their officer, who informed me that if the men were found out they should be severely punished.

September 29th—Went to Israel Pemberton's Plantation where we found a destruction similar to that at our Plantation, 3 closets being broken open, 6 doz. wine taken, some silver spoons, the Bedclothes taken off 4 Beds, 1 rip'd open, the Tick being taken off, and other Destructions about the Plantation. The officers were so obliging as to plant a sentry.... Upon our return home we saw a man hanging.

September 30th—This morning my mother and I went to the commander of the Light Dragoons, near our plantation, to make intercession for the men who are apprehended for ransacking our plantation and house. The Colonel upon my application behaved very unlike a Gentlemen by asking me "what I wanted" in an ungenteel manner, and told me he could not attend to what I had to say.... Some of the British troops came to my mother's pasture...and took away 2 loads of hay without giving a receipt or offering payment.

October 3rd—A foraging party went out last week...and brought in a great number of cattle to the great distress of the inhabitants...

On October 4, 1777, the American soldiers challenged a large body of British soldiers camped in nearby Germantown, halfway on the road between Philadelphia and Reading. Private Martin's Connecticut regiment arrived just in time for the battle. Here is his account:

About daybreak our advanced guard and the British came in contact.... We saw a body of the enemy drawn up behind a rail fence.... Our orders were not to fire till we could see the buttons upon their clothes, but they were so coy that they would not give us an opportunity to be so curious, for they hid.... behind fire and smoke before we had either time or leisure to examine their buttons. They soon fell back and we advanced.... The enemy were driven through their camp. They left their kettles, in which they were cooking their breakfasts, and some of their garments were lying on the ground, which the owners had not time to put on.... Affairs went well for some time.

The enemy were retreating before us, until the first American division that was engaged had expanded their ammunition. Some of the men unadvisedly calling out that their ammunition was spent, the enemy were so near that they overheard them. They made a stand and then returned upon our people who for want of ammunition and reinforcements were obliged to retreat which ultimately resulted in the rout of the whole army.[15]

Two American divisions, lost in the fog and smoke, opened fire on each other. Joseph Martin escaped injury, but 150 of his fellow soldiers were killed and 500 wounded—many in friendly fire by their own countrymen. The day after the battle, the Quaker lad Robert Morton went to Germantown to see the destruction. "Most of the killed and wounded...were taken off before I got there," he wrote, "but.... I apprehend from what I have heard that the loss of the Americans is most considerable.... I went to the [British] headquarters where I saw one of General Howe's aid de camps who is very much enraged with the people around Germantown for not giving them intelligence of the advancing of Washington's Army and that he should not be surprised if General Howe was to order the country for 12 miles round Germantown to be destroyed, as the People would not run any risk to give them intelligence when they were fighting to preserve the liberties and properties of the peaceable inhabitants. "[16]

During the next three days the teenager visited and ministered to some of the wounded soldiers in his city. He noted that "the Americans are... not so much attended to as might be." He witnessed the amputation of an American soldier's leg by a professor of anatomy at the Medical College of Philadelphia, "which he completed in 20 minutes, while the physician at the military hospital took 40 minutes, performing an operation of the same nature." Being a committed Quaker, he also went about to the inhabitants of the city, "seeking for blankets and clothing for the soldiers. From some we received a little, but not generally so. They got one from us."

The Battle of Germantown had been a British victory, but it was also the fifth time that the Redcoats had failed to destroy Washington's army. Two weeks later, on October 17, 1777, General Burgoyne surrendered with some 6,000 British and German troops to the American General Gates at Saratoga. That event turned the tide of the Revolutionary War against Great Britain.

The account of Burgoyne's surrender reached Philadelphia on October 25. Robert noted in his diary that "the terms of capitulation are that the army should march out of their entrenchments [in upstate New York] and pile up their arms on the Bank of the Hudson River, and that the men should march to and encamp as nearly as convenient to the Town of Boston, there to remain at the expense of Congress till transports should be sent to carry them to Great Britain."[17]

Washington's troops were elated at the news of the defeat of Burgoyne's army. Hugh McDonald remembered,

> We rejoiced with great shouting and firing all day, our officers being more joyous than the common soldier—and I think more so than was necessary—prancing and capering about everywhere on their horses and in all places of the camp, among the artillery as well as the infantry.
>
> The results of this irregular bustle was many a hard fall from the horses which were scared by the thundering of the artillery while riding by it, especially by our artillery from Carolina as we discharged our cannon. At the same time, a General Sterling of the New England troops, was riding near our artillery on a likely bay mare, which, springing sideways from under him, gave him a very bad fall. After lying for some time, he got up and shook himself like a great water dog, acknowledged himself not hurt, but walked away directly to his quarters and left off his folly for the night.[18]

In October 1777 the British began a series of assaults on two heavily fortified American forts on the Delaware River that blocked their supply line to Philadelphia over the water route. Fort Mifflin was located on Mud Island, close to the mouth of the Schuylkill River; Fort Mercer was situated slightly higher upriver at Red Bank in New Jersey. For some five weeks the teenager Robert Morton chronicled the progress of their campaign, noting the stubborn perseverance of the Americans against overwhelming odds.

About 400 soldiers from two Rhode Island regiments held Fort Mercer against a force of about 2,000 Hessians, led by Colonel von Donop. Their flag was visible on October 22 when the colonel led his superior force through the woods that ended 400 yards from the fort. Hoping to gain the position without a fight, he sent an officer and a drummer boy under a flag of truce with the message "the King of England commands his rebellious subjects to lay down their arms and they are warned that if they wait until the battle, no quarter will be granted." The demand was rejected.

The Hessians moved forward but soon were mowed down by the bullets from the invisible defenders of the fort. After a second unsuccessful assault, in which von Donop was mortally wounded, his soldiers fled, with a loss of about 300 killed or wounded. "From this instance, we see the folly of despising the American army," noted Robert Morton in his diary. The defenders of Fort Mercer held out until November 18, until the evacuation of neighboring Fort Mifflin.[19]

Fort Mifflin had been defended by Private Martin's Connecticut regiment. "Here I endured hardships," he later wrote, "sufficient to kill half a dozen horses. In the cold month of November...to endure a siege in such a place...was appalling to the highest degree." He continued,

Our batteries were nothing more than old spars and timber laid up in parallel lines and filled between with mud and dirt. The British batteries in the course of the day would nearly level our works, and we were, like the beaver, obliged to repair our dams in the night.... It was utterly impossible to lie down to get any sleep or rest on account of the mud, if the enemy's shot would have suffered us to do so. Sometimes some of the men, when overcome with fatigue and want of sleep, would slip away into the barracks to catch a nap, but it seldom happened that they all came out again alive. I was in this place for a fortnight and can say in [all] sincerity that I never lay down to sleep.... We continued here suffering cold, hunger and other miseries till the fourteenth day of November...[20]

According to Robert Morton's diary, "on the morning of November 15th, at about 11 o'clock the *Vigilant* and about six more ships of war attacked the fort.... The firing continued till 6 P.M. and then ceased... The damage which the Fort sustained by an almost incessant fire for seven hours which burnt the Barracks, knocked down the Block Houses, dismounted the canon and rendered the Fort untenable, obliged the besieged to evacuate."[21]

Private Martin described the conditions inside the fort: "The fire was incessant.... I saw five artillerists belonging to one gun cut down by a single shot. And I saw men who were stooping to be protected by the works, but not stooping low enough, split like fish to be broiled.... Nearly every gun in the fort was silenced by mid-day. Our men were cut up like corn stalks."

The Quaker lad, Robert Morton, though a pacifist by conviction, could not help but pay a compliment to the survivors: "By American perseverance...a British Army of 12,000 men and a fleet of 300 ships had been detained in their operation for weeks by a power far inferior to theirs and which has always appeared contemptible in the eyes of men who have uniformly despised the Americans as a cowardly insignificant set of People."

Private Martin picks up the story of the evacuation of Fort Mifflin:

When the firing had subsided...I found the fort a picture of desolation. The whole area was as completely plowed as a field. The buildings were...hanging in broken fragments, and the guns all dismounted, and many of the garrison sent to the world of spirits. I happened to be left with a party of seventy or eighty men to destroy and burn all that was left in the place. After the troops had left the fort...I went to the waterside to find one of my messmates to whom I had lent my canteen in the morning. I found him lying in a long line of dead men who had been brought out of the fort to be conveyed to the mainland to have the last honors conferred upon them.... He was the most intimate associate I had in the army, but he was gone, with many more as deserving as himself.[22]

The survivors escaped without any further injury and landed, a little after midnight, on the Jersey shore. They left their flag flying when they evacuated the island. Robert Morton noted in his diary on November 16 that "the British entered the Mud Island this morning, and by the appearance of the Fort apprehended, the Americans must have lost great numbers killed and wounded. They found a flock of sheep and some oxen, besides 18 pieces of cannon."

In late November and early December 1777 Robert Morton's diary is filled with continuous accounts of the wanton destruction of property by the occupiers of Philadelphia:

> *November 22nd:* This morning the British set fire to Fair Hill mansion and eleven others, besides outhouses and barns. The reasons they assign for the destruction of their friends' property is the rumor of the Americans firing from these houses.... It is reasonable to assume that men whose property is thus wantonly destroyed under the pretense of depriving their enemy of means of annoying them on their march will soon be converted and become their professed enemies.... Here is an instance that George Washington's army cannot be accused of...
>
> *December 8th:* The Hessians on their march committed great outrages on the inhabitants.... Brot off about 700 herd of cattle, set fire to a house on Germantown Road and committed many other depredations as if the sole purpose of the expedition was to destroy and spread desolation and ruin, to dispose the inhabitants to rebellion by despoiling their property...
>
> *December 14th:* The British Army on their last excursion to Chester County, plundered a number of the inhabitants of everything they had upon their farms, and abused many old, inoffensive men. Some have applied for redress, but have not obtained it.[23]

Clearly the patience of the peaceful Quakers of Philadelphia was sorely tried—and so was the perseverance of the foot soldiers of the Continental Army, moving northwest, in cold, rain, and snow, in search of winter quarters. Wrote Martin, "Starvation seemed to be entailed upon the army and every animal connected with it. The oxen all died; the horses fared no better. Even the wild animals... suffered. A poor little squirrel who had the ill luck to get cut off from the woods and, fixing himself on a tree standing alone and surrounded by several of the soldiers huts, sat upon the tree till he starved to death and fell off."

In mid-December the Continental Congress ordered a celebration of Thanksgiving. Private Martin observed,

> As the army had all the cause in the world to be particularly thankful, if not for being well off, at least that it was no worse, we were ordered to participate in it. We had nothing to eat for two or three days previous, except what the trees of the fields and forests afforded us. But we must now have what Congress said, a sumptuous Thanksgiving to close the year of high living we had now nearly brought to a close.....To add something extraordinary to our present stock of provisions, our country,

ever mindful of its suffering army opened her sympathizing heart so wide, upon this occasion, as to give us something to make the world stare.... It gave each and every man half a *gill* of rice and a *tablespoon* of vinegar! After we had made sure of this extraordinary superabundant donation, we were ordered out to attend a meeting and hear a sermon delivered upon the happy occasion![24]

The Quaker girl Sally Wister, meanwhile, managed to find some rare entertainment in her wintry exile in Montgomery County. "We had brought some weeks ago a [wooden] British Grenadier from Uncle Mile's on purpose to divert us," she wrote in her journal. "It is remarkably well executed, six feet high, and makes a martial appearance. This we agreed to stand at the door [of our house] that opens into the road."

The figure was so lifelike that a young American, come to visit the girl one evening, mistook the statue for a *real* British soldier and fled into the countryside. "Figure to thyself," wrote Sally, "this young man, of a snowy evening, no hat, shoes down at the heel, hair unty'd, flying across meadows, creeks, and mud holes. Flying from what? Why, a bit of painted wood. But he was ignorant of what it was. The idea of being made a prisoner wholly engrossed his mind, and his last resource was to run."

On December 20 Sally entered a wistful passage in her diary—the last for the year 1777: "General Washington's army have gone into winter quarters at the Valley Forge. We shall not see many of the military now. We shall be very intimate with solitude."[25]

CHAPTER 5

⌐⁀ↄ

From Valley Forge to Savannah

Private Martin did not go home for Christmas. General Washington had ordered his army to march some 20 miles north of Philadelphia, to the junction of the Schuylkill River and Valley Creek, to a thickly wooded slope some two miles long, to set up winter quarters. By the time his soldiers arrived at Valley Forge on December 19, 1777, their ranks had been decreased by 2,000 from hardship and exposure. Only some 8,000 men were fit for duty.

"We were now in a truly forlorn condition," wrote young Martin. "No clothing, no provisions, and as disheartened as need be.... Our prospects were indeed dreary."[1] Two days before Christmas, Washington reported to Congress that there was so little f ood that a "dangerous mutiny" had only barely been averted. The common diet shared that Christmas by both officers and men were "firecakes," made from a paste of flour and water cooked upon hot stones. Washington's troops went hungry because most Pennsylvania farmers preferred to sell to the British in Philadelphia for hard cash rather than to the American army for worthless Continental currency.

In response to the General's appeal for supplies, Congress authorized Washington to commandeer them from the countryside. Private Martin received his orders from the quartermaster general: "We understood that our destiny was to go into the country on a foraging expedition, which was nothing more or less than to procure provisions from the inhabitants for the men in the army and forage for the poor perishing cattle ... at the point of the bayonet."[2]

Martin was well treated by the Quakers he met on his expeditions into the countryside: "I do not remember that during the time I was employed in this business, which was from Christmas to the latter part of April, ever to have met with the least resistance from the inhabitants, take what we would from their barns, mills, corn cribs or stalls.... They would generally ask us into their houses and treat us with as much kindness as though nothing had happened."[3]

The teenager Hugh McDonald from North Carolina had not such a pleasant experience on his sallies out into the countryside: "The settlers around Philadelphia took every opportunity of trading [with the British] which made it necessary to send our guards to prevent this unprecedented commerce.... A gentleman by the name of William McKay would be in our camp one day, and in the British the next day, bringing them...every kind of fresh meats they wanted. He was a spy, and he was hung...near the Forge, in the presence of the whole army. He was the first man I ever saw hung. It so affected me that I could not bear the sight, nor did I eat anything for two days afterwards."[4]

But then there arrived in Valley Forge, on February 23, 1778, a German baron who would restore the morale of the Continental Army. He called himself Lieutenant General Friedrich Rudolf Gerhard Wilhelm Augustin von Steuben, aide-de-camp to King Frederick the Great of Prussia. He arrived in a horse-drawn sleigh, with his Italian greyhound and his 17-year-old French interpreter, Pierre Du Ponceau, by his side. Azor, the baron's dog, was reputed to have an excellent ear for music. "Bad singing set him howling and barking, while he listened with apparent pleasure to a good song," remembered Pierre.[5]

The young Frenchman was deeply impressed by the pitiful condition of the soldiers he saw in their miserable huts at Valley Forge. "They were in want of provisions, of clothes, of fodder for the horses, in short every thing." It would take Steuben a month before he could work a transformation in the attitude and appearance of these ragged troops. He composed a standard drill that he first wrote down in French which would then be translated into English by Du Ponceau. On the parade ground the Baron soon attracted hundreds of soldiers drawn by his ability to curse fluently in three languages—German, French, and English. He made them roar with laughter.

His drill squad was a platoon of picked soldiers—grizzled veterans all—who would then become the drill masters for their own units. As they marched, they mimicked Steuben's guttural accent, "Vun—doo—three—four." In four weeks they learned to maneuver with professional precision. By then, Private Martin had returned from his foraging expeditions to his regiment and was "kept constantly .... engaged in learning [the] new Prussian exercises. It was a continual drill," he remembered.[6] By the time spring arrived and the food supply improved, the Prussian had turned Washington's tattered troops into a professional army.

Washington reviewing the troops at Valley Forge. *Courtesy Dover Pictorial Archives.*

Du Ponceau remembered a memorable dinner, hosted by Steuben, that celebrated the spirit of renewal that infused the camp: "With the Baron's permission, his aids invited a number of young officers to dine at our quarters, on conditions that none should be admitted that had on a whole pair of breeches.... Torn clothes were an indispensable requisite for admission and in this the guests were very sure not to fail.... We feasted sumptuously on tough beef steaks and potatoes with hickory nuts for desert.... Such a set of ragged and, at the same time, merry fellows were never before brought together."[7]

Some officers' wives, including Martha Washington and the wife of General Nathanael Greene, had followed their husbands into the camp at Valley Forge and often met at each other's quarters in the evening over a cup of coffee. "There were no formal soirees," young Pierre remembered, "no dancing, card playing or amusements of any kind except singing.... As I had a tolerable voice, and some knowledge of music, I found myself of consequence in those reunions. I soon learned the favorite English songs, and contributed my share to the pleasures of the company."[8] Azor, von Steuben's greyhound dog, was well disposed to the music he heard.

Some 20 miles south, in British-occupied Philadelphia, the entertainment was more lively. A letter, written in the spring of 1778 by 17-year-old

Rebecca Franks, describes the social scene among the loyalists who often entertained British troops at their homes:

> Dear Nancy: You can have no idea of the life of continued amusement I live in…. I spent Tuesday evening at Sir William Howes, where we had a concert and a dance…. No loss for partners, even I am engaged to dance with seven different gentlemen, for you must know 'tis a fixed rule never to dance but two dances at a time with the same person. Oh, how I wish your papa would let you come in for a week or two…. I know you are as fond of a gay life as myself. You'd have an opportunity of rakeing [having a good time] as much as you choose, either at plays, balls, concerts, or assemblies. I have been but three evenings alone since we moved to town. I begin now to be almost tired…. I must go finish dressing as I'm engaged out to tea. God bless you, Becky F.[9]

The good times for the loyalists in Philadelphia came to an abrupt end in May 1778, when news of the French alliance with the Americans was received at Washington's headquarters. The treaty that had been negotiated by Benjamin Franklin in Paris obligated the French to fight for American independence; in turn, America would be obliged to stand by France if war should occur between France and Great Britain. At Valley Forge the news was greeted with universal joy. Pierre Du Ponceau remembered, "I shall never forget that glorious time…. Rejoicing took place throughout the army, dinners, toasts, songs and whatnot…. Wherever a French officer appeared he met with congratulations and smiles. O that was a delightful time! It bound me forever to the country of my adoption."[10]

There was little rejoicing in Philadelphia, where Sir Henry Clinton succeeded Sir William Howe as chief commander of the British troops. The French Navy would become an imminent threat to the British supply lines that stretched more than 3,000 miles across the Atlantic. Comte d'Estaing's fleet was already approaching America with 12 ships of the line and a squadron of frigates. Clinton decided to evacuate his army by land across New Jersey to strengthen the defense of New York. His ships carried his great guns and some 3,000 Philadelphia Tories who had suddenly become destitute refugees. His troops marched to their embarkation point on the morning of June 18, 1778.

The next day, the Quaker girl Sally Wister wrote two entries in her diary. In the morning of June 19 she scribbled hastily, "We have heard an astonishing piece of news! That the English have entirely left the city!" And in the evening, she wrote, "A horseman has just confirmed the intelligence…. He was in Philadelphia. It is true. They have gone. Past a doubt… may they never, never return." Her journal closes on June 20: "I now think of nothing but returning to Philadelphia."[11]

Young Pierre Du Ponceau rode from Valley Forge to Philadelphia as soon as the British had evacuated the city. He encountered mixed emotions about their departure among the Americans along the way. "As I was riding along," he recalled, "I was met by an old Quaker who was traveling the opposite way, and who, as he passed me, asked me whether I was going into Philadelphia? I answered him affirmatively! 'Ah!' said he 'if uncle Howe was still there, thee would not be going so fast.'"[12]

Very different was the greeting the young Frenchman received from a farmer's wife at whose house he stopped a few miles further on to refresh himself. "She no sooner discovered that I was a native of France than she and her family broke out into the warmest expressions of kindness and gratitude. 'And is it possible,' said she, 'that you have come all this way to fight our battles?' Everything they had to give was offered to me, and no compensation was even thought of. 'Too much could not be done,' she said, 'for our good friends and allies.'"[13]

The fastidious Frenchman found that Philadelphia had been left by the occupying troops in filthy conditions. "Such was the filth of the city that it was impossible for us to drink a comfortable dish of tea that evening. As fast as our cups were filled, myriads of flies took possession of them.... Some said they were Hessian flies, and various other jokes were cracked on the occasion, for the evacuation of the city had put us all in good spirits..."[14]

After a 20-month exile in the countryside, Sally Wister was happy to be back in her native city: "I had the satisfaction of finding my friends in possession of health and tolerable spirits. My heart danced and eyes sparkled at the sight of the companions of my girlish days.... I don't expect anything uncommon will mark my future life, therefore I shall not continue this journal," reads the last entry in her diary.[15]

After leaving Philadelphia, Clinton's forces of some 15,000 men marched over difficult terrain, at some five miles a day, in the direction of New York. On June 20 1778 Washington set his army in motion for the New Jersey hills to waylay their progress. Private Martin was among the troops who crossed the Delaware River, above Trenton, to strike the enemy's advance guard. On June 24, as they approached Princeton, the sun was eclipsed— "in the olden days it would have been considered ominous," Martin wrote, "but we took no note of it."

What was more devastating to him was the sight of what the British had left behind along their route: "Cattle killed and lying about the fields and pastures, some just in the position they were in when shot down, others with a small spot of skin taken off their hind quarters and a mess of steak taken out; household furniture hacked and broken to pieces; wells filled up and mechanics' and farmers' tools destroyed. It was in the height of the season of the cherries; the creatures could not climb the trees for the fruit, but universally cut them down."[16]

It was stifling hot—the temperature was in the mid-90s—and the British and Hessian troops were unaccustomed to such enervating heat. The British had only covered 30 miles in the six days since they had left Philadelphia; the rebels had marched 47 miles since they had left Valley Forge. When Washington held a council of war in his camp on the evening of June 24, he concluded that in three days of rapid marching his troops would cross the path of the main part of the British army.

Early in the morning on June 28, 1778, an American advance force, under the command of General Lee, engaged the lead elements of the British army at the village of Monmouth, near present-day Freehold in New Jersey. The 5,000-man force prepared to attack the British, only to receive orders from Lee to retreat after the first hint of British resistance. Private Martin remembered that "grating as this order was to our feelings, we were obliged to comply."

Falling back three miles, they met General Washington advancing with the rest of his troops, some 7,000 men. Private Martin saw him cross the road near a muddy brook. "I heard him ask our officers by whose orders the troops were retreating, and being answered 'by General Lee'...he then road [sic] on the plain field and took an observation of the advancing enemy." Washington quickly took command and, with four regiments and four guns positioned behind a hedgerow, succeeded in delaying the enemy until a main defense could be formed.

With the midday temperature hovering around 100 degrees, General Clinton attacked Washington's left flank. The American troops launched a counterattack that drove the British back. Private Martin remembered,

> When within about five rods of the rear of the retreating foe, I could distinguish everything about them, they were retreating in line, though in some disorder; I singled out a man and took my aim directly between his shoulders, he was a good mark being a broad-shouldered fellow; what became of him I know not, the fire and smoke hid him from my sight; one thing I know, that is, I took as deliberate aim at him as ever I did at any game in my life. But after all, I hope I did not kill him, although I intended to at the time.[17]

Four more attacks by the British on the American right flank and in the center could not break the rebels' position. At dusk, the British moved behind a ravine, and both armies camped on the battlefield. The exhausted and thirsty Americans dropped down from fatigue. After midnight, Sir Henry Clinton ordered a retreat of the British troops and arrived the next day in Sandy Hook, New Jersey, where Admiral Howe's fleet ferried his army to New York.

At Monmouth the Americans showed that they could fight well using standard (European) infantry and artillery tactics. Baron von Steuben's training at Valley Forge had made them an effective, highly disciplined army. But the real hero of June 28 was not a soldier, but a young woman: 22-year-old Mary Ludwig Hayes, wife of a Pennsylvania artillery private. In midday, at the height of the battle, she had rushed back and forth from a stream with pitchers of cool water for the soldiers who were sweating in the sweltering heat. "Molly Pitcher," as the rebels called her, was a welcome sight.

Private Martin saw her in action among the artillery men: "While in the act of reaching for a cartridge and having one of her feet as far before the other as she could step, a cannon shot from the enemy passed directly between her legs without doing any other damage than carry away all the lower parts of her petticoat. Looking at it with apparent unconcern, she observed that it was lucky it did not pass a little higher, for in that case it might have carried away something else."[18] When her husband fell dead at her feet, she fired his cannon.

Casualties in the Battle of Monmouth were heavy, with about 360 men lost on both sides and a large number dying from sunstroke. Most vulnerable were the Hessians, who were accustomed to the cool summers of central Europe. Clothed in thicker wool and bearing heavier equipment than the Americans, their casualty rate was an appalling one out of three. Only half a dozen "rebels" perished the same way because they were accustomed to the torrid northeast summers and had removed their coats and packets before they went into action.

With the British evacuation of Philadelphia this was the last important military engagement in the North. On July 2, 1778, Congress returned to Philadelphia, with a "firing of Cannon on ye occasion." On July 4, Elizabeth Drinker, mother of five children, whose husband had been imprisoned with other Quakers for his refusal to formally pledge his loyalty to the United States government, wrote in her diary, "A great fuss this evening, it being the Anniversary of Independence, firing of Guns, Sky-Rockets &c. Candles were too scarce and dear to have an illumination which perhaps saved some of our windows."[19]

On that very same day the British colonel Sir John Butler, with some 800 Indian allies, struck at the settlements of the Wyoming Valley along the banks of the Susquehanna, near present-day Wilkes-Barre in northern Pennsylvania. Some 2,000 people, mostly settlers from Connecticut and New York, lived on the fertile farmland along the river. They had sent most of their able-bodied men to fight in Washington's army and could muster only some 300 old men and young boys for their defense. They were ambushed and destroyed. Hundreds perished. Men were burned at the stake or thrown on beds of hot coal and held down with pitchforks.

"The women and children who were enclosed in the stockade distinctly could hear and see this dreadful onset," reported Hector St. John Crevecoeur, an eyewitness to the atrocities. "But now a scene of unexpected humanity ensues," he continued. "Happily these fierce people, satisfied with the death of those who had opposed them in arms, treated the defenseless ones, the women and children, with a degree of humanity almost hitherto unparalleled."[20]

St. John Crevecoeur gives a graphic description of the child refugees:

> Many of these young victims were seen bare-headed, bare-footed, shedding tears at every step, oppressed with fatigue too great for their tender age to bear; afflicted with every species of misery, with hunger, surrounding their mothers as exhausted as themselves.... Here you might see a poor starved horse, as weak and emaciated as themselves.... On it sat a wretched mother with a child at her breast, another on her lap, and two more placed behind her, all broiling in the sun; accompanied ... by the rest of the family creeping along.... Such was the mournful procession, which for a number of weeks announced to the country, through which they passed, the sad disaster which had befallen them.[21]

There was one story among the many sad ones surrounding the Wyoming Massacre that had a happy ending. The Slocums, a Quaker family who had been known for their kindness to Indians, had remained unharmed during the first assault in July. But their oldest son had fought in the defense of the settlers, and some Indians returned in the fall to kidnap their youngest daughter, Frances. Fifty-nine years after her capture, her surviving brother and sister learned from an Indian agent that Frances was alive in Ohio and had told the agent that her name was Slocum, that her father was a Quaker, and that she had been taken from the Susquehanna River when she was very young. Her siblings promptly traveled to Ohio and identified her by a mark of recognition that was only known to them: a crushed bone and missing nail on one of the fingers of her left hand.

She told them the story of her life: "The Indians when they took me from the house," she said, "went to a rocky cave in the mountains. They were Delawares. The next morning they departed for Indian country.... I was kindly treated and ... adopted in an Indian family and brought up as their daughter.... I was taught the use of bow and arrow ... and to ride on horseback. When I grew to womanhood, both of my Indian parents died, and I soon afterward married a young chief and moved to the Ohio frontier.... My husband died, and my people have joined the Miamis, I ... married one of that tribe. I have children and grandchildren, and I am very happy."[22]

Washington's troops had been unable to come to the rescue of the settlers in Wyoming Valley. After the Battle of Monmouth, he had given his army a day of rest. Next, he marched his soldiers to New York State, moving them about 10 miles each day until the July heat compelled them to halt. They rested for a few days on the banks of the Raritan River, opposite New Brunswick, and then crossed the Hudson to join General Gates at White Plains, New York. Here Washington established himself in a defensive position.

Private Martin and some of his comrades who had been in the Battle of White Plains in 1776 revisited the ground where they had been engaged with the British two years earlier. "We saw a number of the graves of those who fell in that battle," he wrote. "Some of the bodies had been so slightly buried that the dogs or hogs, or both, had dug them out of the ground.... Here were Hessian skulls as thick as a bomb shell—poor fellows! They were left unburied in a foreign land—they had, perhaps, no near and dear friends to lament their sad destiny as the Americans who lay buried near them."[23]

But pity toward the enemy had its limits. Martin, who had been transferred to a light infantry regiment, reported on an encounter with a group of Hessian horsemen near White Plains in July 1778. Seeing a wounded enemy lying in the road and in danger of being trodden upon by the horses, one of the Americans took pity on him. He put him on his shoulders and staggered off with his load in order to get him to safety. While crossing a rickety bridge over a muddy brook, he jostled the fellow more than usual.

The Hessian cried out, "Good rebel, don't hurt poor Husliman." "Who do you call a rebel, you scoundrel?" said the American and tossed him off his shoulders as though he had been a log of wood. The wounded man fell with his head into the mud, and when Private Martin passed by, he saw him struggling for life. "But I had other business on my hands to stop to assist him," wrote Martin. "I did sincerely pity the poor mortal, but pity him was all I could then do. What became of him after I saw him in the mud, I never knew."[24]

All of Washington's resources were at that moment directed toward recovering Newport, Rhode Island, from the British. Some 10,000 of his soldiers had marched north of the port city to rendezvous with some 4,000 French soldiers that had been brought in on d'Estaing's ships. The city inhabitants braced themselves for a confrontation. Mary Gould Almy, mother of six children, captured their mood during the siege of Newport in her diary[25]:

August 1: All the fleet in motion, everything in consternation; the inhabitants much distressed; the batteries all spirited; all warlike preparation ... by night they were so ready that the foolhardy would wish for nothing more than a movement of the French fleet into the harbor.

August 2: The day passed on with stillness; every person conjectured the meaning of the ships going up the river was to cover the landing of the troops, which we could see had gathered.

August 3: The whole town is in some great confusion…. Every man ordered to be in readiness, the American troops were landing at Howland's Ferry…. When I look over the list of my friends on both sides of the question, my heart shudders at the thought, what numbers must be slain, both so obstinate and determined.

August 4: The French ships before the harbor, the French ships up the river; all riding it out with colors flying.

August 5: The three large French ships up the river made sail, the others at the mouth of the harbor made signals of unmooring …. They ran as near the land as possible …

August 6: All terrified with apprehension … the sound of a cannon most distressing to women and children…. The wretched inhabitants—how are they hurt by every party.

August 7: A solemn silence reigns…. What preparations could I make, had I been endowed with as much presence of mind as every woman was; six children hanging around me, the little girls crying out. "Mamma, will they kill us?" The boys endeavor to put on an air of manliness …. I was roused by a violent firing, I call out for my children to run; we sally forth into the street; there was a scene, men women and children, all in as great consternation as myself, which sight brought me to myself. I directly order my little ones to make the best of their way along, each with a large bundle …. By this time, the ships fired continually, the women shrieking, the children falling down, crying…. The boys had Billy in their arms; the others had such heavy bundles, my heart ached for them…. The largest ship came around [the Point] and gave such a broadside, as I really thought would have sent us to another world. There we all lay flat in a hollow …

August 8: The morning gun of the French admiral had frightened me to death …. Where to fly for shelter? The cellar was determined on…. Cousin's C. 's cherry rum being brought, I grew more and more enabled to bear my sorrows …

August 9: About ten o'clock [William] came to tell me a fleet in sight; it must be Lord Howe. Nothing more transpired during the day …. Various conjectures, everybody turns politician forming and planning schemes for Lord Howe …

August 10: Great expectations from this day; about eight o'clock the French fleet all drew up in a line of battle …. What Count d'Estaing thought, Heavens knows, for his haste was great. He cut all his cables and came firing through the harbor, as if the very Devil was in him, and our batteries returned his favors with a vengeance; one half the town went … to see a grand sea fight, but returned exceedingly disappointed in a few hours…. Lord Howe's strength was not sufficient to cope with such a fleet…. I contented myself down in the cellar till the heaviest firing was over.

August 11: This morning a violent storm came on, before day, and continued thundering and lightening most terribly all day ...

On the night of August 11 the ships of both fleets were scattered by
the storm and both had to sail away for repairs—Howe to New York
and d'Estaing to Boston. A few days later, five-year-old Mary Palmer
Tyler witnessed the appearance of a barge, crowded with officers wearing
cocked hats and shining epaulettes, coming around a point of land below
her home at Germantown, near Boston. "We were clinging to mother in
great terror," she remembered. "But soon she quieted our fears by the
assurance that ... they were our dear friends.... who had come all the way
from France in great ships to help us fight the British ..."[26]

Three months later, Walter Butler, son of Sir John Butler, assisted by
the Indian chief Thayendanega—known as Joseph Brant—struck at the
frontier settlement of Cherry Valley in western New York. Most of its
inhabitants, including women and children, were killed or captured, and
their houses were put to the torch. In revenge, Washington ordered General Sullivan to conduct a campaign of destruction that would devastate
the farms and orchards of the Iroquois the following spring.

After having ravaged the American frontier, the British moved south.
Late in 1778, Clinton sent about 3,500 regulars and Tories against
Savannah. Among the troops that sailed from New York harbor in mid-
November was the Hessian grenadier Johannes Reuber, who had rejoined
his regiment in a prisoner exchange after 22 months of captivity.

On December 13 Reuber noted in his diary, "There arose a whirlwind
that made the sea very restless and our ship was tossed about." A week
later, the British and Hessian troops finally spotted a lighthouse on the
shore, and on December 21 they sailed into the Savannah harbor. Two
days after Christmas, they raised the British flag and prepared to attack.
They were heavily fired upon by the local militia defenders as they sailed
up the river to the center of the city.

On December 29 Reuber wrote, "We Hessians and British landed, and
the city of Savannah was at once surrounded and stormed from three sides.
The two Hessian regiments made the first assault from the water front.
Three regiments of English [soldiers], three regiments of Green Rangers
and a regiment of Scots made the second and third assault .... We captured
a great amount of booty in Savannah from the province of Georgia....
There was a large amount of indigo, rice and a supply of salt ..."[27]

One of the loyalists who returned to Savannah with a regiment of
New York volunteers was a native of Georgia, the father of 14-year-old
Elizabeth Lichtenstein. The young girl, who had lost her mother at age
10, was in the care of an aunt on a nearby plantation. An avid reader and
diarist, she kept a record of the events surrounding the fall of the city.

"The town was taken without loss [on December 29]," she wrote, "though the Americans as they retreated fired on the 71st Regiment of the Highlanders, without attempting a regular stand. This exposed the inhabitants to the fury of the British soldiers.... In consequence, before the officers could have time to stop them, they committed much outrage, ripped open feather beds, destroyed the public papers and records, and scattered everything about in the streets."[28]

Her father, who was with the conquering British troops, sent a passport to his daughter and her aunt to come to town. "Having to stop within a mile of Savannah that the Hessian officer on duty there should examine our pass, I was dreadfully frightened," the girl confessed. "He soon allowed us to go on; and what a sight did the streets present of feathers and papers! The meeting with my father I scarce need add was joyful!"[29]

Up north, both Washington and Clinton had gone into winter quarters. The British remained in and around New York. Washington's main army returned to New Jersey; the Connecticut and New Hampshire troops went to the western part of Connecticut. Private Martin and his comrades arrived at Reading at Christmastime and began to build huts for their winter quarters. Down south, in Savannah, Grenadier Reuber entered his barracks on garrison duty.

"Now the old year has flown away and—with God—we begin again a new year," he wrote in his diary on January 1, 1779.[30]

CHAPTER 6

ঔ৯০

From Savannah to King's Mountain

By 1779, a stalemate had developed in the North. After two and a half years of fighting, both armies were back where they began. Private Martin and his light infantry regiment would spend most of the year marching through Connecticut and along the Hudson Valley, while his commanders were trying to guess where the enemy would strike next. In February 1779 Martin obtained a furlough of 15 days to see his folks—an event he considered the highlight of the year. He had not seen his family since he had reenlisted in the Continental Army in April 1777.

"I prepared for the journey, which was about thirty miles, and started from the camp about nine o'clock in the morning, intending to go the whole distance," he wrote. "I had not a mouthful to eat or carry with me. I had ... two or three shillings of old Continental money, worth about as much as its weight in rags.... I believe the old people were glad to see me.... I was glad to see them and all my other friends."[1]

After Martin returned to camp, his unit was sent to New London to guard the fortifications. They stayed there until the first of May. Then his regiment was sent to dislodge the British from the Hudson River forts at Verplanck's Point and Stony Point—without success. Eventually, Martin and his comrades settled down just below West Point, at the eastern side of the river. Clinton tried to lure Washington out of his new headquarters, but Washington refused to budge. In the fall the British evacuated the two forts on the Hudson River. Clinton sent their garrisons south to help defend Savannah against the French. Washington had waited in vain for the arrival of d'Estaing's fleet to help him capture New York. The count wanted to seize Savannah.

On September 12, 1779, about 3,500 French soldiers came up the Savannah River and landed south of town. First, Count d'Estaing tried to take Savannah by summons. Grenadier Reuber and his regiment had just returned to the city after seizing an American ship near Stono Ferry and recapturing the cannons and flags the Hessians had lost at Trenton. Reuber recorded the British response to the call for surrender in his diary: "The English Field Marshall Prevost requested 24 hours to consider the demand, and during the night the rest of the English army...arrived at Savannah because they were able to pass the French Fleet in the harbor. [Then] General Prevost gave his answer to the Count with a 26-pound cannon shot, which was the same as replying that if you want something you will have to win it with the sword."[2]

On October 3, 50 guns on land and those of three ships in the river began battering the city. Fifteen-year-old Elizabeth Lichtenstein observed, "The streets being sandy and not paved, the shells fell and made great holes in the sand, which often put out the fuse and prevented explosion. The colored children got so used to the shells, that they would run and cover them with sand, and as we were rather scarce of ammunition they would often pick up the spent balls and sell them for seven-pence apiece."[3]

Early in the morning of October 9, when Count d'Estaing and the American General Lincoln sent the main body of the French and American troops hurling against Savannah's defenses, the British and the Hessians greeted them with a hail of rifle fire and artillery shots. "Alas, every heart in our barn [where I was with fifty-eight women and children] was aching, every eye in tears!" wrote Elizabeth. "When they sent their flag to offer terms...the answer the Count received was laconic, 'The King...pays these men to fight, and they must fight, and we decline your terms.' "[4]

Instead, the two sides settled for an armistice to bury their dead. Stunned by losses of about 250 dead and 600 wounded, Count d'Estaing reembarked his troops and sailed away. When Elizabeth Lichtenstein left the shelter of her barn and went into town, it offered "a desolate view." "The streets were cut into deep holes by the shells," wrote the young girl, "and the houses were riddled with the rain of cannon balls. Winter was now approaching, and many houses were not habitable."[5]

Up north, Washington and his troops entered their winter quarters at Morristown. "We arrived on our wintering ground in the latter part of the month of December," wrote Private Martin, "and once more, like wild animals, began to make preparations to build us a 'city for habitation'.... Let it be recollected that this was ... 'the hard winter,' and hard it was to the poor soldiers."[6]

Howling blizzards blew into Morristown. Often, the soldiers of the Continental Army were buried beneath deep drifts of snow after the wind had blown their tents away. "We have never experienced a like extremity at any period of the war," Washington wrote. Meanwhile, his opponent, Sir Henry Clinton, decided on an all-out attempt to conquer the South. He would use Savannah and eastern Georgia as a base to conquer the Carolinas and Virginia. First, he aimed to capture the great port of Charleston. Washington's army, now in New Jersey, was too far away to make a winter's march to South Carolina.

Clinton set sail from New York on December 26, 1779, with a fleet of 90 transport ships carrying 8,500 soldiers—eight British, five Hessian, and five Tory regiments—plus detachments of artillery and cavalry. Among the troops was a young diarist, Johann Valentin Asteroth, a chaplain's assistant, whose duty was to instruct the children of the Hessian soldiers in reading and religion. On December 28 he wrote, "Our ship tilted first to one side, and then the other, lurched forward and backward, and was soon almost totally swallowed by a giant wave. We all lay in our beds in the dark, holding on to whatever we could ... and cursed our fate." On New Year's Day, there was some relief in sight. "The morning of January 1, was quite pleasant and we spent some time on deck. But after sunset on January 2, another storm front arose, and our ship was separated from the rest of the fleet."[7]

It would take them 10 days to rejoin the fleet. In mid-January 1780, nearly half of the transport ships were still missing. (One ship loaded with Hessians was driven all the way across the Atlantic, landing at Cornwall on the coast of England!) It was a full month before the last of the dispersed ships arrived in the bay at the mouth of the Savannah River. Here the damaged ships were repaired and replenished and then changed course to sail north for Charleston.

On February 11 the British anchored at Johns Island, at the south side of Charleston harbor, and embarked two days later. The young German diarist marveled at the "foreign" vegetation that surrounded him: "There were pineapple trees which are exotic looking; and also orange and mulberry trees. Most of the trees were covered with moss ... which we used to cover our huts and as straw for our bedding. The horses liked it very much which suited us since we could use it for fodder instead of hay."[8]

Charleston lies at the narrow end of a peninsula formed by the Ashley River on the west and the Cooper River on the east. The two rivers converge at the tip of the peninsula to flow into Charleston harbor. At the time the British arrived the two forts that constituted the harbor defense had fallen into disrepair. Charleston was also vulnerable on the landside, where it was connected to the mainland by a narrow isthmus called the Neck. A besieging force could simply blockade the harbor, seize the Neck, and then advance on the city. The British proceeded to do just that. Clinton sent part of his fleet to blockade the harbor and then erected artillery batteries on the east bank of the Ashley River.

Meanwhile, in Charleston, morale among the defending militia was low. An epidemic of smallpox had broken out. Because the militias were irregular soldiers, serving when called upon to fight close to home, they had missed out on the mass inoculations that protected regular Continental troops. Many refused to come from the countryside for the city's defense, declaring that "they dreaded that disorder more than the enemy."[9]

Samuel Baldwin, a young schoolteacher from Charleston, kept an anxious eye on the siege of his hometown. On March 20 he reported that "the English ships came over the bar [through the channel] without meeting with any accidents. The naval force of the enemy was now become so superior that it was thought that our ships could not...withstand them." On March 24 he noted, "This day the term of service of the greater part of the North Carolina militia being expired, they marched homewards in the evening.... Very generous offers were made to induce them to stay longer, but to no avail."[10]

On March 29 Clinton's guns and troops were safely in place on the peninsula. "We were surprised to hear of their being on the Neck advancing towards town at no more than three miles distance," wrote Baldwin in his diary the next day. "There was some considerable skirmish afterwards." A week afterward, Charleston suffered its first serious bombardment from the sea.

"The shots from the gallies struck in different parts of the town," reported Baldwin. "A ball went into a kitchen...and fell...into the next yard upon a poor cat whom it cut into two parts.... A man was struck as he stood at his door and...there were two or three horses also killed."[11]

On April 7 Charleston received a much hoped for reinforcement from Virginia and North Carolina. "Thirteen guns were fired soon after [their arrival]...and huzzas echoed along the lines from Cooper to Ashley. This evening the bells have been ringing," observed the young diarist. But the next afternoon brought a shock to the young schoolteacher: "About four o'clock the enemy's ships got under way, and a little after five, they all anchored in the harbor.... Fort Moultrie [on Sullivan Island] fired upon them with all possible spirit as they sailed by successively, but with the advantage of a fine wind and a strong flood they passed without receiving much damage."[12]

The British fleet had now sealed off the city by sea. On April 10, in the evening, Clinton sent a messenger with a white flag to General Lincoln, demanding a surrender. "Both duty and inclination lead me to defend the town to the last extremity," was the reply of the American commander, who had less than half as many troops as his enemy. The next morning, the British began a cannonade that lasted all day. "The houses... have received a good deal of injury from the cannon balls," wrote Baldwin. "A nurse and a young child that was in her arms were both killed by a ball. Another woman and two or three soldiers were also killed."[13] The Americans held out as long as they could. But after a month-long siege, culminating in a night of incessant shelling on May 9–10, they surrendered.

On May 12, 1780, in the morning, the Continentals marched out with colors ceased. Three British regiments and two companies of Hessian grenadiers moved in to occupy the city. The militia were allowed to go back to their homes, the 5,500 Continental soldiers who had defended Charleston were imprisoned—and so was Samuel Baldwin, the young diarist. He was ordered to take the oath of allegiance to Great Britain or "to retire into the country." Baldwin refused and left his hometown, only to return three years later to take up teaching again.

Among the occupying troops in Charleston was the chaplain's assistant, Johann Valentin Asteroth, who started his own school for the children of the soldiers garrisoned in the city. He first gave reading lessons to four eager boys—one a regimental drummer—who came each morning from 8:00 to 11:00 A.M. to his room. As the number of his students grew, he moved next door to a Quaker meeting house, where he received permission to use a room with small benches, suitable for children. Among his pupils were ten Hessian boys, two American children from the city of Charleston, and one little girl—Henriette Schnackin. He tells us in his diary that they all were hard-working students and that he taught them "with much happiness."[14]

They must have been among the lucky youngsters who escaped the ravages of the smallpox. That dreaded illness took a turn for the worse when the British went inland to "pacify" the Carolina backcountry. Always the most susceptible, children fell sick in growing numbers, and the virulence of smallpox increased as summer set in. It also spread among the Americans held aboard the prison ships in Charleston harbor. Andrew Jackson's mother, who went to nurse relatives and neighbors on board ship, died, and so did her son, Robert.[15]

During the British occupation General Clinton adopted a conciliatory policy of granting pardons and paroles, but his underlings did little to assuage the spirit of mutual hatred in South Carolina. In a series of letters to her girlfriend, Eliza Wilkinson, a young widow who had lost her son in infancy, documented life in and around occupied Charleston during a period when she grew to fear the British:

> Now comes the day of terror—the 3rd of June (I shall never love the anniversary of that day).... A Negro girl ran in exclaiming "O the king's people are coming; it must be them for they are all in red.... I had no time for thought—they were up to the house—entered with drawn swords and pistols in their hands; indeed, they rushed in, in the most furious manner, crying out, "Where 're these women rebels?" They then began to plunder the house of everything they thought valuable or worth taking; our trunks were split to pieces, and each mean, pitiful wretch crammed his bosom with the contents.... After bundling all their booty, they mounted their horses.[16]

And in a second letter, she wrote,

> It was likewise on the 3rd of June when they ran into [my father's] house with drawn swords and pistols...searched his pockets and took all they found there.... They then went into the rooms up and down stairs, demolished two sets of drawers, and took all they could conveniently carry off. One came to search Mother's pockets, too.... They even took her two little children's caps.... "Why," said Mother, "I suppose you think you are doing your king a great piece of service by these actions; but you are mistaken—'twill only enrage the people; I think you'd much better go and fight the men, than going about the country robbing helpless women and children."[17]

James P. Collins, age 16, observed a similar pattern of destructiveness among the Tories at the border of South and North Carolina. "Women were insulted," he wrote in his autobiography, "and stripped of every particle of decent clothing they might have on, and every article of bedding, clothing or furniture was taken—knives, forks, dishes, spoons, everything that could be carried off.... They even entered houses where men lay sick of the smallpox, that they knew were opposed to them, dragged them out of their sick beds into the yard and put them to death, in cold blood, in the presence of their wives and children."[18]

But slowly, the scales that had tipped in favor of the British in the spring were beginning to right themselves in the late summer and early fall. Even though they held the coastal cities of Charleston and Savannah, the Redcoats were not trained in guerrilla warfare, which would soon become the predominant style of fighting. The British army was also spread dangerously thin and was decimated by yellow fever and malaria during the long mosquito season.

October 7, 1780, became a turning point in the war in the South. That day, Patrick Ferguson, a British major, and his loyalist militia went down in a surprising defeat at King's Mountain, near the North Carolina border. James Collins was among the American frontiersman who refused

Sergeants Jasper and Newton Rescuing American Prisoners from the British. Painting by John Blake White. *Courtesy U.S. Senate Collection.*

to give quarter to their loyalist foes. "Everything was at stake," wrote the boy, "life, liberty, property, and even the fate of wife, children and friends, seemed to depend on the outcome; death or victory was the only way to escape suffering."[19]

Thomas Young, another 16-year-old who was in that battle, remembered, "Major Ferguson had taken a very strong position upon the summit of the mountain, and it appeared like an impossibility to dislodge him, but we had come there to do it, and we were determined, *one and all*, to do it, or die trying."[20]

After four unsuccessful attempts to scale the rocky, treeless, 60-foot rise, four columns of Americans succeeded in their surprise attack and remained in possession of the hilltop. The enemy was hemmed in on all sides, with no chance of escaping. Ferguson died in the melee. The Battle of King's Mountain lasted only an hour. By the time it was over, the Americans had captured some 700 loyalists and killed and wounded hundreds more. "Awful indeed was the scene of the wounded, the dying and the dead on the field, after the carnage of that dreadful day," remembered Thomas Young.[21]

James Collins had pity on the survivors: "Next morning... the scene became really distressing. The wives and children of the poor Tories came in, in great numbers. Their husbands, fathers, and brothers, lay dead in heaps ... a melancholy sight indeed! While numbers of the survivors were doomed to abide the sentence of a court martial, and several were actually hanged.... We proceeded to bury the dead.... yet not so as to secure them from becoming a prey to the beast of the forests, or the vultures of the air.... I saw myself, in passing the place, a few weeks after, all parts of the human frame, lying scattered in every direction."[22]

The Battle of King's Mountain had shifted the balance in favor of the Americans against the loyalists. "After the results of the battle was known," wrote Collins, "we seemed to gather strength, for many that before lay neutral through fear ... shouldered their guns, and fell in the ranks; some of them making good soldiers." A week later, when the "fighting Quaker," General Nathanael Greene, took command of the Southern Department at the request of Washington, the Continental forces had seized the initiative.

Meanwhile, up north, Joseph Martin's circumstances had considerably improved. He had been appointed sergeant in the Corps of Sappers and Miners, the equivalent of today's Corps of Engineers. It consisted of three companies, led by officers who were knowledgeable in the sciences, and young men who were skilled in building fortifications. Sergeant Martin considered it an honor to become part of the Corps, although he had some doubts whether he was altogether qualified for the appointment. His regiment was stationed near King's Ferry on the Hudson River. "We had constantly to be on the lookout, but never happened to come in contact with the enemy," he remembered.

In the latter part of October his company was assigned to build winter quarters at West Point. "We had to go six miles down the river, and there hew the timber, then carry it on our shoulders, to the river, and then raft it to West Point," remembered Martin. "We were living in the old barracks, where there were rats enough, had they been men, to garrison twenty West Points.... By New Year's Day [the new barracks] were ready to receive us, and we safely stowed away in them."[23]

CHAPTER 7

❧

From Richmond to Yorktown

As he considered his prospects for returning home in 1781, Sergeant Martin saw "no likelihood that the war would ever end." People everywhere were weary of a conflict that had dragged on for six miserable years. The British still controlled the major ports along the Atlantic coast—from New York City in the North to Charleston and Savannah in the South—and Nathanael Greene, the newly appointed commander of the "Grand Army of the Southern Department of the United States of America," could count on only some 2,500 men to fight the enemy. Half were members of the Continental Army; the rest were local militia. Few were properly clothed and equipped. As Greene proceeded south through Maryland, Delaware, Virginia, and North Carolina, his appeals for clothing and arms for his men and for forage for their horses produced little "effectual aid."

On January 6, 1781, the British made a foray into Richmond. Thomas Jefferson, then governor of Virginia, escaped into the mountains on his faithful horse Caractacus. Five-year-old Isaac, one of Jefferson's slaves, later gave an account of what he saw when the British arrived: "There was a monstrous hollering and screaming of women and children.... The British was dressed in red. They formed a line and marched up to the Palace with drums beating, it was an awful sight; seemed like the day of judgement was come.... When the British come in, an officer rode up and asked 'Whar is the Governor?' Isaac's father told him: 'He's gone to the mountains.' The officer asked: 'Whar is the keys to the house?' Isaac's father gave him the keys.... The officer said 'Whar is the silver?' Isaac's father told him, 'It was all sent up to the mountains.'"

Isaac's story continues,

> The British searched the house but didn't disturb none of the furniture;
> but they plundered the wine cellar.... The bottles they broke the necks
> off with their swords, drank some, threw the rest away.... The British next
> went to the corn crib and took all the corn out, strewed it in a line along
> the street...and brought their horses and fed them on it.... While they
> were plundering they took all the meat out of the meat house; cut it up;
> laid it out in parcels; every man took his ration and put it in his knapsack....
> One of the officers came on a horse and ordered us all to go with them....
> There was about a dozen wagons along.... four horses to a wagon...every
> wagon guarded by ten men marching alongside. One of the officers give
> Isaac name Sambo; all the time feeding him, put a cocked hat on his head
> and a red coat on him and all laughed. Coat, a monstrous big thing; when
> Isaac was in it couldn't see nothin of it but the sleeves dangling down.[1]

The British brought Jefferson's slaves to Yorktown [Little York].
"They treated us mighty well," remembered Isaac, "give us plenty of
fresh meat and wheat bread. It was very sickly at York; great many colored people died there [from small pox], but none of Mr. Jefferson's
folks." [2]

On the morning of January 17, 1781, the British had their comeup-
pance. Two small armies—the British under the command of Banastre
Tarleton, the American under the command of David Morgan—met in
a place of sandy hills at the North–South Carolina border where cattle
roamed in open cow pens. Two 16-year-olds, James P. Collins and Thomas
Young, who had fought together at the Battle of King's Mountain, left
us eyewitness accounts of the encounter in which the Americans would
score a dramatic victory.

"We were very anxious for battle," remembered young Thomas. "Two
companies of volunteers were called for.... I attached myself to Major
Jolly's company.... General Morgan...went among the volunteers, helped
them fix their swords, joked with them about their sweethearts, told them
to keep in good spirits. 'Just hold up your heads, boys,' he would say,
'and you are free, and then when you return to your homes, how the old
folks will bless you, and the girls will kiss you....'" [3]

By sunrise, Morgan had placed 150 riflemen on the edge of the woods
out of which the British were to appear. Their mission was to fire two shots
each, then to retreat. They were to regroup at the first crest of a slope that
rose above the grazing fields, where some 300 militia had assembled. When
the British were within 50 paces, the militia would fire again, especially
aiming at officers and sergeants. When the Redcoats readied themselves
for a bayonet charge, the militia would move behind a ravine, near the top
of a hill, where another 400 troops were assembled. About 125 American
cavalrymen remained a half mile to the rear, behind another hill.

James Collins was among the main body of the militia that fended off the British bayonet attack. "In a few moments our cavalry was among them like a whirlwind," he remembered. "The shock was so sudden and violent that they could not stand it, and immediately betook themselves to flight.... They began to throw down their arms, and surrender themselves prisoners of war.... After the fight was over, the sight was truly melancholy. The dead on the side of the British exceeded the number of those killed at the battle of King's Mountain.... That day I fired my little rifle five times, whether with any effect or not, I do not know."[4]

Tarleton's defeat was nearly total: Nine-tenths of his force had been killed or captured against only 12 Americans killed and 60 wounded. American morale rose dramatically, and large numbers of local militia rallied to the American cause. Among them was a 14-year-old farm boy who rode out in the spring of 1781 with Colonel Davie's regiment to fight the British in the Waxhaw District of South Carolina. His name was Andrew Jackson.

He was captured in April 1781 and confined to a pox-ridden jail in Camden. His memories of prison time were grim. "No attention was paid to the wounds or the comfort of the prisoners," he later wrote, "and the small pox having broken out among them, for want of proper care, many fell victims to it. I frequently heard them groaning in the agonies of death."[5]

Andrew Jackson, brave boy of the Waxhaw. *Courtesy North Carolina State Archives.*

When Andrew and his ailing brother were finally exchanged, he walked barefoot back to his home. In quick succession his brother and all his remaining family members succumbed to the illness, and he became an orphan. Decades later, when he had become the seventh President of the United States, he would still recollect with fury the pain and sorrow that the war had inflicted on his kinfolk.

During the spring and summer the British suffered a series of defeats by American guerilla forces. Nathanael Greene proved himself to be a master of unconventional warfare, but the British greatly outnumbered his army, and the Southern countryside was still full of loyalists. In the summer Greene had settled his troops near the Broad River in South Carolina. He needed a messenger to take a letter requesting reinforcements for his troops to General Sumter, who was camped some 100 miles away by the Wateree River.

When he asked for a volunteer who knew the countryside, 16-year-old Emily Geiger, daughter of a local German planter and owner of a spirited horse, offered her services. Greene wrote out a message to Sumter and Emily memorized it. Then she took off. The first day and night of her ride was uneventful. But on the second day, when she was riding through an open dry swamp, she was confronted by a Tory scout with a gleaming bayonet. She was taken prisoner and led to a farm house nearby. The British sent for a neighbor woman and her teenage daughter to search young Emily. She had to undress, and every inch of her clothing was turned inside out. No incriminating message was found.

The British let Emily go on her way "to visit some friend." It took her an extra day to reach General Sumter's camp. She recited to him the message she had memorized. She also described her encounter with the Tory scouts. "I have only one question," said General Sumter. "When you were alone in the room, what did you do with the letter?" "I ate it," replied Emily.[6] General Sumter gave orders to his troops to break camp and join up with Greene's soldiers. When the British discovered that reinforcements for the Continental Army were on their way, they retreated.

Lord Cornwallis and his soldiers had spent the summer of 1781 in Virginia. When he reached Williamsburg, he received a directive from his superior, General Clinton, to establish defensive positions near the Chesapeake Bay. Cornwallis choose Yorktown, placing some of his troops across the York River at Gloucester. By mid-August he was fully established in his new headquarters.

On August 14 George Washington, who was still in New York, received a message from the French Admiral Comte de Grasse, who informed him that he was en route to the Chesapeake Bay with 29 warships carrying three regiments of 3,000 men, plus 100 dragoons and 100 artillerists with 10 field pieces, siege cannons, and mortars. Cornwallis had barely settled in when the French fleet arrived off the Virginia coast on August 26 and began landing troops. Two weeks later, French ships slipped into Chesapeake Bay. The outmaneuvered British fleet sailed off to New York, leaving Cornwallis without a navy and in a difficult spot.

Because of the coastal location of Yorktown, a general evacuation of its residents had begun years earlier. When the British arrived in 1781, only about 400 civilians had remained in the once thriving seaport. Among them was 16-year-old Mildred Smith, who wrote to her friend Betsy Ambler, age 15: "When you left our dear little town, I felt as if every ray of comfort fled. Oh, my dearest loved Betsy, (now what would I give if you had a name a little more romantic!) how shall I exist without you? Life seems a dreary waste since deprived of your loved society."[7]

A concerned Betsy replied from Richmond, "I have just received yours of last night.... Oh, my dearest girl, I tremble for your safety. Where were you hid when the enemy passed your door? How dreadful the idea of an enemy passing through such a country as ours, committing enormities that fill the mind with horror... without meeting one impediment to discourage them!"[8]

But the impediments to discourage the enemy were on the way: Leaving half his army, mostly militia, on the Hudson River, Washington took the other half and Rochambeau's French force from Newport, Rhode Island, to Virginia. As Washington's army traveled overland through New Jersey, it picked up ammunition and other military stores in Philadelphia and went by boat down the Delaware River for about 10 miles in a schooner that had her hold full of gunpowder. Then the artillery was hauled overland 12 miles to Head of Elk, Maryland, on the upper part of Chesapeake Bay.

At Elk Landing the army contracted for 64 civilian ships to take the troops to Virginia. Although the journey took 18 days, the water route was much faster than an overland march. Sergeant Martin of the Corps of Sappers and Miners was on a small schooner, called the *Birmingham*. Also aboard were six officers and a commissary who had in his keeping a small store of provisions and a hogshead of rum, which the officers had placed in a cabin, walled off by a bulkhead. But the soldiers contrived to loosen one of the boards at the lower end. "While the officers in the cabin thought they were the sole possessors of its content," wrote Martin, "the soldiers in the hold had possession of at least as good a share as themselves."[9]

Their "mosquito fleet" passed down the bay to Annapolis and in sight of the French fleet, lying in Lynnhaven Bay. "They resembled a swamp of dry pine trees," remembered Martin. The Americans landed at Burwell's ferry, on the James River side of the peninsula, and marched to Williamsburg, where they joined General Lafayette and his troops. "We prepared to move down and pay our old acquaintances, the British, a visit," mused Martin. "I doubt not that their wish was not to have so many of us come at once, as their accommodations were rather scanty. They thought, 'The fewer, the better the cheer.' We thought, 'The more, the merrier.'"[10]

The teenager Ebenezer Denny from Pennsylvania kept a journal of the preparations for the Yorktown campaign:

> *September 14th:* General Washington arrived (he had come overland); our brigade was paraded to receive him; he rode along the line—Army in high spirits.
>
> *September 15th:* Officers all pay their respects to the Commander-in-Chief…. He stands in the door, takes every man by the hand—the officers all pass in, receiving his salute and shake. This is the first time I had seen the General…. The presence of so many officers, and the arrival of a new corps seem to give additional life to everything. In all directions troops seen exercising and maneuvering…. The guards attend the grand parade at an early hour, where Baron von Steuben is always found waiting with one or two aides on horseback.
>
> *September 25th:* Joined by the last of the troops from the east. French encamped a few miles on the right; busy in getting cannon and military stores from aboard the vessels.
>
> *September 28th:* The whole army moved in three divisions toward the enemy who were strongly posted at York. …. We changed ground and took a position within one mile of York on a high sandy plain, on a deep navigable river of the same name. Americans on the right; French on the left, extending on both sides of the river; preparations for a siege. This business reminds me of a play among the boys, called Prison-base.[11]

As the Americans' heavy siege artillery began moving over the sandy roads to Yorktown, the British withdrew their most vulnerable outposts. Cornwallis brought in cannons and sailors from the few ships on the York River to strengthen his positions. But his defensive perimeter around Yorktown was too long to be manned adequately by his limited number of troops.

John Hudson, at age 13 one of the youngest members of the New York Regiment, recalled his first day and night of the siege:

> We left the camp a short time before sundown…. The night approaching when we were halted, every man was directed to sit down, and neither to talk nor leave his place. As I had been sick throughout that day, and had, like the rest, my knapsack on my back, I laid my cartridge box under my head, and with my musket in my arms, soon fell asleep…. A sudden and violent rain came on, falling in torrents, which failed, however, to wake me. In the course of the night…the non-commissioned officers came along the ranks, and without saying a word, woke us all and got us to our feet. I rose up with the rain dripping from my clothes. We were directed to…put the right hand on the shoulder of our file leader, marching in two ranks…nothing was visible—no man being able to even see his comrade.

We finally halted, and every man had a spade put into his hands. Shortly afterwards... a party of men with *gabions* [baskets] came along.... We were then directed to shovel up earth sufficient to fill them.... We finished by throwing up a bank in front of [the baskets, filled with wet sand]. Not a single cannon-ball penetrated this defense during the whole siege.... It ceased raining just as the day was about to dawn, when we observed that our artillery had thrown up a battery to our right, on the bank of the river, and had raised a lofty flag staff with the star spangled banner streaming to the wind upon it.[12]

Sergeant Martin, watching the hoisting of the American flag in the 10-gun battery, confessed, "I felt a secret pride when I saw the 'star spangled banner' waving majestically in the faces of our implacable adversaries; it appeared like an omen of success to our enterprise."[13]

After dark, on October 6, the Americans began digging the first trench, or parallel, about 2,000 yards in length and from 1,200 to 800 yards from the British defensive position. "It was a very dark and rainy night," remembered Martin. His Sappers and Miners began to lay out laths of pinewood end to end upon the line marked out by the engineers for the trenches. After a while, the officers departed, and a stranger came along. "He inquired what troops we were; talked familiarly with us a few minutes, when, being informed which way the officers had gone, he went off in the same direction, after strictly charging us, in case we should be taken prisoners, not to reveal to the enemy what troops we were."[14]

In a short time the engineers returned with the stranger, who turned out to be General Washington. "Had we dared," mused Martin, "we might have cautioned him for exposing himself so carelessly to danger at such a time, and doubtless he would have taken it in good part if we had. But nothing ill happened to him or ourselves." The next night the work of building the first trench was completed, and General Washington struck a few blows with a pickaxe to commemorate the event.

Heavy guns were dragged into place, and on October 9 a French battery on the left opened fire, then the American battery on the right began blasting. Ebenezer Denny, who watched the display from camp, jotted in his diary, "The scene... was grand, particularly after dark—a number of shells from both parties passing high in the air, and descending in a curve, each with a long train of fire exhibited a brilliant spectacle."[15] The American artillery fire was devastating and caused much destruction in town. Many of the local residents took shelter near the beach, behind cliffs, and some even in caves.

During the night of October 11 the Americans began digging the second parallel, 300–500 yards closer to the British. It would allow the allies to move their heavy guns even closer to the main British defense works. Two British redoubts (temporary defensive positions) were captured just before sunset on October 12, before the second parallel was completed.

Sergeant Martin witnessed several casualties caused by hand grenades that the retreating British threw into the trenches. "Immediately after the firing ceased," he wrote, "I went out to see what had become of my wounded friend and another that fell in the passage. They were both dead. In the heat of the action I saw a British soldier jump over the walls of the fort next to the river and go down the bank, which was almost perpendicular and twenty or thirty feet high. When he came to the beach, he made off for the town."[16]

Ebenezer Denny noted in his diary on October 15 that there was "heavy fire from our batteries all day…. Shot and shell raked the town in every direction." On October 16, "firing continued without intermission."[17] That night, Cornwallis tried to ferry his troops across the river to Gloucester, but he had too few boats, and a sudden storm caused him to call off his effort. On the morning of October 17 the Americans and the French continued their cannonade. One by one, the British works collapsed. The enemy had no ammunition left.

Johann Döhla, who had joined the Ansbach-Bayreuth Regiment at age 18 and now found himself at the receiving end of the cannonade, wrote in his diary, "At daybreak, the bombardment resumed, more terribly strong than ever before. They fired from all positions, without letup…. There was nothing to be seen but bombs and cannonballs raining down on our entire line."[18]

Just after reveille, a red-coated drummer boy mounted the British parapet and beat a parley. Immediately, a British officer, holding up a white handkerchief, made his appearance. The drummer accompanied him, beating. The American batteries ceased firing. An officer from the Continental troops ran and met his British counterpart and tied the handkerchief over his eyes. The drummer was sent back and the British officer was conducted to the rear of the American lines. Firing ceased altogether.

Ebenezer Denny, who witnessed the event, noted in his diary, "Had we not seen the drummer in his red coat when he first mounted, he might have beat away till doomsday. The constant firing was too much for the sound of a single drum; but when the firing ceased, I thought I never heard a drum equal to it—the most delightful music to us all."[19]

The British officer asked for a 24-hour armistice. Washington granted him two hours. In the early afternoon the officer returned with Cornwallis's surrender terms, asking that his army be paroled to Britain. Washington insisted that the enemy troops surrender as prisoners of war, and Cornwallis submitted.

In accepting the surrender of the British at Yorktown, Washington granted them the same honors of war that Cornwallis had granted to the

Surrender of Cornwallis. Painting by John Trumbull. *Courtesy National Archives.*

American garrison at Charleston. At 2:00 P.M., on October 19, 1781, the scarlet-coated British and their Hessian allies, brilliant in blue and green, marched out of Yorktown with colors furled and laid down their arms. Sergeant Martin watched the surrender ceremony. "The British did not make so good an appearance as the German forces; but there was certainly some allowance to be made in their favor; the English felt their honor wounded; the Germans did not greatly care whose hands they were in."[20]

The Germans strode briskly and stacked their arms neatly. Then the British came, moving along slowly, avoiding the eyes of their captors. Their arms went down in a disorderly crash as infantrymen smashed their musket butts and stomped on their cartridge cases. Above all the clutter rose the music of the British bands, with the tune of "The World Turned Upside-Down." The next day, American troops escorted their prisoners into the interior—to Virginia and Maryland. After the prisoners had been marched off, 13-year-old John Hudson visited Yorktown:

> I walked through it until I came to the road leading to the river.... The road ... descended gently to the beach; and on that side were several cellars which had been covered with frame buildings, of at least four rooms to the floor. The buildings had been blown to pieces and no sign of them left; and the cellars were all filled with dead bodies, rounded over the level of the cellar walls and covered with earth.
>
> When I arrived at the beach I found ... cots, mattresses, blankets, and sheets, saturated with blood .... The beach itself had been thrown up as in

rows of corn, with graves dug in the sand. I walked along the beach down the river and then I found Tarleton's light horses, lying dead and washed up to the foot of the bank. They had been tied head and tails, four and five together, and forced into the stream, and thus drowned and floated ashore, having the ropes still on them at this time. They were such beautiful animals as I have never seen. At right angles...a stockade which reached to the river bank had been constructed.... Somewhere near the angle had been a marquee with nine officers sitting around the table at dinner. One of our shells had fallen into their midst and killed the whole party.[21]

Ebenezer Denny, who also entered Yorktown on October 20, was repelled by what he saw: "Glad to be relieved from this disagreeable station," he wrote in his diary. "Never was in so filthy a place—some handsome houses, but prodigiously shattered. Vast heaps of shot and shells lying about in every quarter, which came from our works. The shells did not burst, as was expected."[22]

Both Denny and Martin were appalled by the sight of many Negroes, lying about, "sick and dying, in every stage of the small pox." Martin found them in the nearby woods "after Lord Cornwallis had turned them adrift, with no other recompense for their confidence in his humanity than the smallpox for their bounty and starvation and death for their wages. They were scattered about in every direction... with pieces of ears of burnt Indian corn in their hands and mouths, even of those that were dead."[23]

After the siege was ended, many of the former slave owners came to the American troops, offering a guinea a head for Negroes who were still alive. Martin's regiment refused to deliver them unless the owners promised not to punish them. Among those rescued alive was five-year-old Isaac Jefferson and his family. He remembered, "General Washington brought all Mr. Jefferson's folks...back to Richmond with him and sent word to Mr. Jefferson to send down to Richmond for his servants. Old master sent down two wagons right away and all of em that was carried away went up back to Monticello. Old master was mighty pleased to see his people come back safe and sound."[24]

For his part, Johann Döhla was glad to be alive. "I had good reasons to thank God that he was my Protector who during the siege had so graciously saved my life and protected my body and all my limbs from illness, wounds, and all enemy shots," he wrote in his diary after the capitulation.[25]

News of the surrender of Cornwallis at Yorktown reached the Continental Congress in Philadelphia two days later. During the early hours of October 22, 1781, a night watchman cried out, "Basht dree o'clock and Cornwallis isht daken!" Two days later, Washington's official report arrived, and the entire Congress went to the Lutheran Church for a Thanksgiving service. On October 24 a broadside encouraged all Philadelphians "to illuminate on this glorious occasion between six and nine o'clock in the evening." Decorum and harmony were recommended to every citizen. But it didn't quite work out that way!

Elizabeth Drinker, a prominent Quaker and mother of five small children, noted in her diary, "We grievously suffered on ye 24th by way of rejoicing. A mob assembled about 7 o'clock and continued their insults until near 10, to those whose Houses were not illuminated. Scarcely one Friend's House escaped. We had nearly 70 panes of glass broken .... Some fared better and some fared worse. Some Houses, after breaking the door, they entered and destroyed the furniture. Many women and children were frightened into fits, and'tis a mercy no lives were lost."[26]

And Anna Rawle, another Quaker women, wrote to her exiled mother in New York on October 25, "I suppose, dear Mammy, thee would not have imagined this house to be illuminated last night, but it was. A mob surrounded it, broke the shutters and the glass of the windows, and were coming in, none but forlorn women here. We listened to their attacks in fear and trembling. Coburn and Bob Shewell called us not to be frightened, and fixed lights up at the windows which pacified the mob, and after three huzzas they moved off.... At last they were victorious, and it was one general illumination throughout the town."[27]

As the news of Cornwallis's surrender reached British-occupied Charleston, the young widow Eliza Wilkinson could not contain her joy. "Yes, joyful indeed," she wrote to her friend. "Cornwallis—the mighty British hero—the man of might and his boasted army are conquered, subdued by the glorious Washington! .... Our red and green birds, who have been, for some time past, flying about the country, and insolently perching themselves upon our houses will [shortly] be all caged up in Charlestown. Oh, how they will flutter about and beat their plumes in mere fright! Do you not think [it is] a little spiteful to laugh at them? I cannot help it—I will ... and I have even ventured to laugh at some to their faces, out of a little sweet revenge." [28]

But perhaps most moving is a letter by 16-year-old Mildred Smith from Yorktown to her friend Betsy, still in exile in Richmond. It was written after the end of the siege:

> My dear Betsy—Again we are quietly seated in our old mansion. But oh! how unlike it once was! Indeed, were you to be suddenly and unexpectedly set down in the very spot where you and I have often played together—in that very garden where we gathered flowers or stole your father's choice fruit—you would not recognize a solitary vestige of what once was. Ours is not totally annihilated, being more remote from the battery. Others that remain are so mutilated—as to grieve one's very soul. But it is over! Our individual sufferings are nothing—now we can reflect that the great end is accomplished. Peace is again restored, and we may yet look forward to happy days.[29]

The news of the surrender of Cornwallis at Yorktown arrived in London on November 25. The prime minister, Lord North, exclaimed, "Oh, God it is all over!" King George III, also shocked by the disaster, was not yet willing to admit defeat. Anticipating a renewed effort by the British in the following season, Rochambeau and his French troops wintered in the Yorktown area and then marched back to Newport, Rhode Island. Washington and the Continental Army returned to the banks of the Hudson River. By December 7, 1781, the New York and New Jersey troops, among them Private John Hudson and Sergeant Martin, were in their winter quarters in Burlington, New Jersey. Ebenezer Denny and his Pennsylvania Regiment went to South Carolina to reinforce General Greene's troops.

Washington's victory over Cornwallis did not immediately end the war, but it greatly weakened the resolve of the English public to pour more men and money into losing battles overseas. After Yorktown, the British debt had doubled, the navy was weak, and both army and navy needed great numbers of men to bring them up to minimum strength. The war dragged on for 17 more months, but there was no more major fighting on American soil.

PART III
Transatlantic Travelers

CHAPTER 8

❧

Boys at Sea

In May 1777 young Christopher Hawkins, an indentured apprentice from Providence, Rhode Island, had run away to sea. He signed up on an American schooner, a privateer, that hailed from New Bedford, Massachusetts, bound for a cruise in quest of British vessels and their cargo. "This was the first time I was engaged in any sea service," he wrote later, "and being only in the thirteenth year of my age, of course I knew nothing of a seafaring life."[1]

Christopher was not alone. Boys as young as 11 and 12, from New England and the Mid-Atlantic states, took to the sea during the Revolutionary War. They served as cabin boys, mess boys, powder boys, boatswains, and midshipmen on board the ships of the fledgling Continental Navy and, more often, on privately owned armed merchant vessels. They sailed north along the Atlantic coast to Newfoundland and Nova Scotia and south to Bermuda, the Caribbean Sea, and the British West Indies. They ventured east across the Atlantic to the Irish coast, the English Channel, and the Bay of Biscay, along the western shores of France and the northern shores of Spain.

During the War of Independence, the Continental Congress issued nearly 2,000 letters of marque, giving the owners of private vessels the right to capture enemy vessels and goods on the high seas. As the war progressed, Congress set strict rules around the distribution of prizes and the treatment of prisoners for the commanders of the privateers and required that one-third of their crew must be landsmen—to protect the small Continental Navy from losing its sailors to the more lucrative privateering.

The boys who wrote eyewitness accounts of their exploits at sea came from the four states that contributed the bulk of the privately armed vessels: Massachusetts, Pennsylvania, Maryland, and Connecticut. Some, like 12-year-old Israel Trask and 15-year-old Henry Yaeger, had served several years as foot soldiers before they signed up on privateers. Others, like 14-year-old Andrew Sherburne and 15-year-old John Blatchford, had served in the Continental Navy. Still others manned the gunboats and whaleboats that patrolled the coast of Connecticut and New Jersey.[2]

All the boys who ventured on the high seas and later wrote about their exploits were captured at least once. Some were imprisoned five times by the British during their years of service. Most managed to escape or were released in prisoner exchanges. Others spent extended periods of time in overcrowded prisons, in the Old Mill, near Plymouth, England, or on the infamous prison ship *Jersey* in New York harbor.

Despite their hazardous duties, the privateers managed to capture some 2,283 enemy ships during the Revolutionary War, more than 10 times as many as the Continental Navy. Together, with the Continental Navy, they also captured some 16,000 British prisoners, a thousand more than the number of prisoners taken by the entire Continental Army before the British surrendered at Yorktown. Every newspaper rushed to print the latest adventures of the "boys at sea" from their hometown, and people took great pride in how well they succeeded in thwarting the British merchant ships and the mighty British Navy.

Boston newspapers also printed advertisements for volunteers:

An Invitation to all brave Seamen and Marines, who have an inclination to serve their country and make their fortunes. The grand Privateer ship DEANE, commanded by ELISHA HINMAN, Esq., and prov'd to be a very capital Sailor, will Sail on a Cruise against the Enemies of the United States of America, by the 20th instant. The DEANE mounts thirty Carriage Guns, and is excellently well calculated for Attacks, Defense and Pursuit— This therefore is to invite all those Jolly Fellows, who love their country and want to make their fortunes at one Stroke, to repair immediately to the Rendezvous at the Head of His Excellency Governor Hancock's Wharf, where they will be received with a hearty Welcome by a Number of Brave Fellows there assembled, and treated with that excellent Liquor call'd GROG which is allow'd by all true Seamen to be the LIQUOR OF LIFE.

Ebenezer Fox first ran away to sea at age 12—on the night of Paul Revere's ride to Lexington and Concord. He served for a while as a cabin boy on a cargo boat that hauled molasses and coffee from the West Indies to Providence, Rhode Island. Four years later, he signed up on the new 20-gun ship *Protector*, the largest ship in the Massachusetts state navy.[3] This is how it happened:

Recruiting privateersmen to serve the American cause in the Revolutionary War.
Courtesy Dover Pictorial Archives.

A rendezvous was established for recruits at the head of Hancock's wharf where the national flag…was hoisted. All means were resorted to which ingenuity could devise, to induce men to enlist. A recruiting officer, bearing a flag and attended by a band of martial music, paraded the streets…. He possessed the qualifications requisite to make the service appear alluring, especially to the young. He was a jovial good-natured fellow, of ready wit…. Crowds followed in his wake when he marched the streets, and he occasionally stopped at the corners to harangue the multitude in order to excite their patriotism and their zeal for Liberty. When he espied any large boys in the crowd around him, he would attract their attention by singing:

> All you that have bad masters,
> And cannot get your due,
> Come, come, my brave boys,
> And join with our ship's crew.

A shout and huzzah would follow…. My excitable feelings were roused; I repaired to the rendezvous, signed the ship's papers, mounted a cockade, and was in my own estimate already more than half a sailor.

Andrew Sherburne, who was 15 at the time, describes the makeup of the crew of the schooner on which he signed up. "She had a full complement of officers, two or three ordinary seamen before the mast, and between twenty and thirty boys, scarcely one of them as large as myself, and some of them not a dozen years old."[4]

In order to increase the size of the crew, the captain staged a frolic at a public house. "Suitable persons were employed," wrote Andrew, "to invite the lads and lasses for a country dance. Rum, coffee, sugar, biscuit, etc., were taken on shore for that purpose. I was selected by some of the officers to sing for some of the dancers. Every art and insinuation was employed by the officers to obtain recruits."

Once on board, the new recruits soon learned the habits of the older sailors. Remembered Andrew Sherburne, "My aversion to swearing rendered me an object of ridicule to those profane chaps. I was insulted and frequently obliged to fight. In this I was sometimes victorious. I soon began to improve in boxing, and to indulge in swearing. At length I became proficient in this abominable practice. To counterbalance my guilt.... I became more constant in praying."

Others had a harder time findings their bearings. Wrote Christopher Hawkins, age 13, "After the vessel had sailed from the sight of land, she seemed to me as steering in the same direction as when she left the Harbour, and the illusion was not dispelled even when the sun rose above the horizon on a clear day." By the time his vessel was taking fish

Mrs. Washington prevails upon her son not to go as midshipman. *Courtesy Library of Congress.*

along the Newfoundland coast, the boy finally knew they were heading northeast.[5]

Among the most widely traveled young sailors during the Revolutionary War was John Blatchford, who wrote a narrative of the "remarkable occurrences" in his seafaring life in 1788, five years after the war had ended.[6] In June 1777, at the age of 14, he shipped out as a cabin boy on the frigate *Hancock,* one of the first ships built for the Continental Navy. Under the command of Captain John Manley, the *Hancock* sailed along the Newfoundland coast, where she was captured on July 8 by the *HMS Rainbow.* Thus the *Hancock* was lost to the American cause after just 48 days of active service. Her crew was taken to a makeshift prison in Halifax, Nova Scotia.

For 12 days, young John and his cell mate dug a small passage underground that extended into a garden behind the prison wall. On the day they had planned their escape, they were betrayed by another prisoner, a midshipman from the Continental frigate *Boston.* The crew of the *Hancock* was placed in irons, under close confinement. Two of John's cell mates died within days. After some time had passed, the boy was put on a British frigate bound for Boston for a prisoner exchange, but the ship detoured to Antigua in the West Indies after the main mast was damaged in a severe storm. After repair, the ship returned to Halifax.

Undaunted, John Blatchford made a second unsuccessful escape attempt and ended up in confinement on the very ship he had run away from. This time, the *HMS Greyhound* was bound for England. Her captain, "being a humane man," saw to it that John was freed from the irons and ordered to perform the duties of a cabin boy. As the ship approached the Irish coast, the boy made his third attempt to escape: He jumped overboard and was promptly picked up by British Marines, who carried him back to his ship. He spent the next 18 days in the carpenter's berth with a broken right leg, thigh, and arm. The ship's captain cared enough to procure a doctor for the boy.

Upon arrival in Portsmouth, the principal naval station in England at the time, John found an unexpected advocate. Thomas Diggers, a Maryland merchant residing in London at the time, spoke up on his behalf at the Admiral's Court. "I was asked if I was not sorry I had undertaken the rebellion against my king," the boy remembered, "and Mr. Diggers then spoke and said it was hardly fair to ask me such a question…considering my youth." The verdict of the court was duly recorded: John Blatchford was to be sent back to Halifax from hence he had come to be exchanged as a prisoner of war.

But it was not to be: John Blatchford mistakenly boarded the *Princess Royale,* bound for the East Indies, in the company of 82 other American "rebels." For the first time he resigned himself to his fate: "I now found my destiny was fixed—that whatever I could do, would not in the least alter my situation, and therefore was determined to do the best I could, and make myself as contented as my unfortunate situation would admit."[7]

It took the *Princess Royale* some 17 weeks until they reached the island of St. Helena in the South Atlantic. They sailed around the Cape of Good Hope and then on to Batavia, the capital of the island of Java, where they arrived 10 weeks later. After a brief stay, their ship headed for the island of Sumatra. They arrived in the port of Bencouloo six weeks later. Here the Americans were put ashore and put to work on the pepper plantations of the East India Company.

Wrote John, "Picking peppers from morning till night and allowed but two scanty meals a day—this together with the amazing heat of the sun was too much for an American constitution. The Americans died daily with heat and hard fare which determined my…companions and myself in an endeavor to make our escape…. We resolved upon trying our fortune again."[8]

They had been on the pepper plantation for about four months when John and two other American prisoners made their first attempt to escape. After four days of wandering about in the dense jungle, they were captured, tried by a court at Fort Marlborough, and condemned to death. The oldest of the trio was promptly executed, but the others were pardoned "in consideration of their youth" and received several hundred lashes as punishment. After a three-week stay in a hospital, John Blatchford and his companion managed to escape again, setting out for the Dutch settlement of Croy on the opposite side of the island, some 300 miles distant.

The two boys subsisted on fruit and turtle eggs, but John's companion eventually sickened and died. Blatchford continued on his journey for 15 weeks (he made notches for each day he traveled on a stick he hung around his neck) until he arrived at a village where he was fed by natives and provided with a guide to the harbor of Croy. There the boy boarded a Dutch vessel bound from China to Batavia. In Batavia he was able to find passage on a Spanish ship bound for Brazil. Eventually, he managed to make it back to St. Helena, where he found the vessel on which he had come out from England on her return from her second voyage.

The captain of the *Princess Royale* took the boy back on board and treated him kindly—so did his old shipmates. John worked as a boatswain until the ship arrived in England on March 1, 1782—about two and a half years from the time he had left it. About two weeks, after arriving in London, he shipped out on the *King George,* bound for Antigua in the West Indies. There he made his escape to the French-occupied island of Monterrat and managed to get passage on a French brigantine bound for Philadelphia.

But John was to experience one more misfortune. The French vessel was captured by two British cruisers off Cape Delaware, and he and the crew were put on the prison ship *Jersey* in the New York harbor. After being on board for a week, he was sent back to France in an exchange of French prisoners and arrived at the port of St. Malo a month later. There he procured a pass to go overland to Port L'Orient and signed up on an American privateer, the *Buccaneer*. Three weeks afterward, he learned that Congress had declared peace. The privateer was promptly dismantled, and her crew was discharged.

Blatchford found a space on board a brig bound for Beverly, Massachusetts. On May 9, 1783, John finally set foot on American soil: "I immediately...went to my father's house, and had an agreeable meeting with my friends after an absence of almost six years"—so ends the narrative of his epic journey.[9]

Israel Trask's seafaring adventures were equally dramatic. He wrote about them in his pension application to Congress kept at the National Archives in Washington, D.C. Israel was only 12 years old when he signed up as a privateer on the schooner *Speedwell* in 1777. He had quite a story to tell.[10]

Israel's first voyage, from Gloucester, Massachusetts, to Newfoundland, was successful and yielded many prizes captured from the British. So did his second voyage to Martinique in the latter part of 1777. In the spring of 1778 Israel entered service on board the privateer *Black Prince*. A few days out at sea, his ship captured a British brig of 16 guns. Cruising off the coast of Ireland, the crew captured many prizes and returned safely to their home port in Salem, Massachusetts. In the autumn of the same year his ship seized another English vessel, cruised in the Bay of Biscay and along the west coast of Ireland, and returned with their prizes to their home port one year later.

Israel's fortunes took a turn for the worse when his ship and the *Protector* (with Ebenezer Fox on board) participated in the ill-fated Penobscot Expedition, the biggest naval disaster in the Revolutionary War. A small American naval fleet sailed to the Penobscot River in present-day Maine in a daring attempt to drive the British out of Penobscot Bay. Ill equipped, understaffed, and without a cohesive leadership, the expedition ultimately failed. The Americans were surrounded by the British forces and ran their ships aground or burned them to keep their vessels from falling into the hands of the enemy.

Remembered Israel, "With many others, I escaped to the dense forests and traveled through the wilderness about three hundred miles with a pack on my shoulder, containing a light blanket, a small piece of rusty pork, a bottle of wine and one shirt; wending my way across streams and through underbrush until the second day's march my shoes gave way. The rest of the way I performed on my bare feet until I reached home."[11]

Late in October, 1779, Israel volunteered on the ship *Rambler* and cruised the Atlantic and the Bay of Biscay. In December, in the port of Bilbao, his ship was visited by John Adams and his two oldest sons, Charles and John Quincy Adams, who were traveling from Spain to Paris on a diplomatic mission.

Early in April 1780, Israel sailed on the brig *Wilkes,* looking for prizes along the Newfoundland coast. After some success, his crew was captured, and the boy spent some time on a prison ship in St. John's, Newfoundland, and then was "forced at the point of the bayonet" to do duty on the British ship *Vestal.* Soon after, Israel was returned home in a prisoner exchange. He was captured again the following year when he signed up on the privateer *Garland.* On her return trip he was seized by a British vessel, detained for some months in Bermuda, and then returned in yet another prisoner exchange. Undeterred, he made two more voyages to Martinique on the *Ranger.*

In the spring of 1782 Israel signed up on the ship *Betsy* and was promptly captured on the second day out. The prison ship in which he found himself in Halifax "was a large old condemned East Indiaman. On her three decks were housed, or entombed, some hundred of our countrymen, many of whom had been her occupants for three long years. The gloomy aspect of the ship, the cadaverous appearance of the prisoners, made death preferable to a lengthy abode."[12]

On the eighth day of their confinement, two of the imprisoned crew members swam two miles to a fortified island, where they seized two boats and brought them back "in the obscurity of a foggy evening." Israel and his companion took off in a volley of gunfire. They hid their boats on uninhabited islands during the daytime and rowed under the cover of darkness. After two weeks of "great suffering," they managed to get on board an American cruiser. They reached their home one month later.

Israel would sail on two more privateers, the *Congress* and the *Ruby,* on three more voyages to the West Indies. He learned about the outbreak of peace in 1783 in the port of Gouadeloupe. By then, he had served his country for eight years: two on land and six at sea. He was barely 18 years old when the war ended.

When the crew of an American ship fell into British hands, they were often brought back to England. Old Mill prison, near Plymouth, was the largest prison established by the Lords Commission of the Admiralty to hold the American rebels. It was fitted up for 400 men, and the prisoners' daily rations were, on the whole, plain but adequate. Prisoners even received small weekly allowances of 18 pence from a welfare fund to buy necessities.[13]

Two American teenagers spent several years in the confines of Old Mill prison: Andrew Sherburne was imprisoned between November 1781 and November 1782; Henry Yaeger was imprisoned from 1781 until 1783. Andrew Sherburne had been captured on the privateer *Greyhound* off the coast of Newfoundland and had spent some time on a prison ship in St. John's before being transported to England. Henry Yaeger was captured on the merchant ship *Franklin,* bound for a port in France, and was taken first to Weymouth and Portsmouth in England and then to the Old Mill in Plymouth.

Andrew, in his *Memoirs,* described his first impressions as he entered the outer prison yard: [14]

> The commissary's office and the cook rooms made two sides of this yard, and it was separated from the larger prison yard by a strong wooden gate. In this yard a sentinel stood continually, and "Old Aunt Anna" was there constantly with her hand cart (drawn by a boy) to supply the prisoners with bread, butter, tobacco, needles, thread and every other article for which they might call. Several milk men had their station there.

The moment a group of new prisoners entered the inner courtyard, they would be accosted by their countrymen and asked, "How fare ye shipmates? Where are you from?" Strong bonds of friendship formed among townsmen who supplied the newcomers with necessary clothing and an occasional special treat. The prisoners—not withstanding that they were located within the absolute dominion of the British Majesty— formed themselves into a mini-republic, framed a constitution, and laid down laws of acceptable behavior—with suitable penalties.

Andrew Sherburne, who had little schooling, found a tutor among the prisoners who taught him how to read and write. "My friends were much gratified with my improvement," he wrote later. "I very soon became entirely indifferent to all kinds of gaming, and found sufficient entertainment with my pen and pencil.... I diligently pursued my studies of arithmetic and geometry, with a design to enter upon navigation [when I was free]."

Other prisoners engaged in handicraft, building ship models and making punch ladles from apple tree wood that they sold for a small sum to supplement the donations that Benjamin Franklin, American Minister to France, had managed to procure for the prisoners' welfare. But their main occupation was not engaged in handicrafts, writing, or games, but in hatching escape plans. Andrew Sherburne described one of these attempts:[15]

> They, by some means, got one of the grates out of the chamber window which was directly over the west end door of the long prison; they took a loose beam and ran it out of the window in an oblique direction, so as just to make it reach over the north wall of the yard; they lashed hammocks together, suspended down from the end of the beam and lowered themselves down, and … they all made their escape.

Other escapees tunneled under the wall, some walked out dressed as clerics, others bribed guards. Benjamin Franklin is said to have helped fund such ruses as "oiling the sentry's conscience," often after the fact. He also reimbursed sympathizers who helped the escapees get to France. Those prisoners who were recaptured faced a term of 40 days in the "black hole," a small, dark cell apart from the other prisoners, on half rations.

The escapees who were brought back automatically went to the bottom of the list for prisoner exchanges. Franklin, operating from France, was the chief negotiator with the British government for the exchange arrangements. Reasoning that if he produced a number of British prisoners in France, the British government would agree to an exchange, he set to work organizing a small number of privateers working from French ports with the object of capturing British prisoners.[16]

After many delays, an agreement was reached. All prisoners still had to receive the Royal Pardon before they could be exchanged. These pardons were sent to the agents at the prison who solemnly read out the list of names to the Americans held at Old Mill. One of the names was that of Andrew Sherburne, who had languished in the prison hospital for some weeks. He remembered, "My doctor, in order to raise my spirits, told me the ship had arrived that would take us to our country; that she would sail in two or three weeks, and that I must take the best possible care of myself that I might go on her."

A determined Andrew managed to board the ship with the help of two small canes. When he returned to Marblehead, Massachusetts, he met his family and old friends. "My mother, brothers and sisters had despaired of ever seeing me again…. I was to them almost as one rose from the dead."[17]

As soon as Andrew had regained his health, he signed up as a boatswain on the brig *Scorpion,* together with his former tutor in Mill prison. They sailed for the West Indies to deliver a cargo of lumber and returned with pineapples and other fruit, luxury items in New England. On their way back, off the coast of Virginia, two days away from their home port in Massachusetts, they were captured by the British ship *Amphion.* It was the third time that Andrew had fallen into the hands of the enemy. This time, he would find himself on board the prison ship *Jersey.*

Reports of the wretched conditions on the *Jersey* are confirmed by the independent accounts of Andrew Sherburne, Christopher Hawkins, James Forten, and Ebenezer Fox, all of whom were captured when they were still in their teens. Fox, who had been captured when his ship, the *Protector,* had surrendered to two enemy warships in 1780, recalled his first impression upon being lowered into the hatch that housed the inmates of the *Jersey:*[18]

> Here was a motley crew covered with rags and filth; visages pallid with disease, emaciated with hunger and anxiety, and retaining hardly a trace of their original appearance. Here were men who had once enjoyed life while riding over the mountain wave or roaming through pleasant fields, full of health and vigor. Now shriveled by a scanty and unwholesome diet, ghastly with inhaling an impure atmosphere, exposed to contagion and disease, and surrounded with the horrors of sickness and death.

It is estimated that between 8,000 and 11,000 prisoners died in captivity on the *Jersey,* an old, converted, 64-gun man-of-war, stripped of its fittings, anchored in New York harbor. That would account for about 30 to 40 percent of all Americans killed during the Revolutionary War. Andrew Sherburne put it succinctly: "The death of a man in that place, and at that time, excited but little notice; for a day did not pass without more or less deaths."

This is what Sherburne saw as he entered the *Jersey:* "I now had to commence a scene of suffering almost without a parallel. The ship was extremely filthy, and abounded with vermin. A large proportion of the prisoners had been robbed of their clothing. The ship was considerably crowded; many of the men were very low spirited; our provisions … very scanty. They consisted of worm eaten ship bread and salt beef … that … had been condemned in the British Navy."[19]

Christopher Hawkins, whose schooner had been captured and sunk by the British, ended up on the *Jersey* as well. Here are his impressions of the conditions on the prison ship:[20]

> We were all put between decks every night before dark … our situation was extremely unpleasant. Our rations were not sufficient to satisfy the calls of hunger …. We had a great deal of sickness on the *Jersey* and many died on board. The sickness seemed to be epidemic which we called the blood flux or dysentery. After the prisoners had been driven below at dusk … many of the prisoners would become sick the fore part of the evening and before morning their suffering would be ended by death.
>   The situation of the prisoners was truly appalling…. Boxing was tolerated without stint. Pilfering food was another evil that prevailed…. Another thing which added to the horror of this prison ship was the filth. It was permitted to such an extent that every prisoner was infected with vermin on his body

and wearing apparel. I one day observed a prisoner...with his shirt in his hands, having stripped it from his body and deliberately picking the vermin from the plaits, and putting them into his mouth.... He had been so sparingly fed that he was nearly a skeleton, and all but in a state of nudity. After our crew were put on board, the roll was called, and the regulations of the ship with respect to the conduct of the captives were read.... From these it appeared that every captive who should be detected undertaking to effect his escape from this "floating hell," either by swimming, taking the ship's boat, or any other way, should suffer instant death, and should not even be taken on board alive.

Christopher Hawkins was not intimidated. Only three days after arrival on the *Jersey,* he escaped at night through an open gunport, suspended to a rope from an old cable that was stretched under the forecastle of the ship. He swam for some two hours before he spotted land. Eluding the Hessian sentinels on the shoreline of Long Island, he found refuge in a barn. The farmer's wife who discovered him in the morning provided him with food and clothing. He managed to get back home unharmed.

Andrew Sherburne was not so lucky. He became ill and ended up on the hospital ship *Frederic* that was anchored near the *Jersey.* "The ship on which I was placed was...very much crowded," he remembered, "so that two men were obliged to lie in one bunk.... At this time my mind was very fluctuating and occasionally deranged. My bed fellow was running down very fast.... He finally died stretched across me."[21]

The prison ship *Jersey. Courtesy Library of Congress.*

Whatever property or clothing was left by the deceased fell into the hands of the male nurses who lived in the steerage of the hospital ship. It was taken off the corpse and sold to pay for the drinking and gambling they indulged in at night, when the sick were left unattended and many died. Andrew survived. He later credited his recovery from the fever to the daily pints of Bohea tea, sweetened with molasses, provided by the citizens of New York to the sick prisoners on board the hospital ship.

The boy had to wait some weeks after the outbreak of peace before he was finally released from his captivity: "It was exceedingly trying to our feelings to see our shipmates daily leaving us, until our ship was almost deserted.... There were but seven or eight of us on board when we left.... In the morning, before sunrise, we gladly set our feet once more upon the land of liberty."[22]

Ashbel Green, the son of a clergyman from eastern New Jersey, was in his early teens when he saw the "wretched contents" that were disgorged from the prison ship:[23]

A large proportion of those who were released were sent into the adjacent countryside, to seek relief where they could find it from the humanity of their countrymen.... A number of them were so debilitated by famine and disease that they fell down and died in the streets of New York before they could even reach the vessels appointed to transport them. When they were landed, a considerable part of them were sent forward in wagons, being unable to travel on foot. Those who were able to walk, followed the wagons; and such a company of miserable human beings—pallid, emaciated, begrimed with dirt and smoke, and in every way squalid in the extreme—my eyes never beheld.

James Forten, the 15-year-old whose name was entered on the muster of the *Jersey* as prisoner number 4102, was an exception. He was on the prison ship *Jersey* by choice. A free black from Philadelphia, Quaker educated, he had signed up on the *Royal Louis* under the command of Captain Stephen Decatur as a powder boy in the summer of 1781. The fact that he was black did not set him apart. Another 19 sailors "of color" had volunteered for the ship's first voyage as a privateer. What *did* set him apart was that he was literate and could sign his name. He was tall, athletic, and had some knowledge of how to repair sails.[24]

The first cruise of his ship in July 1781 was a success. The *Royal Louis* sailed between New York and Charleston and took four British vessels. He returned to his widowed mother and sister unscathed, with prize money in his pockets. On his 15th birthday, on September 9, he watched a day-long parade of George Washington's troops through his hometown in Philadelphia on the way to Virginia's Yorktown peninsula. Years later, he wrote, "I well remember that when the New England regiments passed through this city on their way to attack the English Army under Lord Cornwallis, there were several Companies of Colored People, as brave Men as ever fought."[25]

James Forten was eager to go to sea again, but the second cruise of the *Royal Louis,* in October 1781, ended disastrously. She was captured by the British warship *Amphion* after a chase of seven hours. Taken as prisoner aboard the British ship, James Forten's mind was "harassed with the most painful forebodings, from a knowledge...that rarely...were prisoners of his complexion exchanged; they were sent to the West Indies and there doomed to a life of slavery." But fate was kind to him.

The *Amphion* had a complement of boys barely in their teens, training for careers in the Royal Navy. It was the responsibility of the captain to see to it that they were properly taught English grammar, writing, arithmetic, and the elements of navigation. Among them were the two sons of Captain Bazely, 14-year-old John, a midshipman, and 12-year-old Henry. The captain asked James Forten to keep an eye on his youngest son, and they soon became friends.

During a game of marbles between the two, Forten displayed such unusual skill and dexterity that young Henry called his father's attention to it; afterward, the British captain granted the young Philadelphian a great deal of freedom. "Thus," James Forten wrote later, "did a game of marbles save me from a life of West Indian servitude." As the *Amphion* approached New York harbor, Captain Bazely proposed to send Forten with his son to England.

To his surprise, Forten rejected the offer, telling him, "I have been taken prisoner for the liberty of my country, and never will prove a traitor to her interest." The British captain then wrote a letter to the commander of the prison ship *Jersey* requesting that James should be treated decently in captivity and be speedily exchanged. It would take some seven months before that would happen. In the meantime Forten joined a mess of old shipmates from the *Royal Louis* who had arrived a week earlier.

His messmates helped him find his way around the ship and encouraged him to join one of the work parties that washed the upper deck, unloaded food and drinking water from the supply ships, moved the sick from the lower deck to the hospital ships nearby, and hauled out the dead for burial in the sand dunes. A member of the work parties was entitled to more food and more time and air on the upper deck—away from the vermin and stench of the interior of the ship.

Like most prisoners on board, Forten considered the possibility of making a break for freedom. An officer of the Continental Navy was to be exchanged for a British officer, and James asked the man's permission to hide in his sea chest. But in the last moment he gave up his chance for escape to a 13-year-old white boy from Philadelphia, Daniel Brewton, "his companion in suffering." The younger boy was hidden by him in a "chest of old clothes" that was lowered down the side of the prison ship. The black sailor and his white shipmate became lifelong friends.

In April 1782 the pace of prisoner exchange quickened. Together with his companions, Forten was called on deck, told to get his belongings, and rowed ashore. After his release, James walked barefoot from New York to Trenton, where he was given shoes and food by a kind stranger. Having lost almost all his hair by the time he arrived in Philadelphia, he was nursed back to health by his mother and sister, who had long since given him up for dead.

Years later, when James Forten was encouraged to petition for a pension from Congress, he replied, "I was a volunteer." He did not want a pension but the status of a full-fledged citizen of the United States. He had believed in the cause of liberty ever since that hot and humid day in July 1776, when—as a nine-year-old—he had heard the Declaration of Independence read to the people of his hometown.

After an unsuccessful attempt to escape from the *Jersey*, Ebenezer Fox and 12 of his fellow prisoners had chosen a different road to freedom. "To remain an indefinite time as prisoners, enduring privation and sufferings beyond what human nature could sustain... and in despair of any improvement being in prospect for our liberation, we concluded that we would enlist... for the West India service, and trust to Providence for finding an opportunity to leave the British for the American service."[26]

Soon after the young American sailors had formed this "desperate solution," a recruiting officer came on board the *Jersey* to enlist men for the 88th Regiment, to be stationed at Kingston, Jamaica. "We stared at each other, and felt we were about to do a deed of which we were ashamed." They were assured that they would not be called upon to fight against their countrymen.

After some month of "easy and agreeable duty," Ebenezer and four of his comrades managed to escape from Kingston, capture a small sailboat, and head for Spanish-controlled Cuba and Santa Domingo. After three nights at sea, they arrived in the harbor of Cape Henri and boarded an American privateer, the 32-gun frigate *Flora*. They set sail for the coast of France and remained in the harbor of Bordeaux for nine months until news of the signature of the preliminary peace treaty reached their ship.

In April 1783 Ebenezer Fox sailed back to Boston. When he arrived home, his master, to whom he had been apprenticed at the beginning of the war, took the 80 dollars that were his share of the prize money that the boy had earned as privateer. It became of no value in his hands as he took it in the paper currency of the times.

That same month, Captain Bazely, Forten's friend and benefactor, boarded the *Jersey* for the last time and read the prisoners the King's proclamation that hostilities were at an end. Eventually, everyone was released, and the ship was left to sink into the mud of the East River.

In 1803, when work began on the Brooklyn Navy Yard, the banks of Wallabout Bay were cut away, and the skeletons of many prisoners buried by the British were discovered. Five years later, "the bones were interred under the direction of the Tammany Society of New York, attended by a solemn funeral procession, in the presence of a vast concourse of citizens; and the cornerstone of a Monument was laid honoring 'the spirits of the departed free. '"

CHAPTER 9

☙

The Riedesel Girls on a Transatlantic Tour of Duty

O n the 14th of May, 1776, three little girls began a journey that
would lead them from their hometown in Wolfenbüttel in northern
Germany to the wilderness of the Canadian province of Quebec and the
battlefield of Saratoga in upstate New York. The oldest, Augusta (nicknamed Gustava) was three months short of her fifth birthday; her sister,
Frederika, was two years old; and baby Caroline had been born only 10
weeks earlier.

The girls were the daughters of Major General Friedrich Adolph
Riedesel, the commanding officer of the Brunswick troops that were
serving with the British forces in North America. His wife, Baroness
Charlotte Luise Friederike, chronicled their transatlantic "tour of duty"
in a series of letters and journals, written in the period between 1776
and 1783. They represent an extraordinary account of Revolutionary
America from the vantage point of a woman who had the courage
to travel with her small children thousands of miles into an unknown
theater of war.[1]

In January 1776 the Duke of Brunswick, a notorious spendthrift, had
contracted with the British Crown to send some 4,300 fighting men to the
wilds of America. They included both foot soldiers and light cavalry. The
first regiment departed from its garrison some six weeks after the treaty
was signed. When they sailed from the port of Stade in mid-March, 77
women accompanied the soldiers. All were married: A few were officers'
wives; most were wives of common soldiers. Some women carried babies
in their arms; others led older children by the hand. The women on the
regimental muster were entitled to half a man's ration; the children to a
quarter.[2]

The Baroness was in her last month of pregnancy when her husband left with his regiment. But immediately after Caroline's birth, she made preparations to join him in America. Her friends at the Brunswick Court tried to dissuade her from the journey. They told her that the Native Americans were cannibals and that she and her little girls might be eaten alive. They also assured her that the English in North America ate horse-meat and cats. "Yet all this frightened me less than the thought of going into a country where I could not understand the language," she confided in her journal.[3]

As soon as she received her husband's orders to go by way of Calais and Dover, she began to plan her trip. They would take the Post Road through Brussels and use sturdy horses. The baroness would travel in a carriage that was high off the ground, with big wheels because the roads would be deeply rutted. The carriage was covered with oilcloth to keep out the rain, and it had steps to let down so she and the two older children could climb in and out. Within the carriage, there was room for Madame Riedesel, her two women servants, and her three little girls. She carried and nursed the baby Caroline all along the way.

Their luggage was on the outside, with a musket strapped firmly under the seat of the coachman, an old retainer by the name of Rockel, who was utterly devoted to "Lady Fritz" and her children. At their first stopping place on the first day's journey he reassured her, as he lifted the children out of the carriage, "See how God blessed our journey; our children are looking much better!" After two weeks travel by coach, the Baroness and her party reached Calais on June 1, 1776, the same day Major General Riedesel landed with his troops in Quebec. "I had promised [the children] that they should see their father after we had crossed the channel," she wrote in her journal. "I pretended to be very courageous in order to dispel all their fears."

The journey by boat across the English Channel took five hours. The Riedesel girls made fast friends with the sailors on board. Their mother observed, "I looked around for the children and found, to my great astonishment, that they were already…playing among the sailors…. My daughter Frederika, became so well acquainted with the sailors, that when she wished to go up or down, she always called: 'Husband! Your arm!' These people are very fond of children, and know well how to wait upon them. One of them was in the habit of taking up little Caroline, carrying her about, and taking care of her. It was very droll to see him, a large brown complexioned fellow, with a little child constantly laughing at him."[4]

After crossing the Channel, the Baroness stopped in London on her way to Bristol. She quickly learned the importance of feminine fads in the British capital. Walking with her daughters, she was acutely embarrassed when passersby cried, "French women. Pretty girls." She had put ribbons on her daughters' hats, which were differently shaped from English hats for children. Fortunately, she found quarters with the family of one of her husband's friends. The Russells taught her children English and introduced her to the royal family. German-born Queen Charlotte complimented her on her courage to travel with small children and invited her back for informal visits.[5]

After 11 months in England, the little family finally succeeded in boarding a ship headed for Canada. On April 16, 1777, Madame Riedesel, her daughters, and her servants sailed from Portsmouth on a merchant ship in a convoy of 31 vessels. They arrived at the Gulf of St. Lawrence on June 3, her husband's birthday. "My heart," she wrote, "was filled with a mixture of joy and sadness, with a longing to be with him again…and to bring him our dear children." On June 11 they arrived in Quebec, where "all the ships in the harbor fired their cannons in welcome."[6]

General Riedesel was not there to meet his family. He was deep in the Canadian wilderness, preparing an attack on the American rebels in upstate New York. His wife refused to spend the night in Quebec. She wanted to push on to her husband's headquarters. After a dinner party given by General Carlton's wife, the Baroness, her children, and her servants boarded a galley and were rowed 20 miles up the river to the village of Point aux Trembles. At two in the morning she woke her little girls, and they were set ashore.

At Point aux Trembles they hired three two-wheeled carriages—"very small and uncomfortable," she wrote, "but very fast." The Baroness tied Frederika, age three, into one corner of her single seat, held baby Caroline in her arms, and had Augusta sit on the floor—to guard her mother's purse. In the afternoon of June 12 they reached a small town at the conflux of a river that entered the St. Lawrence. There was no bridge across the river. They had to go in a birchbark canoe.

"Seated on the bottom of the boat, in one corner, I had my three children upon my lap while my three servants sat on the other side," Madame Riedesel reported. "We were overtaken by a severe hailstorm." Three-year-old Frederika was frightened and wanted to jump up. The boatman told her mother that the canoe could be overturned by even the slightest movement. The Baroness held the girl tightly. Eventually, they reached the town of Trois Rivieres. Wet and frightened, the three children, the three servants, and the Baroness climbed ashore.

The bad weather continued through the night, but the indomitable "Mrs. General" set out again in the morning—this time in a carriage provided by the local vicar. It went so fast and jolted so much that she had to clutch her children tightly lest they fell out. She felt "completely beaten to pieces."

Traveling almost continuously after they had left Quebec, the Baroness and her children reached Montreal on June 14 in the evening. Setting out early in the morning, they arrived at Chambly, her husband's headquarters, on June 15. "My children and my faithful Rockel kept watch on the highway," she wrote. But General Riedesel had left town by another road to meet his family, and they had missed each other. He returned the next day, after learning from local villagers that a German woman with three little girls had passed their way the day before.

On June 16 the Baroness saw from a distance a carriage coming down the road to Chambly. It stopped at the spot where Rockel and the girls were posted. "I saw him come nearer and fold the children in his arms. It was my husband!" she reported. Augusta cried for joy. But little Frederika did not want to come near her father. She did not recognize the man who was wrapped in a Canadian coat. "No, no," she cried. "This is an ugly Papa! My Papa is pretty." She remembered her father only from a miniature her mother carried with her—a man with a white wig in a brilliant uniform of blue and gold. General Riedesel threw off the Canadian coat, and now Frederika recognized his uniform and embraced him. Baby Caroline was seeing her father for the first time and laughed when he took her in his arms.

"My happiness," wrote the Baroness, "was indescribable." The general stayed with his wife and children for two days, but on the third day he pushed south with his troops. "Mrs. General" watched the departure of the troops against the enemy and then went back to Trois Rivieres. She felt "alone and deserted with her children, in a foreign land among strangers." But she soon made the acquaintance of the Ursuline nuns who worked in the local hospital. She ate dinner with them at the convent and enjoyed their company. The sisters sensed her loneliness and tried to cheer her up.

"The wish to divert me often enlivened them so much," she wrote, "that they would dress themselves up and dance a kind of Cossack dance, dressing me up at the same time like the nuns. Little Gustava began to weep as soon as she saw me in this costume, and said 'Dear Mamma! Do not become a nun, I beg you!' In order to quiet my children, I was obliged to take off my nun's habit quickly."[7]

They left the hospitable nuns after the fall of Fort Ticonderoga (in July) when her husband wrote that they could join him on the advance toward Albany, New York. Guided by an aide-de-camp, the little family traveled through the wilderness by boat up the St. Lawrence River, then up the Richilieu River to Lake Champlain and across the lake to the port of Lake George. On August 14, 1777, the Baroness and her children reached Fort Edward on the east bank of the Hudson.

The Riedesel family stayed in a little house, known as the "Red House," by the river. There was a large yard around it and a big barn where the girls could play. "I had one room for my husband, myself, and my children," wrote the Baroness. Other rooms were occupied by the general's aides. In mid-August, after the defeat of the German forces at Bennington, Vermont (who had been dispatched there by Burgoyne against Riedesel's advice), the general returned to Fort Edward. His wife and children spent "three happy weeks with him in peace and quiet."

When the British troops finally proceeded toward Albany, the Baroness persuaded her husband that she and the girls need not return to Canada but could follow the army. On October 7, 1777, British and American troops engaged in heavy fighting in upstate New York. General Burgoyne's soldiers were repulsed by American forces under the command of General Horatio Gates. Fatigued and short of supplies, the British and Brunswick troops retreated to Saratoga. Baroness Riedesel and her girls moved with them.

In her letters and journals she gives an eyewitness account of what it was like for the noncombatants, caught between the warring factions:

> About two o'clock in the afternoon, we heard the firing of cannons and small arms, and there was much alarm and confusion [among our troops]. My husband sent me a message that I should immediately retire into a house which was not far off. I got into my calash with my children, and when we were near the house, I saw, on the opposite side of the Hudson River, five or six men with guns, which were aimed at us. Almost involuntarily, I threw the children on the bottom of the calash and myself over them. Immediately after our arrival, a frightful cannonade began, principally directed against the house in which we sought shelter, probably because the enemy believed, from seeing so many people flocking around it, that all the generals made it their headquarters. Alas! It harbored none but wounded soldiers and women! We were finally obliged to take refuge in a cellar, in which I laid myself down in a corner not far from the door. My children laid down on the earth with their heads upon my lap, and in this manner we passed the entire night. A horrible stench, the cries of the children and.... my own anguish prevented me from closing my eyes.[8]

The next morning, the Baroness made their temporary shelter more livable. She swept and fumigated the cellar and laid the most dangerously wounded soldiers in the space farthest from the entrance. Women and children were told to stay in the second section of the cellar, and she sent her own little girls into the space under the stairs. Soon "a fresh and terrible cannonade" threw the occupants of the cellar into alarm. "Eleven cannon balls went through the house," wrote Madame Riedesel, "and we could plainly hear them rolling around. One poor soldier whose leg was about to be amputated had the other leg taken off by another cannon ball in the middle of the operation." The moans of the wounded and dying filled the night. On the third day of the cannonade the Baroness "got things better regulated." She had some straw brought in, on which she slept with the children in a corner, and some of the other occupants of the cellar hung curtains from the ceiling to create partitions to ensure a modicum of privacy.

Little Frederika, who cried a lot during the night, was cheered up by one of the wounded officers who could imitate the bellowing of a cow and the bleating of a calf. When he mimicked these animals, "she would at once become still." The most distressing part of cellar life was the want of fresh water. "I was often obliged to drink wine," the Baroness would later confess, "and give it also to the children.... I had lost all appetite, and had the whole time taken nothing but crusts of bread dipped in wine."

On October 17 Burgoyne and his troops surrendered to the Americans. General Riedesel sent a message to his wife to join him with the children. In the passage through the American camp the Baroness observed that "no one cast at us scornful glances. On the contrary, they all greeted us, and seemed touched at the sight of a captive mother with her little children.... When I drew near the tents, a good-looking man advanced towards me and helped the children from the calash and kissed and caressed them. He then offered me his arms.... 'You tremble,' said he, 'do not be alarmed.' 'Sir,' I cried, 'the kindness which you have shown towards my children are sufficient to dispel all apprehension.' He then ushered me into the tent of General Gates."[9]

The surrender of the British and Brunswick troops took place at two o'clock in the afternoon of October 17, 1777. After the official ceremony was completed, Madame Riedesel and her children were invited to dinner by General Schuyler—the handsome gentleman who had first welcomed her in the American camp. The Baroness and the little girls set down to a "frugal" dinner of smoked tongues, beef steaks, potatoes, fresh butter, and bread—delicacies they had not tasted for a long time. "Never did a dinner give me so much pleasure as this," she wrote. "I was at ease, after many months of anxiety."

General Riedesel and his family began the long trek to Boston, where his captive troops were to await transportation to Great Britain "under Condition of not serving again in North America during the present Contest." They spent three days in Albany visiting General Schuyler and his wife and daughters, who showed them "the most marked courtesy." As the Riedesels were about to leave for Boston, they discovered that the general's entire camp equipment had been stolen. They set out with a minimum of luggage in a small carriage, covered with coarse linen

General Schuyler and Baroness Riedesel and her children. *Courtesy North Wind Picture Archives.*

varnished with oil. "It had the appearance of a wagon in which they carry around rare animals," noted the Baroness, who had kept her sense of humor.

The journey to Boston was long and tedious. "I was often obliged to halt because the people insisted upon seeing the wife of the German general with her children," she reported. "The people were very friendly, and were particularly delighted at my being able to speak English." Her arrival in Boston must have escaped the critical eye of Hannah Winthrop, the wife of a Harvard professor of astronomy who described the march of the defeated British troops and their ancillaries through Cambridge in a letter to her good friend, Mercy Warren:[10]

Cambridge, November 11, 1777

Last Thursday which was a very stormy day, a large number of British troops came thro the town via Watertown to Prospect Hill. On Friday we heard the Hessians were to make a procession in the same rout; we thought we should have nothing to do with them but view them as they past. To be sure, the sight was truly astonishing. I never had the least idea that the Creation produced such a sordid set of creatures in human figure—poor, dirty emaciated men, great numbers of women, who seemed to be the beasts of burden, having a bushel basket on their back, by which they were bent double—the contents seemed to be pots and kettles.... children peeping through gridirons and other utensils, some very young infants who were born on the road; the women with bare feet, clothed in dirty rugs.... The Hessian general gave us a polite bow as they passed. Not so the British.... The generals and other officers went to Bradishs, where they quarter at present. How mortifying is it—they in a manner demanding our houses and colleges for their genteel accommodations. Did the brave General Gates ever mean this? Some polite ones say, we ought not to look at them as prisoners, they are persons of distinguished rank. Perhaps too we must not view them in the light of enemies. I fear this distinction will soon be lost. Surprising that our general or any of our colonels should insist on the first University in America being disbanded for their more genteel accommodation, and we poor oppressed people seek an asylum in the woods against a piercing winter!

The Riedesel family found temporary quarters at Bradish's Tavern, just off Harvard Square, "a filthy place" in the opinion of "Lady Fritz," whose pen could be as sharp as that of Hannah Winthrop's. They made do with one attic room and a field bed. The children slept on the floor on straw.

One evening, the British officers celebrated the birthday of the Queen of England and on this occasion drank a great deal of wine. Six-year-old Augusta and three-and-a-half-year-old Frederika noticed that some of the wine that was left over had been placed under the stairs. They decided that it would be a fine thing for them to do to toast the queen's health. When their mother found them by the door, "they had toasted so much that their little heads could bear no more." They became sick, and Madame Riedesel gave them a scolding. But they promptly told her that they also loved the king and queen and felt obliged to wish them happiness.

After a three-week stay at the tavern, the Riedesels were moved to a house in Cambridge. The Continental Congress had changed its mind about the captive British troops. The Americans feared that if these troops returned to England, they would be rotated to new posts in Europe and replaced in America with the troops they relieved. Hence their embarkation was postponed indefinitely.

The Riedesels stayed in Cambridge until November 1778. By then, supplies had become scarce in Massachusetts. When it became clear that the Convention troops were to stay in America "for the duration," Congress ordered their transfer to Virginia, where supplies were more plentiful. In the midst of winter the general and his troops were on the march again. His wife and daughters traveled nearly 12 weeks before they reached their destination at Colle, near Charlottesville, in the middle of February 1779.

They proceeded by carriage through Connecticut, New York, New Jersey, Pennsylvania, and Maryland, crossing the Blue Mountains into Virginia. Their journey was slowed down by bad weather and bad roads. Augusta, the oldest of the Riedesel girls, saw to it that they would be accompanied by one of her father's adjutants, on whom they could rely for assistance when their wagon got stuck on impassable roads.

Occasionally, they ran out of provisions, and sometimes they were not welcome among the local people from whom they sought to buy supplies. One woman, who first refused to sell the Baroness any foodstuff because she considered her an enemy, changed her mind when three-year-old Caroline came up to her, seized her by the hand, and pleaded with her in English, "Good woman, I am very hungry." She was about to give an egg to the child when the little girl told her, "I have still two sisters." The woman promptly gave her three eggs, saying, "I am just as angry as ever, but I cannot withstand this child."[11]

Not everyone changed his mind about the captive foreigners. In Virginia, when they were only one day's journey from the place of their destination, the Baroness and her children had no more food left. "At noon we came to a dwelling where I begged for something to eat," wrote Madame Riedesel. "They refused me with hard words, saying that there was nothing for dogs of Royalists.... My children were exhausted by hunger, very wan, and I for the first time was thoroughly disheartened."

Finally, the driver of one of the baggage wagons gave them a piece of old bread that was so hard that no one could bite off the smallest piece. When the Baroness was about to give the piece to her youngest daughter Caroline, the child refused. "No," she said, "my sisters are more hungry than I." Augusta and Frederika also refused to take it, wishing to leave the bread for their little sister. With tears in her eyes, their mother divided it, as best she could, in three equal pieces and gave it to all three to eat.

From Monticello, Thomas Jefferson could see the arrival of the British and German prisoners of war. "There could not have been a more unlucky concurrence of circumstances than when these troops first came," he wrote. "The barracks unfinished for want of laborers, the worst spell of weather ever known within the memory of man, no stores of bread laid in, the roads by the weather and number of wagons soon rendered impassable."[12]

General Riedesel had moved on ahead to find some accommodations for his family. He was finally able to locate a plantation house that was owned by Jefferson and paid him rent for two years, adding an additional building for the accommodation of his family. In April Thomas Jefferson sold his pianoforte to the German general, who gave it as a present to the

Baroness, who was a fine musician. That same month, the Jeffersons and
their daughter Martha received a formal dinner invitation to meet their
new neighbors.

Six-year-old Martha Jefferson often played with the "three young
ladies from Colle." Augusta was now eight years old; Frederika was
five, and Caroline was three. The Jeffersons and Riedesels became good
friends. After Jefferson's election as governor of Virginia took him to
Williamsburg, he wrote to the general that he missed "the agreeable
society I have left, of which Madame Riedesel and yourself were an
important part. Mrs. Jefferson in this particular sympathizes with me,
and especially on her separation from Madame Riedesel."¹³

In the fall the Riedesel girls were on the move again. Their father
and General Phillips, the ranking officer of the captive British troops,
were to be exchanged in New York for captured American officers.
When his family left Virginia, General Riedesel sent Jefferson a farewell note, expressing his "heartiest thanks for every mark of Friendship
which you have so kindly testified to me from the first moment of our
acquaintance, and for the assistance and hospitality which you have
shown the Troops under my Command since you have assumed the
Government of Virginia."¹⁴

The general and his family spent several weeks among the German
Moravians in Bethlehem, Pennsylvania, under orders from General
Washington and the Congressional Continental Congress, until the
British had settled debts incurred for the maintenance of the Convention troops. When the Continental Congress finally released Riedesel
to go to New York on parole, he left his family in Bethlehem. Little
Caroline had developed a "choking cough" and was very ill. The other
children came down with it later. Their mother was "far advanced in
pregnancy" and "in constant pain."

Finally, at the end of November 1779, the Baroness and her three girls
set out for New York. "The journey fatigued me exceedingly," she wrote
in her journal. They settled in a house that was furnished with carpets
and furniture confiscated from wealthy rebels. Residing with the Riedesel
family was Pastor Mylius, the regimental chaplain, "who gave the children instructions in everything useful. He was a man of character and
good humor, and the children ... loved him very much."

On the seventh of March, 1780, Madame Riedesel gave birth to
another daughter. "My husband wished very much for a son," the
Baroness wrote later, "but the little one was so pretty that we are soon
consoled for its not being a boy. We had intended, in case it had been a
boy, to have named it Americus, which we now changed for the little girl
into America. The same day my eldest daughter was seized with a dangerous illness, called *asthma infantile,* and some days afterward my third

child became also very sick; and I, therefore, lay in bed between both my almost dying children. But if my heart suffered deeply, my body had by this time become endured to any hardships."[15]

Six weeks afterward, when the Baroness and the older girls had recovered, she accompanied her husband to a dinner given by General Tryon. Unknown to Mrs. Riedesel, an English physician inoculated baby America against the smallpox while her mother was out of the home. "When the baby became so ill that we were afraid we would lose her, my poor husband was inconsolable," she wrote. "I had all I could do to keep up his spirits. But God be praised, it came out all right in the end." Jefferson, meanwhile, had sent a letter of condolence to the Riedesels on account of the birth of yet another daughter![16]

On October 13, 1780, General Riedesel was restored to active duty in exchange for General Benjamin Lincoln, captured by the British at Charleston during the summer. He was given a command on Long Island, and in spring 1781 he and his family moved to his Brooklyn headquarters, a farmhouse across the East River from New York. That spring, eight people in the Riedesel household fell dangerously ill, among them the general and 10-year-old Augusta. "Augusta had such violent paroxysms of fever," reported her mother, "that she begged me to hold her tightly, and when the chills and the fits of shaking came she shook me with her in the bed."

At last, Augusta and her father recovered. By early summer, the general requested a transfer to Canada and was relieved of his Long Island assignment in July. After an eight-week journey, the Riedesel family reached Quebec in September. The girls were fluent in English and German, and now they would have to learn French as well. The governor of Canada appointed their father to command all German troops in Canada and assigned him to Sorel in the province of Quebec, where the Richelieu River joins the St. Lawrence. They moved into their new home a few days before Christmas.

On Christmas Eve they invited some English officers for a dinner to celebrate the holiday, partly in the English and partly in the German manner. Under the illuminated Christmas tree—its branches lit with candles—was placed the Christmas pie or "plum pudding"—"an article inseparable among Englishmen from this festivity." The Riedesel's "young ladies"—Augusta, Frederika, Caroline, and America—marveled at the feast. The general's house in Sorel would henceforth be known by the local population as the Christmas Tree House.[17]

The Riedesels lived a bucolic life: In the winter the Baroness used her attic as a gigantic freezer, where she stored frozen fish, fowl, beef, and lamb. The Indians brought her cranberries—"a tasty red fruit the size of a small cherry, but without the stone." In the spring the general planted a garden and hundreds of fruit trees. "I had my cows, many fowl, and

Baroness Riedesel celebrates Christmas at Sorel, Quebec, 1781. *Photographed by Simon Menard.*

Virginia hogs," wrote the Baroness in her diary. "I also made my own butter." She was pregnant again.

The Riedesel girls and their mother were alone a lot on their "magnificent farm." General Riedesel spent much of the summer and fall with his troops at the Isle aux Noix. The girls practiced duets on the harpsichord their father had bought for their mother. Madame Riedesel went riding in the countryside.

On November 1, 1782, another daughter was born. General Riedesel returned to Sorel on November 5 and "found the little maiden so handsome that he was consoled for his disappointment [of not having a son]." The baby was christened by Pastor Mylius, the tutor of the Riedesel girls. They named the little girl Luisa Augusta Elizabeth Canada. But "Canada"—the name they would call her by—died at the age of five months from a violent attack of diarrhea. Her mother had not been able to breast-feed her, and she was malnourished. Augusta, the baby's 11-year-old godmother, was taken ill as well—from sorrow, her mother surmised.

Baby Canada was buried in the cemetery at Sorel. The officers at the garrison promised her mother that they would mark the grave with a stone "which would prevent the inhabitants from taking up the heretic child from the consecrated earth." But the local parish priest assured Madame Riedesel that she need have no fear. Her child was now "one of God's angels."

By the middle of March 1783, news from London reached Quebec that the war was finally winding down. The Baroness was homesick. Her children were now more fluent in English and French than in German and had forgotten the faces of their relatives in Germany. "Had it not been for this homesickness," she wrote in her journal, "I should have been perfectly contented in Canada; for the climate agreed well with my children, and we were beloved by, and on very pleasant footing with the people." But it was time to go back to Europe.

The Riedesel family and the surviving members of the Brunswick regiment sailed for home in August 1783. Their ship was a large West India three-decker in good condition, "a pretty ship," according to nine-year-old Frederika. Her parents partitioned off two staterooms, one for the children and one for themselves. The governor had a cow and a calf put on board so that the children could have fresh milk, and "a place on the upper deck he had filled with earth to make a garden for growing salad plants." The Riedesels brought "many fowls, sheep and vegetables" on board because they had to feed 22 officers each day who were part of their "official family." Twelve-year-old Augusta received a beautiful hunting dog as a farewell gift from Governor Haldimand, a bachelor, who adored the girl and had taken to calling her "my little wife."[18]

The voyage to England took some five weeks, alternating between calm weather on the St. Lawrence and a fierce storm in the North Atlantic. They reached Portsmouth in mid-September, shortly after the Definitive Treaty had been signed between the United States and Great Britain. They went first to London, where the general made a report to the king. Queen Charlotte assured the Baroness, who felt not properly dressed for an audience at St. James, that the royal family did "not look at clothes when we are happy to see the people." The children had a tearful reunion with the Russells, who had taught the three oldest daughters to speak English during their first stay in England in 1776–1777.

By October 1783, Riedesel's regiment was back in Germany. The Baroness and her children went immediately to their residence in Wolfen-büttel. On October 8 General Riedesel marched his troops to Brunswick, where they were surrounded by a "partly happy, partly pathetic bustle of fathers, mothers, wives, children, brothers, sisters, and friends who all pressed about to see their loved ones again." Only 2,400 of the 4,300 Brunswick soldiers returned home from America.[19]

CHAPTER 10

John Quincy Adams on a Diplomatic Mission to Europe

The boy who had boarded the 24-gun frigate *Boston* on February 13, 1778, bound for Europe, was 10 years old. John Quincy Adams was the only family member to accompany his father, who had been appointed by Congress to serve as a commissioner to the Court of France. John Adams was to work with Benjamin Franklin and Arthur Lee in negotiating an alliance with the French.

Abigail Adams had intended to accompany her husband, but that plan had been considered "too hazardous and imprudent." Now, her oldest son would have the chance of his lifetime. Father and son embarked with a mountain of baggage for the long journey. They brought two fat sheep; two hogs; six dozen chickens; 14 dozen eggs; five bushels of corn; a barrel of apples; a barrel of Madeira; a keg of rum; four dozen bottles of port wine; tea; chocolate; sugar; and a box of wafers—for nourishment. Their cabin contained a double mattress, comforters and pillows to rest on, and quill pens, ink, and paper.[1]

Abigail and John Adams were inveterate correspondents, and their eldest son soon used his pen to relate his experiences in letters and diaries that span the period from 1778 to 1785. During that time John Quincy visited more than half a dozen countries in Europe. He traveled to Spain, France, Holland, Russia, Sweden, Denmark, Germany, and England and crossed the Atlantic four times before his 18th birthday. He would dine with Benjamin Franklin and Thomas Jefferson, witness the splendor of the Royal Courts of Versailles and St. Petersburg, and attend a debate in the British Parliament in London. He would "bear down" on his lessons in Latin, Greek, French, German, and Dutch—and yearn to own a pair of ice skates, riding boots, and a penknife for he was still a child when he first ventured abroad.

Born on July 11, 1767, John Quincy Adams was seven years old when his father went to Philadelphia to participate in the first meetings of the Continental Congress. Despite his busy political life, John Adams was concerned about his oldest son, "what school to send him to—what measures to take with him." "And above all, he must write," he told Abigail—and write the boy did.

On October 13, 1774, John Quincy sent a note to his father:

> Sir,—I have been trying ever since you went away to learn to write you a letter. I shall make poor work of it; but, sir, mamma says you will accept my endeavors, and that my duty to you may be expressed in poor writing as well as good. I hope to grow a better boy, and that you will have no occasion to be ashamed of me when you return. Mr. Thaxter says I learn my books well. He is a very good master. I read my books to mamma. We all long to see you. I am, sir, your dutiful son, JOHN QUINCY ADAMS[2]

Abigail had persuaded "little Johnny" to read her each night a page or two from Charles Rollin's *Ancient History,* popular among patriots. She hoped that her eldest son would develop a fondness for it. One month before his eighth birthday, on June 12, 1775, she had taken the boy to witness the Battle of Bunker Hill. That experience nurtured his patriotic spirit as much as his father's advice that, despite his tender age, he should study the histories of revolutions to help throw some light on the American conflict with the British.

In a letter of August 11, 1777, John Adams urged his 10-year-old son to read Thucydides's *History of the Peloponnesian War*—in the original Greek! Such a work, he told him, would afford "the most solid Instruction and Improvement for the Part which may be allotted to you to act on the Stage of Life." John Quincy—precocious, serious, and eager to please—responded:

> Dear Sir—I love to receive letters very well, much better than I love to write them. I make but a poor figure at composition, my head is much too fickle, my thoughts are running about birds' eggs, play and trifles till I get vexed with myself.... I wish, sir, you would give me some instructions with regard to my time, and advise me how to proportion my studies and play, in writing, and I will keep them by me and endeavor to follow them. I am, dear sir, with a present determination of growing better, Yours JOHN QUINCY ADAMS[3]

When father and son embarked on their 3,000-mile voyage on the North Atlantic on February 14, 1778, winds were gathering to gale force. They were departing for France in the most treacherous season of the year, and neither John Adams nor his small son knew of the perils that lay ahead of them. Both would allude to this, their first ocean voyage, more frequently than to any of the later crossings—and tell of the savage storm, the misery, and the terror they experienced.

During that voyage, after they lost their main topmast in the storm, John Adams began to regret that he had brought his son along. But "Johnny's Behavior gave me a Satisfaction that I cannot express—Fully sensible to our Danger, he was constantly endeavoring to bear it with a manly Patience, very attentive to me and his Thoughts constantly running a serious Strain."

They reached the coast of France after a six-week voyage and landed in Bordeaux on April 1, 1778.

A week later, they arrived in Paris. John Quincy Adams, in his first letter to his "Honored Mamma," expressed the heartfelt feelings of both father and son: "I hope I shall never forget the goodness of God in Preserving us Through all the Dangers That We have been exposed to in Crossing The Seas, and that by his almighty Power we have arrived Safe in France after a Troublesome Voyage."[4]

"Johnny" promptly entered a boarding school at Passy, a suburb of Paris. His schoolmates included Benjamin Franklin Bach and William Temple Franklin, grandsons of Benjamin Franklin. Soon the boy from Puritan New England acquired a taste for the French theater. His favorite was the Theatre des Petits Comediens du Bois de Boulogne, "where a company of Children performed two or three times a week."

On April 20, 1778, John Quincy Adams informed his mother about the important political development that had taken place after his father's arrival. "I suppose before this reaches you, you will hear of the Treaty concluded between France and America which I believe will rouse the hearts of the Americans exceedingly, and also of the desire of the English To make Peace with us and the Commissioner dispatched from England for that purpose."[5]

The alliance between France and America designated each partner "a most favored nation" for trade and friendship. From now on France would be obliged to fight for American independence, and America would be obliged to stand by France. Shortly after John Quincy's letter, Britain and France were at war, and the British commissioners returned home, their peace mission a failure.

On June 5, 1778, John Quincy wrote to Abigail, "Yesterday, my pappa received a large number of papers from America, but the two armies were then in the same posture as they were when we came but I hope they have done Something by this time."[6] As the months passed, John Adams became increasingly disenchanted about any prospect for peace.

While John Quincy was attending school, his father admonished him to keep a journal or diary, but the 11-year-old had some doubts about this enterprise. He confided them to his mother in a letter, written on September 27, 1778:[7]

> Honoured Mamma—My Pappa enjoins it upon me to keep a journal, or a diary of the events that happened to me, and of objects that I see, and of characters that I converse with day to day, and altho I am convinced of the utility, importance and necessity of this exercise, yet I have not patience and perseverance enough to do it so constantly as I ought. My Pappa, who takes a great deal of pains to put me in the right way, has also advised me to preserve copies of all my letters, & has given me a convenient blank book for this end; and altho I shall have the mortification a few years hence to read a great deal of my childish nonsense, yet I shall have the pleasure and advantage of remarking the several steps by which I shall have advanced in taste, judgement & knowledge. A journal book and a letter book of a lad of eleven-years-old cannot be expected to contain much of science, literature, arts, wisdom, or wit, yet it may serve to perpetuate many observations that I may make & may hereafter help me to recollect both persons & things that would otherwise escape my memory.

In the spring of 1779 John Adams started making plans to return home. His work as a commissioner was terminated. Congress had appointed a single minister to France, Benjamin Franklin. On June 17, 1779, he and his son embarked for America in the French king's frigate *La Sensible*. On August 2, 1779, John Quincy Adams and his father were rowed from the *Sensible* to the shore at Braintree, Massachusetts. No one was expecting them—their arrival back home was a complete surprise. When they met Abigail and the three children, they talked day and night about their experiences abroad and about the news of the war at home.

The war was at a stalemate. In June the British had evacuated Philadelphia, and Washington's forces had fought them at Monmouth, New Jersey, in a major battle. But the British were still holding New York and had made successful forays in the South. No one knew how the struggle would be resolved. Suddenly, in October 1779, Congress sent word from Philadelphia that John Adams had been chosen to return to France as Minister Plenipotentiary to negotiate treaties of peace and commerce with the British.

From the captain of the *Sensible* came the offer of a return passage. John Adams accepted it and, a little more than three months after he arrived home, he was again on his way across the Atlantic Ocean. This time, he was accompanied by two of his sons: John Quincy Adams, now 12 years old, and nine-year-old Charles Adams. "Johnny" had wanted to remain at home and prepare for entry to Harvard, but his mother convinced him to return to France.

One of the first letters John Quincy would receive from Abigail after he left home bears her admonitions:

It will be expected of you, my son, that as you are favored with superior advantages under the instructive eye of a tender parent, that your improvements should bear some proportion to your advantages. Nothing is wanting with you, but attention, diligence, and steady application. It is your Lot, My son, to be an eye witness of these calamities in your own native land, and at the same time to owe your existence among a people who have made a glorious defence of their invaded Liberties, and who, aided by a generous and powerful Ally, with the blessing of heaven, will transmit this inheritance to ages yet unborn. Your ever affectionate Mother[8]

On November 13, 1779, John Adams, his sons John Quincy and Charles, his secretary, Francis Dana, and John Thaxter, tutor for the boys, went aboard the *Sensible*. The wind seemed favorable. John Quincy Adams wrote his first entry into his new diary.[9] Suddenly, two days out of Boston, with a stiff northeast wind blowing, the *Sensible* sprang a leak. A pump was put in service, but the leak grew worse day by day. Then, the second week off the Grand Banks, the wind began to blow from the northwest. For one day, in a violent gale, the frigate labored only under her foresail.

By the time the storm passed, the ship was leaking so badly that two pumps had to be manned day and night. All hands took part in the unrelenting work, including young John Quincy Adams. In the event of another storm or an encounter with an enemy ship, the *Sensible* would be utterly defenseless. The only chance they had was to head for the nearest friendly port in Spain. The ship labored across the ocean until she reached El Ferrol, on Spain's northwestern tip, on December 8, 1779.

That day, John Quincy Adams noted in his diary, "I thought that the fort saluted us at twelve o'clock, but I find it is the Spanish Admiral's birthday, and they have a great festival of it."[10] Faced with the prospect of having to wait weeks while repairs were made on the ship, his father decided to proceed overland, east across Spain and over the Pyrenees to the French border. The distance to Paris was 1,000 miles; the terrain was extremely difficult, especially in the winter.

On the morning of December 15, John Adams, his two sons, Francis Dana, John Thaxter, and a couple of Spanish guides and muleteers set off on scraggy mules across mountains that were covered with fog and snow. On the last day of 1779 John Quincy Adams scribbled in his diary, "We had nothing worth remarking today except we kept ascending." The next day's journey was "almost perpendicular." The boys were sick with colds, but they persevered across the Pyrenees. From Bordeaux they traveled by coach to Paris. "It was the worst three weeks that I ever passed in my life," wrote Johnny.[11]

Despite fog and icy roads, they reached the French capital on February 9, 1780, nearly two months after they had departed from El Ferrol and three months after setting sail from Boston. On February 17 John Quincy

Adams wrote to his "honoured mamma," "I have wrote you a small account of my Voyage and that we were obliged to put into Ferrol in Spain. After a terrible journey from thence to Paris of about 1,000 miles, we have at last once more reached Paris. The day after we arrived Pappa put me [in]to one of the Pensions where I was before, and I am very content with my situation. Brother Charles begins to make himself understood in French and, being as he is, he will learn that Language very soon."[12]

A month later, Abigail wrote to her eldest son a letter of "gratitude and thankfulness to Heaven for the preservation you experienced in the imminent Dangers which threatened you." She continued,

> If you have a due sense of your preservation, your next consideration will be, for what purpose you are continued in Life? Every Mercy you receive is a New Debt upon you, a new obligation....Justice, humanity and Benevolence are the duties you owe to society in general. To your Country the same duties are incumbent upon you, with the additional obligation of sacrificing ease, pleasure, wealth and life itself for its Defense and security.... Behold your own Country, your Native Land suffering from the Effects of Lawless power and Malignant passions, and learn betimes from your own observation and experience to govern and control yourself....Having once obtained this self-government, you will find a foundation laid for happiness to yourself and useful to mankind.[13]

After half a year in Passy, the boys left with their father for Holland, where John Adams was to negotiate a loan for the United States. On July 27, 1780, they were on their way north by coach, traveling through the finest farmland they had ever seen. "We passed by Mons which is a city and a very pretty one," wrote John Quincy Adams in his diary. "I never saw a more beautiful one in my life."

In a new country and in an unfamiliar city, the boy diligently copied into his diary long passages from guidebooks about points of interest in Amsterdam and marveled at the tidiness and order of the Dutch countryside. When winter came, the days turned bitterly cold and raw, and the air was filled with chimney smoke. But John Quincy loved the spectacle of the skaters on the ice of the frozen canals.

In September 1780 John Adams had enrolled his sons in the Latin School in Amsterdam. The school was an unhappy experience for John Quincy. He was placed with elementary students because he spoke no Dutch, and he resented being taught at a level below his abilities. He grew restless and discouraged. "How long we shall be here," he wrote, "I cannot tell." The rector of the Latin school thought him impertinent and in need of a thrashing.

The headmaster wrote to John Adams, "The disobedience and impertinence of your older son, who does his best to corrupt his well-behaved brother can no longer be tolerated, as he endeavors by his bad behavior to bring upon himself the punishment he deserves, in the hope of leaving school as a result." "Send the boys to me this evening," was John Adams curt reply. To Abigail, he wrote angrily, "The masters are mean-spirited wretches, punching, kicking, and boxing the children upon every turn." He did not want his sons subjected to "such littleness of soul."[14]

In December 1780 their tutor, John Thaxter, took the boys to Leyden, where they were to study Latin and Greek and attend lectures at the university (which were given in Latin). "You are now at an University, where many of the greatest Men have received their Education," wrote John Adams to his oldest son on December 20. "Many of the most famous Characters, which England has produced, have pursued their Studies ... at Leyden. Some, tho not many of the Sons of America have studied there.... As I know you have an Ardent Thirst for Knowledge and a good capacity to acquire it, I depend upon it, you will do no Dishonour to yourself nor to the University of Leyden."[15]

Thirteen-year-old John Quincy's expressed desires were more appropriate for a boy his age. On December 21 he wrote to his father in Amsterdam:

> Honoured Sir—I should be glad to have a pair of Scates they are of various prices from 3 Guilders to 3 Ducats those of a Ducat are as good as need to be but I should like to know whether you would chuse to have me give so much.... For riding I must have a pair of leather breeches and a pair of boots. I should be glad if you would answer me upon that as soon as you receive this for there is a vacancy here ... and in the vacancy is the best time to begin to learn to ride.... I continue writing in Homer, the Greek Grammar and Greek testament every day. I am your most dutiful Son, JOHN QUINCY ADAMS[16]

John Adams replied two days later. "Mr. Thaxter may purchase each of you a Pair of Scates. He may go to what Price he thinks proper—but be careful and moderate in the Use of them. You may get the Leather Breeches and Boots, but have them made large, otherwise, you grow so fast, that you will not be able to wear them many months. I would have you all take some Lessons at the Riding School."[17]

The boys were separated from their father during Christmastime, but there would be another letter for John Quincy before the year ended. On December 28 John Adams wrote to him, "The ice is so universal now that I suppose you spend some Time in Skating every day.... As your Constitution requires vigorous Exercise, it will not be amiss, to spend some of your Time in Swimming, Riding, Dancing, Fencing and Skaiting, which ... is easy to learn by a little attention to perform them all with Taste.... Everything in Life should be done with Reflection, and

Judgement, even the most insignificant Amusements....That you may attend early to this Maxim is the Wish of your affectionate father."[18]

The new year brought a letter from Abigail Adams. "'Tis nine months since a single line from your own hand reached me," she began her letter of January 21, 1781. She seemed unaware of the painful adjustments her sons had to make in moving from France to Holland, from one strange city (Amsterdam) to another (Leyden), and their struggle to learn another foreign language. Instead, she set forth, once again, her demanding expectations for her oldest boy:[19]

> You are now in a Country famed for its industry and frugality, and which has given Birth to many Learned and great Men....You must not be a superficial observer, but study Men and Manners that you may be Skillful in both....The earlier in life you accustom yourself to consider objects with attention, the earlier will your progress be, and more sure and successful your enterprizes....Let your ambition be engaged to be eminent, but above all things support a virtuous character and remember that "an Honest Man is the Noblest Work of God."

The correspondence between John Quincy Adams and his parents during the first half of 1781 reveals their deep concern about his education and his "good Morals" and the boy's constant desire to please them as best he could. With few amusements to describe, his diary entries become perfunctory, then stop altogether. He would not resume his diary until a half-year later, on the day his father came to take him and his brother from Leyden. Meanwhile, he bore down on his lessons—according to his tutor, "with a constancy rarely seen at that age."

His father sent him a gift of several volumes of Pope and a volume of his favorite Roman author, Terence—"remarkable for good morals, good taste, and good Latin." "I hope you will not forget your mother tongue," John Adams advised him. "Read Somewhat in the English Poets every day. You will find them elegant, entertaining and instructive Companions through your whole Life.... You will never be alone with a Poet in your Pocket.... You will remember that all the End of study is to make you a good Man and a useful Citizen. This will ever be the Sum total of the Advice of your affectionate Father."[20]

Abigail expressed the hope that the cleanliness and neatness of the Dutch would cure her "dear boy" of his slovenly tricks and teach him industry, economy, and frugality. "I would recommend it to you," she wrote in her letter of May 26, "to become acquainted with the History of their Country; in many respects it is similar to the Revolution of your own. Tyranny and oppression were the original causes of the revolt of both Countries."[21]

John Quincy, in turn, reported dutifully on his academic exercises— "I learn a Greek verb through the Active, Passive and Medium Voices every day" he wrote to his father. "The last letter that I received from you contained some excellent advice for which I am very much obliged to you," he told his mother. But more typical of a boy his age was a request he made from John Adams: "I should be much obliged to you if you would be so good as to desire Stephens to buy me a penknife, I want one very much, and can't get one here."[22]

In the early summer 1781 Francis Dana was notified by Congress to proceed from Amsterdam to St. Petersburg to seek recognition of the United States of America by the imperial government of Catherine the Great of Russia. Dana spoke little French and needed secretarial help. He asked Adams if John Quincy might accompany him on a 2,000-mile journey to a capital city that few Americans had ever visited. Adams consented, thinking this extraordinary experience would be an asset for his son's political future.

"Johnny" was gone on a "long journey with Mr. Dana...as an interpreter," he reported to Abigail in a letter from Paris, written on July 11, 1781, John Quincy's 14th birthday. Young Charles, whose health had been precarious throughout his stay in Holland and who was home-sick for his mother, would be returning to Massachusetts. "I consented to the departure of both boys ... and thus deprived myself of the greatest pleasure I had in life," Adams wrote later.[23]

John Quincy Adams left with Francis Dana from Amsterdam on July 7, 1781; Charles sailed on the *South Carolina* in mid-August. By the end of August, John Quincy wrote his first letter to his father from St. Petersburg. Their trip had taken them from Amsterdam through northern Germany to Berlin, "the capital of the King of Prussia's Dominion which is a very pretty town." The king, according to young Johnny's observations, "treats his subjects like slaves." They then passed through Danzig, Königsberg, and Riga into Poland, "where all the farmers are in the most abject slavery; they are bought and sold like so many beasts." St. Petersburg, in John Quincy's opinion, was even handsomer than Berlin, with large streets and very well built houses.[24]

Once settled in St. Petersburg, John Quincy Adams mentioned only the routine features of his daily life in his correspondence. Contrary to expectations, Francis Dana never received acknowledgment as the representative of an independent nation, and he was treated as an outsider by the empress and her ministers. John Quincy's role as Dana's secretary and interpreter proved to be a minor one. He was reduced to continuing his studies, including German (the native language of the Russian empress), without proper schools, tutors, or books.

The boy's letters to his father are filled with references to his limited opportunities to pursue new knowledge. In October 1781 he wrote from St. Petersburg, "I can't get here any good dictionary either French and

Latin or English and Latin.... This is not a very good place for learning the Latin and Greek Languages, as there is no academy or school here, and but very few private teachers who demand at the rate of 90 pounds Sterling a year, for an hour and a half each day. Mr. Dana don't chuse to employ any at that extravagant prize."[25]

His father responded in mid-December, "I think the Price for a Master is intolerable. If there is no Academy, nor School, nor a Master to be had, I really don't know what to say about your staying in Russia. You had better be at Leyden.... You might come in the Spring in a Russian, Swedish or Prussian Vessell, to Em[b]den perhaps or Hamb[oro]urg[h], and from thence here."[26]

In his letter of February 5, 1792, John Adams expressed his concern about his son's social isolation: "Do you find any Company? It must be an unsociable dull Life to a young Man, if you have not some Acquaintances. Alas! I regret that the Friendships of your Childhood cannot be made among your own Countrymen. And I regret your Loss of the glorious Advantages for classical studies at Leyden."[27]

Abigail Adams, in turn, challenged John Quincy to make the best out of his stay in St. Petersburg: "You are confined in your studies, you tell me and have little opportunity for observation. But you cannot reside among a people, without learning Something of their Laws, customs, and Manners. Nor can you ... omit comparing them with those of your Own country.... It will be of advantage to you to compare the Monarchical governments with the Republican to reflect upon the advantages and disadvantages, arising from each."[28]

After a 14-month stay, John Quincy Adams left St. Petersburg in the last week of October 1782. He arrived back in Holland in mid-April 1783. In a letter to his mother he sent his apologies to her and his friends in America for having been "a little bit behind" in writing to them. "I have been all that time almost at the world's end," he continued, "in such an *out-of-the-way* place."[29]

On his return journey he stopped in three countries, Sweden, Denmark, and Germany. Of the three, he liked Sweden the most. "I stayed in Stockholm about six weeks," he wrote to his mother, "and was much pleased with the polite manner in which the people of the Country treat strangers, Sweden is the country in Europe which pleases me most ... of those I have seen. Because their manners resemble more those of my own Country than any I have seen. The King is a Man of great Abilities.... He is extremely popular and has persuaded his people that they are free."[30]

"They are in general good friends to America," he wrote to his father from Gotheborg, where he stayed in January 1783. "They are well disposed for carrying on Commerce with America.... They talk a great deal

John Quincy Adams at age 15. *National Portrait Gallery, Smithsonian Institution.*

here about peace.... Of all men, the King of Sweden knows the best how to seize upon opportunities and I think we might have a considerable commerce with Sweden."[31]

By mid-February, John Quincy found himself in Copenhagen. "The people of Denmark treat strangers with a great deal of Politeness and Civility," he wrote to Abigail, "but not with the same open-heartedness, which they do in Sweden. The government is entirely Monarchical. It astonishes me that a whole people can place at the Head of their government such a Man as the King of Denmark.... The hereditary prince it seems is at least possessed of common sense and is considered in the Country as a prodigy as indeed he is, if he is compared to his father."[32]

John Quincy had originally planned to sail from Copenhagen to Kiel in Germany, but the harbor of Copenhagen froze up, and so he traveled by land to Hamburg. He informed his mother, "I arrived in Hamborough the 11th of March. I stayed there near a month. It is a large city; quite commercial and will, I dare say, carry on hereafter a great deal of Trade with America.... The last city where I made any stay ... was Bremen which is another commercial Republic ... one of the Hanseatic league. There are at Bremen some publick cellars which are famous, I drank there some Rhenish wine—about 160 years old."[33]

He arrived back in Holland on the 15th of April, on the day Congress ratified the Preliminary Articles of Peace, and warfare between America and Britain formally ceased. His father had gone to Paris to work on the Definitive Peace Treaty. A week later, John Adams wrote to his son:

> Mr. Hartley is arrived here, as Min. Plen, from his Brittanic Majesty to finish the Peace, and I hope it will be not many weeks before I shall see you at The Hague.... It is my hope and expectation to return to America as Soon as the Definitive Treaty is signed and I can go to The Hague to exchange Ratifications [of the Treaty of Amity and Commerce between the United States and the Netherlands] and Take Leave. If we could embark by the Middle of May or beginning of June We should have a Prospect of a Pleasant voyage....You and I don't yet know what it is to cross the Atlantick without fear of Enemies.[34]

John Quincy reported to his father from The Hague in mid-May: "The 4th of this month a vessel from Philadelphia arrived.... Tis said here that the Preliminary articles between Great Britain and the Republick are about to be signed, and that the Definitive Treaty will soon be finished; if so, I hope you will soon be here."[35]

On July 3, 1783, a dispirited John Adams wrote from Paris, "My dear Son, I can tell you nothing with Certainty when the Peace will be finished, I hope it will not be long....I long to See you, but can as yet form no Judgement when I shall have that Pleasure. We have no News from Congress, a Neglect which is to the last degree astonishing and inexplicable."[36]

By the end of July, the elder Adams went to Holland to take his son back to France to serve as his personal secretary. On August 11, 1783, John Quincy noted in his diary, "This morning, Mr. Hartley, the British Minister for making Peace, came to pay a visit to my Father, but as he was out he desired to see me. I had some Conversation with him. He says he hopes the Peace will be soon signed."[37]

On September 4 the boy wrote to his mother, "Mr. Thaxter who will deliver you this [letter] expects to sail for New York in the course of this Month. He will probably carry the Definitive Treaty (which was at last signed yesterday) to Congress....I suppose we shall soon leave this Place, and return to The Hague, as the business which called my Father here is now all finished."[38]

But John Adams would not yet be free to return with his son to America. Instead, his stay abroad was prolonged by more diplomatic assignments from Congress. John Quincy remained with his father in Europe for another 20 months. He returned to the United States a week after his 18th birthday. On July 4—still at sea—he wrote in his diary, "I wish'd very much to arrive in America before this day, which is the greatest day in the year for every American: The anniversary of our Independence. May heaven preserve it..."[39]

PART IV
At Liberty in a New Nation

CHAPTER 11

Peace at Last

Congress ratified the Preliminary Articles of Peace on April 15, 1783. After eight long years of fighting, the colonies were granted their freedom from Great Britain, and warfare formally ceased. The news traveled quickly from "the highways and housetops and firesides, from Province to Province through the land." In Boston, where the struggle for independence had begun, eight-year-old Mary Palmer was playing on the floor in the family's parlor when her father opened the door and rushed into the house. He caught his daughter up in his arms and danced around the room, "singing and whistling in an extraordinary manner."

"Mother sprang up from her work table," the girl remembered, asking, "Mr. Palmer, what is the matter? What does ail you? He dropped me instantly, clasped her in his arms, flew around the room kissing her over and over again, and at last exclaimed 'Peace is declared! Hurrah!' And away he flew to spread the joyful news. Mother, as was her wont, expressed her joy by a copious shower of tears. We children were too much astonished by the behavior of our parents to say anything, but ran out of the house to hear more about the great event."[1]

In Lebanon, Connecticut, nine-year-old Dan Huntington was roused by his parents from a comfortable nap in the chimney corner to partake in the general joy. "Not knowing what it all meant, I sought relief, as soon as possible, by returning to the quietude in which the uproar found me."[2]

On Long Island, Mary Titus Post wrote in her diary, "The cry of peace resounds! The news came today [on April 23, 1783]. The children ran from school, dismissed by the teacher, that all might share in the general joy. They are told that some great good has happened, they know not what. The time will come when they will treasure it as the highest favor vouchsafed by a kind Providence. God be praised!"[3]

In his winter quarters in New York, Hessian Grenadier Johannes Reuber, of the Rall Regiment, suddenly received orders from the English headquarters that there was peace. "Shortly thereafter this was also read to us and that we were no longer to treat the Americans in a hostile manner," he noted in his diary.[4]

And in Frederick, Maryland, a prisoner of war from the Ansbach-Bayreuth Regiment heard the news from the city's commandant, General Lincoln. Wrote Johann Döhla,

> To-day ... the happy restoration of peace between England and America was announced to the joy of all the residents of the city. Thereupon a peace celebration bonfire was built by the regular troops and the militia stationed here, and they paraded behind the resounding sounds of the fifes and drums through all the streets ... firing their weapons. With each volley, old and young gave an extraordinary loud cheer: "Hyroh for peace! Hyroh for liberty! Hyroh for Washington! Hyroh for Congress! For Hancock! For ourselves! God save the General Washington!"
>
> At night a beautiful firework display took place, which was prepared for the Americans by our Artillery Captain and his artificers and cannoneers.... It was very beautiful to see. When all of this was finished, a splendid ball was held in a large hall, attended by all of the American officers and all of the gentlemen and rich merchants of the city. They ate, drank, and danced the entire night to the music of ... the Hessian hautboists. All the officers of the captive regiments here were invited to this dance of joy and celebration of peace.[5]

In his barracks at West Point Joseph P. Martin received the news of peace with mixed feelings. He was joyous that "the war was over and the prize won for which we had been contending through eight tedious years." But there was little celebrating among the common soldiers of the Continental Army. "Their chief thoughts were more closely fixed upon their situation ... upon leaving the army starved, ragged and meager, not a cent to help themselves with, and no means ... to remedy or alleviate their condition.... All that they could do was to make a virtue of necessity and face the threatening evils with the same resolution and fortitude that they had for so long a time faced the enemy in the field."[6]

Washington tried to get three months' back pay for his men. Congress did not grant his request. Instead, it offered the troops certificates that promised they would be paid when money was available and let the soldiers keep their arms. Joseph P. Martin, like many others, eventually sold his certificate and his weapons "to procure decent clothing and money sufficient to enable us to pass with decency through the country and to appear something like ourselves when we arrived among our friends."[7]

The Continental Army marches down the Old Bowery. *Courtesy Library of Congress.*

Joseph and thousands of other soldiers were officially released from the army on June 11, 1783. Some of the soldiers went off for home that same day. He lingered several days, reliving his many adventures and narrow escapes with his comrades. He had seen his first battles as a 15-year-old on Long Island. He had survived the hungry winters at Valley Forge and Morristown. He had fought the British to a draw at Monmouth Courthouse and witnessed the surrender of Cornwallis and his troops at Yorktown. And now that it was time to leave, he experienced a curious mixture of joy and sorrow on the occasion:

> We had lived together as a family of brothers for several years, setting aside some little family squabbles, like most other families. Had shared with each other the hardships, dangers, and sufferings incident to a soldier's life; had sympathized with each other in trouble and sickness; had assisted in bearing each other's burdens or strove to make them lighter by council and advice; had endeavored to conceal each other's faults or make them appear in as good a light as they would bear. In short, the soldiers, each in his particular circle of acquaintance, were as strict a band of brotherhood as the Masons, and I believe, as faithful to each other. And now we were to be ... parted forever; as unconditionally separated as though the grave lay between us.... I question if there was a corps in the army that parted with more regret than ours did ...[8]

"Disbanding of the Continental Army." *Courtesy Dover Pictorial Archives.*

The news of peace, so highly prized in the United States, turned out to be a source of some distress among the American sailors stranded on privateers in foreign ports in France, Spain, and the Caribbean. Only a small number of seamen were necessary to navigate the ships upon their return; the remainder of the young men, many of them teenagers, like Ebenezer Fox, John Blatchford, and Israel Trask, were discharged and left destitute of means to return to their own country. Most eventually obtained work on merchant ships bound for Boston or New York, glad to set sail for their native land. "Every little service I could perform was a pleasure to me," wrote Ebenezer, "as it helped my onward course … HOME."[9]

There were thousands of noncombatants on the move as well. At the close of the war, half a million loyalists in the United States faced an uncertain future. Both American and British signatories to the Paris Peace Treaty, recognizing that the treatment of the loyalists would be a key issue in the newly independent country, pleaded for "a spirit of reconciliation which, on the return of the blessings of peace, should universally prevail." But these pleas went generally unheeded. In many communities the victorious patriots made it clear that the loyalists would find no peace among them.

Between 80,000 and 100,000 loyalists became permanent exiles when the war ended. They gathered whatever belongings they could

"Tory Refugees on Their Way to Canada." *Courtesy Library of Congress.*

fit in a cart and hastened to the ports of New York, Savannah, or Charleston. Evacuations on board British ships proceeded quickly and on a massive scale. Most émigrés, lacking the resources to establish themselves in England, traveled to other British outposts in North America—the maritime provinces of Canada, the Bahamas, and the Caribbean islands.[10]

Hannah Ingraham was among the children who had to leave the United States because her father, a farmer in upstate New York, had fought for the British. She was just a baby when the war began. When her father left, the local patriots confiscated their farm. The family was allowed to keep four sheep, one heifer, and her four-year-old brother's pet lamb. Everything else was taken. When the war ended, Benjamin Ingraham relocated his family to Nova Scotia.

Hannah was 11 years old when they set out on the journey. The family packed their clothing and household utensils and set off with 20 bushels of wheat, some candles, a tub of butter, a tub of pickles, and a good store of potatoes. They went down the Hudson River on a sloop. In New York City they transferred to the British transport ship *King George*. Several babies were born on their ship on the way to Canada. A fierce snowstorm was raging when they arrived in Nova Scotia. For a while they lived in a tent provided by the British government.

"The melting snow would soak up into our beds as we lay," remembered Hannah. "Mother got chilled and developed rheumatism and was never well afterwards." Her father built a new house while his family lived in the tent and the winter grew colder. "One morning, when we awoke father came wading through [the snow] and told us the house was ready.... Father carried a chest and we all took something and followed him up the hill through the trees."[11]

At the new house they found "no floor laid, no windows, no chimney, no door, but we had a roof at least. A good fire was blazing and mother had a big loaf of bread and she boiled a kettle of water and put a good piece of butter in a pewter bowl. We toasted the bread and all sat around the bowl and ate our breakfast that morning," and Mother said, "Thank God we are no longer in dread of having shots fired through our house. This is the sweetest meal I have ever tasted..."

Sarah Scofield Frost was pregnant during her journey from New York to New Brunswick. She sailed with her husband, her nine-year-old son, and her little daughter on a ship called *Two Sisters*, part of a convoy of 14 vessels, accompanied by a British warship. Conditions were extremely crowded. Seven families shared the cabin with Mrs. Frost and her family.[12]

On June 9, 1783, she wrote in her diary,

> Our women, with their children, all came on board today, and there is great confusion in the cabin. We bear with it pretty well through the day, but as it grows towards night, one child cries in one place and one in another, whilst we are getting them to bed. I think sometimes I shall be crazy. There are so many of them.... I stay on deck to-night till nigh eleven o'clock, and now I think I will go down and retire for the night if I can find a place to sleep.

On June 10 her diary entry reads, "I got up early not being able to sleep the whole night for the noise of the children. The wind blows very high. My little girl has been sick all day, but grows better toward evening." Conditions had not improved by June 13: "It is now about half after three in the morning. I have got up, not being able to sleep for the heat and I am sitting in the entry way of the cabin to write. My husband and children are still sleeping. Through the day, I am obliged to sleep in my berth, being quite ill."

Finally, on June 15, at half-past 12, the ship was getting underway for Nova Scotia.

"Our people seem cross and quarrelsome today," wrote Sarah, "but I will not differ with anyone if I can help it." She kept her vow throughout the two-week journey at sea, but when Sarah and her family were finally able to go ashore in Nova Scotia, she thought, "it is the roughest land I have ever seen."

A fellow passenger recalled her feelings as she saw the convoy of ships that had brought them to Canada sailing away: "I climbed to the top of the hill and watched the sails disappearing in the distance and such a feeling of loneliness came over me that, although I had not shed a single tear through all the war, I sat down on the damp moss with my baby in my lap and cried."[13]

Few of the loyalists had lived in such primitive frontier conditions in their homes in America. They had come from well-kept farms or had lived in comfortable homes in town. It took years for the adults to feel at home in the Canadian wilderness, but the children were more adaptable. One little loyalist girl could look back at those early days as happy times: "Mother used to help to chop down trees....We were very useful to her, tended the cattle, churned the butter, making cheese, dressing the flax, spinning, made our own clothes....Fish could be had by fishing with a scoop. I have often speared large salmon with a pitchfork ..."[14]

About half of the loyalists exiled from America after the Revolution ended up in Canada. Many of the southern loyalists fled to east Florida which grew from a population of 4,000 to 17,000 in a single year. Among them was Elizabeth Johnston, born and raised in Georgia, who at age 15 had married a medical student from a loyalist family. In December 1782 the British regiment in which her husband served was transferred from Charleston to New York. His teenage wife traveled with her two small children, Andrew and Kate, to her in-laws' home in St. Augustine, Florida.

On April 20, 1783, Elizabeth wrote to her husband, "A packet arrived from London with the accounts of peace being made, with terms most shameful to Britain. The war never occasioned half the distress which the peace has done to the unfortunate loyalists. No other provision has been made than recommending them to the clemency of Congress which is casting them off ..."[15]

Pregnant with her third child, the young mother counted on finding a permanent home in St. Augustine. But the British returned Florida to Spain after the definitive peace agreement was signed, and the loyalists had to move again. Elizabeth's husband sailed back to England with a ship full of wounded soldiers under his care. On February 3, 1784, his wife reported in some distress, "This has been a day of sad confusion and has occasioned many long faces, as the people here were quite sanguine in the expectation of … Florida being held. The arrival of a packet, however, has dashed their hopes and made their disappointment unspeakable. Your father remains … at loss what to determine with regard to his next movement …"

Two months after the birth of her third child, the young mother sailed with her little family to Great Britain, where her husband finished his medical studies. In 1786 the Johnstons settled in Kingston, Nova Scotia.

The harsh treatment of the loyalists during and after the Revolutionary War was never formally repudiated. But once the war was ended, many Americans recoiled at the popular fury they had witnessed. Civil liberties, once denied to people called Tories, were guaranteed to everyone by the new federal government.[16]

In general, the suffering of the loyalists did not last beyond one generation. The great majority of the exiles prospered in their new homes in Canada and the Caribbean, and some of their children and grandchildren would eventually return to the United States.

Among those who left the new country permanently were the British troops and their Hessian auxiliaries. Seven years to the day of their arrival in New York harbor, the Hessian foot regiments boarded the transport ships at Brooklyn Ferry "in order to … return to Germany … because now there was Peace between England and the Free States of America."

On November 29, 1783, Johannes Reuber, veteran of the Battles of Long Island, White Plains, Trenton, Savannah, and Charleston, wrote in his diary, "The Rall Regiment was disbanded and we all marched home. On this date, the American Campaign had ended with God's help."[17] Among those who returned home to "the fatherland" were hundreds of women and children who had accompanied their husbands and fathers to the war. During their stay in America the children had all been baptized, received religious instruction, and were confirmed. Educated soldiers, and field chaplains and their assistants, like Valentin Asteroth, had done their best for their education.

One of the returning youngsters, Philipp Hunold, had gone to America at age 11 with his father. The regimental chaplain continued the boy's education, and he was confirmed at Newport in the winter quarters of 1777. The chief surgeon of the Hessian hospital in New York had taken the youth on as his assistant because of his interest in medicine. His parents were too poor to support his studies after his return to Hessen. Several benefactors whose favor he had won in America made it possible for him to continue his medical studies at the Collegium Carolinum in Kassel. After a period as a company surgeon, he completed his medical studies at the University of Marburg and received his M.D. degree on May 6, 1790.[18]

End of hostilities: The British leave New York.
Courtesy Library of Congress.

Also traveling with the Hessian regiments were a group of "black Hessians," former slaves from South Carolina, Virginia, Georgia, New Jersey, and New York who had served in Hessian regiments as drummers and fifers and had been recruited when they were in their early teens. The military records of the Hessian State Archives in Marburg and the church records that contain baptismal, marriage, and death records for black soldiers (and their children and wives) in the Hessian regiments in Kassel offer some tantalizing glimpses into their lives before and after they left America "in pursuit of freedom:"[19]

Yorck, Jean: A Negro Yorck, age 14, from Charleston, South Carolina; enlisted on July 1, 1779 as drummer in the company of Major Goebel; In 1785, drummer in the company of von Benning, in Kassel; transferred on November 16, 1786 to the company of von Rotsman, First Bataillon. Died on February 14, 1784: Susanne, age 6 months; daughter of the Negro drummer Yorck. Baptized on January 16, 1785: Christoph, son of the Negro Drummer Yorck; wife: Nancy; godfather: corporal Sommer. Died on December 5, 1786: (Daniel) Christoph, age 11 months, son of the Negro drummer Yorck. Died on June 16, 1787, Negro drummer Jean Yorck, age 22.

Jean Yorck, like most "black Hessians," came from the southern colonies. His home state, South Carolina, furnished the largest contingent of recruits for the Hessian regiments. His hometown, Charleston, provided more black enlisted men than any other coastal city in the areas occupied by the British and Hessian troops. Since most of the "black Hessians" were drummers, they tended to be very young: Jean was 14 when he enlisted; others joined the German regiments when they were only 10, 11, or 12 years old.[20]

The opportunity to escape from slavery must have been a major factor in their decision to join the Hessians. Some of the black youth may also have been attracted by the colorful Hessian uniforms that made them look quite "exotic." The Hessian pay, furnished by the British crown, was relatively high, and the British currency was sounder than the currency with which Congress paid its own army.

Even more inviting than the uniforms and the financial benefits must have been the tolerant attitude of the Hessians, who had not been brought

Black drummer boy in regiment of Hessian sovereign. *Courtesy Anne S. K. Brown Military Collection, Brown University Library.*

up with any racial prejudices. Nowhere in the Hessian letters and military records do we find any condescending attitudes toward the blacks. The common Hessian soldier judged them by their performance rather than their skin color. Few, if any, Hessians had ever seen a black man before coming to America, except for the figure of Caspar, one of the wise men from the Orient who followed the star to Bethlehem in the German Christmas play—and who was usually the most sumptuously costumed of the three kings who approached the Christ child in the stable.

There was a popular song among the Hessian troops that showed their compassion for the runaway slaves they met in America: *Es traf bloss eine grosse Zahl von Negern bei uns ein. Doch ohne Kleidung, ohne Brot, sind sie vergnuegt mit Reis. Der Schwarze kennt keine Not weil er vom Glueck nichts weiss* (A large number of Negroes came to us, in rags, barefoot, and without bread. They were satisfied with rice. The black folks did not need much, since they had known little happiness).

Many black soldiers served out their time loyally during the war, and more than 40 accompanied their units to Germany. There they were baptized with German names, usually with an officer as their sponsor, and assigned to a new regiment, as Jean Yorck was when he arrived in Kassel, the capital of the Hessian sovereign. Some took wives and had their children baptized in the Lutheran church, as did Jean Yorck when his son Daniel Christoph was born. Usually, the company commander became the godfather of their children. One of the "black Hessians," who married well and prospered, had such an excellent reputation in the town of Kassel that the Hessian Landgrave himself was a sponsor at his children's baptisms.

But the transition from the tropical climate of the Carolinas to the colder climate of Hessen was not easy for many of the young musicians who arrived in their new environment at the beginning of a harsh winter. Many soon sickened and developed respiratory ailments (pneumonia or tuberculosis), which proved to be lethal (as they still are today!) for youths who had been malnourished as children. Nearly half of the former slaves who had enlisted in the Hessian regiments eventually died from "consumption." Their average age at the time of death was 22, the age recorded for the Negro drummer Yorck in the church records in Kassel.

His wife and daughter survived, as did many of the older black musicians who remained in the service of their sovereign until they reached their mid-forties. Upon his death, one of the black Hessians was dissected in the anatomy theater of the Collegium Carolinum at Kassel, proving to the assembled witnesses that under his dark skin, he was just like a white man!

Back in the United States, the last remnants of the British troops had left New York by the end of 1783. In November General Washington entered the city and formally bade farewell to his officers. Soon after, he resigned his commission. In December, nine-year-old Eliza Q. Morton, whose family had fled New York in 1776 when the British had occupied the city, returned to her home.

"The city looked ruinous," she remembered. "My mother took me to our home in Water Street. I accompanied my mother to visit Mrs. Smith, the wife of Chief Justice Smith (a loyalist) who received us very kindly, and brought in her daughter ... a few years younger than myself. 'This child, said Mrs. Smith has been born since the *Rebellion*'—'Since the *Revolution*,' replied my mother. The lady smiled and said, 'Well, well, Mrs. Morton, this is only a truce, not a peace; and we shall all be back again in full possession in two years.' ... A few months afterwards Mrs. Smith accompanied her husband to Quebec; and he became Chief Justice of Lower Canada."[21]

Four and a half years later, after the Federal Constitution was adopted, General Washington returned to New York on April 23, 1789. "I was at a window in a store on the wharf," remembered Eliza, now 15 years old. "Carpets were spread to the carriage prepared for him, but he preferred walking through the crowded streets.... He frequently bowed to the multitude, and took off his hat to the ladies at the windows, who waved their handkerchiefs, threw flowers before him, and shed tears of joy and congratulation."[22]

First in Peace: Washington at home with his family. *Courtesy Library of Congress.*

The grave of Joseph P. Martin, a soldier of the Revolution. Sandy Point cemetery overlooking Penobscot River in Maine.

A week later, on April 30, 1789, Washington took the oath of office as President of the United States on the balcony of the old Federal Hall. Eliza witnessed the event from the roof of a house in Broad Street:

> I was so near to Washington I could almost hear him speak. The windows and roofs of houses were crowded; and in the streets the throng was so dense, that it seemed as if one could literally walk on the heads of the people. The balcony of the hall was in full view of the multitudes. In the center of it was placed a table, with a rich covering of red velvet; and upon this, on a crimson velvet cushion, lay a large and elegant Bible.... Washington's entrance on the balcony was announced by shouts of joy and welcome. Advancing to the front of the balcony, he laid his hand on his heart, bowed several times, and then retired to an armchair near the table.... After a few moments he arose

and came forward. Chancellor Livingston read the oath according to the form prescribed by the Constitution and Washington repeated it, resting his hand upon the Bible. Mr. Otis, the Secretary of the Senate, then took the bible to raise it to the lips of Washington who stooped and kissed the book. At this moment, a signal was given, by raising a flag upon the cupola of the Hall, for a general discharge of the artillery at the Battery. All the bells in the city rang out a peal of joy and the assembled multitude sent forth a universal shout. The President again bowed to the people and then retired from a scene such as the proudest monarch never enjoyed ...[23]

But the long struggle for independence had taken its toll: Approximately 25,324 Americans out of a population of 2.5 million had died in the pursuit of liberty. Nearly 7,000 soldiers died in battle; the rest perished from disease and starvation in camps and prisons. An even larger number of noncombatants—mostly infants under the age of one and people of color—died in the great smallpox epidemic that spread from Boston in the North to the Carolinas in the South in the years between 1775 and 1782. The proportion of deaths to the size of the population in the Revolutionary War would be higher than in any other subsequent armed conflict in which Americans fought—except for the Civil War![24]

Young Joseph P. Martin summed up his experience in the Revolutionary War as eloquently as any common soldier in the Continental Army could—had he his wit and way with words:

I never learned the rules of punctuation any further than just to assist in fixing a comma to the British depredations in the state of New York; a semicolon in New Jersey; a colon in Pennsylvania, and a final period in Virginia—a note of interrogation, why we were made to suffer so much in so good and just a cause; and a note of admiration to all the world that an army voluntarily engaged to serve their country, when starved and naked and suffering everything short of death (and thousands even that) should be able to persist through an eight years war, and come off conquerors at last![25]

CHAPTER 12

Fruits of Liberty

After his discharge from Washington's army, Joseph Plumb Martin spent some months teaching the children of Dutch farmers in upstate New York before he settled in the wilderness of the new state of Maine. Land was being offered to Revolutionary War veterans at low prices to encourage settlers in what was then the "western frontier" and to act as buffers against Indian excursions.

Joseph farmed the rocky soil as best he could, married the daughter of a neighboring farmer, and raised five children. In 1818 President Monroe signed the first pension act, designed to help needy Revolutionary War veterans. Any officer, soldier, mariner, or marine who served for a "term of nine months ... on the continental establishment" or served until the war ended and was "in reduced circumstances" was eligible for the pension.[1]

Joseph P. Martin, now 58 years old, applied for a pension of $8 a month. In support of his claim he wrote, "I have no real or personal estate, nor any income whatever, my necessary bedding and wearing apparel excepted, except two cows, six sheep, one pig. I am a laborer, but by reason of age and infirmity I am unable to work. My wife is sickly and rheumatic and I have five children.... Without my pension I am unable to support myself and family."[2]

Approximately 30,000 applications were submitted under the 1818 Act and its amendments by Revolutionary War veterans in "reduced circumstances." Among them was William Diamond, who had beat the call to arms that had begun the War of the American Revolution. After Lexington, he had fought at the Battle of Bunker (Breeds) Hill and under Washington at Trenton. He returned to Lexington after the war and married a local girl, whose father had been among the minutemen who had marched off to Cambridge to pursue the British. They had six children.

In later years Diamond and his family went to New Hampshire, where he purchased 60 acres of wilderness. For eight years he worked as farm laborer and wheelwright while converting the land into a farm capable of sustaining his family. In 1817, at age 62, Diamond retired. In 1818 he applied for the pension. He reported that he was "very destitute of property." In 1820, when Diamond had to list his assets, he claimed that he owned no real estate (he had deeded his farm to his sons), possessed only $42 worth of livestock, and paid $6 annually for a life lease he held to a small portion of his farm. He also told the court that he was unable to work and owed $50 in debts.

Continued on the pension rolls and guaranteed an income for life, Diamond's pension helped sustain his intergenerational household, which he shared with his wife, a daughter who had been abandoned by her husband, and her children. The veteran paid for his lease and contributed income from his pension to sustain his household. Following his death in 1828, during the presidency of John Quincy Adams, Diamond's estate of $163 was reduced to $4. As he had claimed in his pension application, the veteran had owed as much as he owned, but his children had gained independence as owners of their land.

By the time of drummer William Diamond's death, the youngest veterans of the War for Independence were in their late sixties, and their new nation felt secure and wealthy enough to show its gratitude for their services on behalf of their country. In 1832, during the presidency of Andrew Jackson, the U.S. Congress passed the first comprehensive federal pension act, providing a yearly grant to every man who had served in the Revolutionary War for six months or more.[3]

To be eligible, a veteran had no longer to be disabled or poor; service in any military organization was satisfactory, as long as this service could be proved beyond a reasonable doubt. An individual with two years of active duty was eligible for full pay during the remainder of his lifetime, and a proportion of this was awarded for any service of more than six months. Widows married at the time were also eligible.

The 1832 act resulted in some 33,000 claims submitted by veterans. Nearly 23,000 additional applications were submitted by widows under laws passed in 1834 and later. All together, the Revolutionary War pension files, located in the National Archives, contain some 88,000 applications that provide a remarkable cross section of data from one of the most unusual armies in history: They come from members of voluntary corps, Continental units, state militia units, companies of Indian spies and coast guards, and from men serving in the United States Navy, state navies, and on privateers.

Some of the applicants, like Henry Yaeger and Israel Trask, who joined the army at age 10, later served at sea as well and experienced the war both as combatants and as captives. To qualify for a pension, they had to indicate the time and place of their service, the names of their units and officers, and the engagements in which they had participated. Their narratives were presented and sworn to in a court of law and had to be supported by two character witnesses.

The war itself and the subsequent half century had already weeded out the less healthy and the older soldiers. Four out of five among the applicants for pensions in the 1830's had been teenagers in the Revolutionary War. At the time of their service they were impressionable, enthusiastic, and observant of the everyday details of the life of an ordinary soldier or sailor. They also provided data on their geographic and occupational mobility after they had returned to civilian life.

"Where and in what year were you born?" was one of the questions posed to all who sought pensions under the Act of 1832. A second, three-part interrogatory dealt with mobility: "Where," the applicants were asked, "were you living when called into service; where have you lived since the Revolutionary War, and where do you now live?" Over 15,000 men responded to these queries. Nearly two-thirds moved more than once, and many of those who had been in their teens during the war moved four, five, or six times.[4]

Fully half of the men who would ultimately relocate made their first move before 1785—within three years of the end of hostilities—as did Joseph P. Martin. The others moved before 1795—as did William Diamond. Over half of the young veterans ultimately made state-to-state moves: Diamond went from Massachusetts to New Hampshire; Martin went from Connecticut to the new state of Maine. For many young veterans the wilderness lay only a few days' walk to the west—and with it the promise of land that one could claim. No longer indentured servants on someone else's farm, they would bequeath their children land of their own.

Wealthier men did not generally apply for pensions, even though they were eligible if they had served in the war. Some of the young veterans had become successful professionals and businessmen, making use of the special skills or education they had acquired in their youth. Among them were John Greenwood, James Forten, and Peter Stephen Du Ponceau.

Greenwood, son of a Boston ivory turner and part-time dentist, had enlisted in a Massachusetts militia regiment at age 15. In his journal he recorded his impressions of the Battle of Bunker (Breeds) Hill, the siege and evacuation of Boston by the British, and his engagement with the Hessians in the Battle of Trenton. Concluding his service on land at age 18, Greenwood joined the war at sea in 1779 and was captured by the British and taken prisoner to Barbados. After being released, he engaged in trading activities as a privateer in Port-au-Prince, the Chesapeake Bay, and Kingston, Jamaica. During that time he was imprisoned twice more but each time managed to escape.

In 1786 John Greenwood, following in his father's footsteps, opened a dentistry practice in New York. He had no formal education, but he had learned from his father how to carve ivory dentures. In 1789, when Washington became the first president of the United States, John Greenwood became his favorite dentist. That year, Greenwood prepared the first of four sets of dentures for Washington—a lower denture from hippopotamus ivory inlaid with eight human teeth. A hole carved into the denture accommodated Washington's lower teeth.

By the time of his death in 1819, Greenwood had become the "father of American dentistry." He formulated the use of foot power drills and developed adaptable springs for dentures. Throughout his professional life he remained thankful for the opportunity to serve his country and his president.[5]

James Forten, the free black sailor from Philadelphia who had fought and suffered imprisonment in the name of a new nation, returned to his native city after the war and to a remarkable opportunity—the chance to achieve the economic independence that was denied to so many of his contemporaries. Forten was to become one of the best-known men of his hometown.

Quaker educated and a master of the craft of sail making, he soon became the head of a thriving business, employing scores of people—black and white. He was a shrewd investor and amassed a fortune. He gave much of his wealth to poor and struggling blacks and became a founder of the abolition movement to help end American slavery.

During his lifetime James Forten witnessed the death of slavery in his home state of Pennsylvania. A firm believer in the principles of the Declaration of Independence, he became one of the most powerful black voices in the North. He knew how to use the press and the speaker's podium. He lived to see his sons and grandson become leaders in the antislavery crusade.

When he died in March 1842, the funeral cortege that set off from his home to St. Thomas African Episcopal Church was followed by hundreds of black and white citizens walking together to honor a "gentleman of color" who never lost the faith that "the spirit of Freedom is marching with rapid strides and causing tyrants to tremble."[6]

The spirit of Freedom did not move fast enough to free Isaac Jefferson, the young slave who had been captured by the British, taken to Yorktown, and returned to Monticello by Washington's troops after Cornwallis's surrender. In 1790, at age 15, when Thomas Jefferson became Secretary of State, he accompanied his master to Philadelphia. He returned to Monticello for about nine years and then lived for more than 25 years with Jefferson's son-in-law, Thomas Mann Randolph, and his wife. (He and Patsy Randolph had grown up together as children and had been nursed by the same mother.) Later, he helped nurse the ex-president in his old age. The last years of Isaac Jefferson's life were spent in Petersburg, Virginia, where he dictated his memoirs in the 1840s.[7]

Peter Stephen Du Ponceau, the French interpreter of Baron von Steuben, who had shared the tribulations of Washington's troops in their winter quarters at Valley Forge, became a citizen of the United States of America. After the end of the Revolutionary War, he studied law under the tutelage of a prominent Philadelphia lawyer and was admitted to the bar in 1785. He became one of the nation's most respected lawyers. His services before the Supreme Court of the United States were in frequent demand because he was one of the few lawyers in the country at that time who knew anything of foreign and international law. He also played an important part in establishing the Law Academy of Philadelphia in 1821.

His flourishing practice as a lawyer did not keep him from spending time in the study of foreign languages, a subject that had fascinated him since childhood. He read and spoke fluently a number of European languages, but he also immersed himself in the study of Native American languages. He wrote numerous articles on American history and constitutional law.

He lived quietly and unobtrusively, but his scholarship was so respected that by the time of his death in 1844 he had been granted membership in 23 American learned societies. Those he valued most were the American Philosophical Society (founded by Benjamin Franklin) and the Historical Society of Pennsylvania. His greatest single ambition throughout his long life was to prod the Europeans to recognize the worth of American literature, science, and scholarship.[8]

The Revolutionary War had disrupted normal patterns of existence for young women as well as men. Betsy Ambler Brent, the teenage correspondent from Yorktown who had fled to Richmond before the battle of 1781, would look back at her youthful wartime experience and write in 1810, "Necessity taught us to exertions which our girls of the present day know nothing of. We were forced to industry … to make amends for the loss of fortune."[9]

During the postwar period, women who had managed competently, despite severe hardships, began to question the prevailing stereotypes of feminine weakness and delicacy. Their daughters, who had watched their mothers cope independently and successfully with a variety of challenges during the Revolution, no longer felt a pressing compulsion to marry early and to have large families. Some, like Sally Wister, the author of the journal that described the exile of her family from Philadelphia during the British occupation, chose not to marry at all. Other households were more willing to relinquish the parental veto over children's selections of marital partners and displayed more egalitarian marital relationships.[10]

In 1790 Thomas Jefferson wrote to a French acquaintance about his older daughter Patsy's wedding to Thomas Mann Randolph, commenting that "according to the usage of my country, I scrupulously suppressed my wishes, that my daughter might indulge her own sentiments freely." Anna Rawle, who had left us an account of the trashing of the Quaker homes in Philadelphia during the celebration of the Yorktown victory, simply informed her mother of her plans to marry John Clifford, a local merchant, asking her opinion only about the timing of the wedding.

The average life span in Philadelphia at the time was 45, and Anna was 25 years old when she married. She relished her individuality and privacy, even after she wed. "I used to say if I ever married I hoped my spouse and I would not be forever together, and I have my wish, for we never are but at meals and in the evening, so that I have plenty of time for contemplation," she wrote later. "He is constantly engaged at the store and with his vessel that he cannot possibly be much with me." An English visitor commented that Anna had a reputation for "wearing the breeches in the Clifford household" but added that the couple was "esteemed by some the Superior Male and Female for understanding in the city."[11]

The formal education of women had received little attention prior to the American Revolution. In her letters Abigail Adams, wife and mother of future presidents, repeatedly acknowledged the deficiencies of her own untutored writing; in 1785 she wrote to her niece, "It is from feeling the disadvantages of it myself, that I am the more solicitous that my young acquaintance should excel me."[12]

During the postwar period, public education at the elementary level was opened to female as well as male children, and private academies greatly expanded the curriculum previously offered to girls. Daughters from middle-class and well-to-do white families could now attend schools at which they were taught grammar, rhetoric, history, geography, mathematics, and some of the natural sciences.

One of the best known of these schools, and one with a rigorous curriculum, was the Friends Girl's School, founded in Philadelphia by Anthony Benezet. Among Benezet's pupils were Elizabeth Sandwich Drinker, who wrote in her journal about the Independence celebrations during the Revolutionary War, and Deborah Norris Logan, Sally Wister's friend, with whom she had kept up a correspondence during the British occupation.[13]

Deborah Norris was the daughter of a Quaker merchant whose home was just two doors down from the State House. At age 14 she had heard the public reading of the Declaration of Independence, and at the Friends Girl's School she had created her own curriculum in which history and belles lettres were highlighted. After the war, her husband, George Logan, a Quaker doctor who had become a gentleman farmer, became active politically. Meanwhile, Deborah became fascinated with the politics of the past.

She first published the transcripts of correspondence between two giants of Pennsylvania history, William Penn and James Logan, her husband's grandfather, in 1814. When her husband died in 1821, she wrote a memoir about him. Her book features letters and personal accounts of George Washington, Thomas Jefferson, and John Randolph.

The largest and best known of the republican academies was the Moravian Young Ladies Seminary in Bethlehem, Pennsylvania. From its founding in 1742 until 1785 it had served only the daughters of the small German sect. But Congressmen and army officers who visited the school during the Revolution were impressed by what they saw and asked the seminary's trustees to open their school to non-Moravians. The trustees agreed to the proposal and announced in 1785 that they would teach girls "reading and writing in both the German and English languages, also arithmetic, sewing and knitting and other feminine crafts. Likewise they will be instructed in history, geography and music, with great care and faithfulness." From then on, many of the leading families of the young republic sent their daughters to the Moravian Seminary.[14]

John Adams was an exception. He had admired this "Institution for the Education for Young Ladies" but explained in a letter to his only daughter Nabby that he did not want her to live there because "the young Misses take too little exercise and fresh air to be healthy." By the time the academy opened its doors to outsiders, young Nabby was already engaged to be married. It was left to her father to impress on her another postwar maxim concerning the changing role of women—that they should use their influence on their children to imbue them with principles of patriotism as well as morality.

He wrote to her when she was 18, "It is by the female world that the greatest and best characters among men are formed.... There can be nothing in life more honorable for a woman than to contribute her virtues, her advice, her example, or her address to the formation of a husband, a brother, or a son, to be useful to the world."[15] And when she had become a young matron with four children of her own, he reminded her, "There is ... a young generation coming up in America. You, my dear daughter, will be responsible for a great share of the duty and opportunity of educating a rising family, from whom much will be expected." And so the founders of the new republic defined a woman's public role not in direct participation in politics but in her duty to raise sons who would love their country and preserve its liberty as had Nabby's mother, Abigail Adams.

Nabby's younger brother, John Quincy Adams, had returned in 1785 from Europe to complete his formal education at Harvard and to study law. He settled down to practice in Boston in 1790, but not for long. George Washington appointed him to be United States minister to the Netherlands from 1794 to 1797. When John Adams became president, John Quincy was appointed United States minister to Berlin (from 1797 to 1801). Returning to countries he had known as a child (and whose languages he understood), John Quincy Adams reported faithfully to his government about the escalating cycle of European revolutions and wars.

After Jefferson's election in 1801, John Quincy Adams returned to Boston and resumed the practice of law. Eight years later, the new president, James Madison, appointed him as the first minister of the United States to Russia, where he served from 1809 to 1814 and witnessed Napoleon's invasion of Russia and his subsequent retreat and downfall. After the peace treaty with Britain at Ghent was concluded, he served as minister of the United States to England.

President Monroe recalled Adams from England to become Secretary of State in 1817. He held the office throughout Monroe's two administrations until 1824. His greatest diplomatic achievement was the Transcontinental Treaty with Spain, in which both east and west Florida became officially a part of the United States and through which Spain agreed to a frontier line running from the Gulf of Mexico to the Rocky Mountains and thence along the 42nd parallel to the Pacific Ocean. It has been called "the greatest diplomatic victory ever won by a single individual in the history of the United States."[16]

John Quincy Adams's presidency was decidedly less successful. He was a minority president, chosen by the House of Representatives in preference to Andrew Jackson, who had received the greatest number of votes, both at the polls and in the state electoral colleges, but lacked a constitutional majority. Henry Clay, one of the two other candidates in 1824, threw his support to Adams in the House. But John Quincy Adams had no real party to back him up, and his call for strong national (i.e., federal) policies under executive leadership did not appeal to most politicians, who wanted the least government possible.

Andrew Jackson, hero of the Battle of New Orleans and a populist from humble origins, defeated John Quincy Adams for reelection in 1828. Determined to open up new territories, Andrew Jackson pursued an expansionist policy that removed Native Americans from their tribal lands east of the Mississippi and gave voice to an aggressive nationalism that appealed to workers and farmers, particularly in the south and west. Throughout his life Jackson continued to harbor a bitter resentment toward the British for the way he and his brother had been treated when they were imprisoned as child soldiers during the Revolutionary War.[17]

John Quincy Adams embarked on yet another career in public service—as a member of the House of Representatives and an opponent of slavery. In November 1830 the voters of the Plymouth District of Massachusetts elected the former president to Congress. He was reelected nine more times by his fellow citizens and died in the House of Representatives on February 23, 1848.

During his long years in Congress he worked for universal emancipation and tried, but failed, to introduce resolutions in Congress for a constitutional amendment so that no one could be born a slave in the United States after 1845. He also spoke on behalf of the Miami Indians, who had adopted Frances Slocum, the child captive of the Wyoming Valley Massacre. She was regarded as a queen among her tribe, and when the Miamis were to be forcibly removed from Indiana, he pleaded her cause and that of her Indian relatives so eloquently that Congress gave her and her descendants a tract of land a mile square to be held in perpetuity.[18]

Perhaps John Quincy Adams's greatest legacy was that of a diplomat who foresaw the leading role that the United States would one day play among the nations of the world and his awareness of the dangers of unilateral intervention in world affairs. On July 4, 1821, when he was Secretary of State, he issued a warning that is as relevant today as it was on the 45th birthday of the new republic:

> America ... well knows that by once enlisting under other banners than her own, were they even the banners of foreign independence, she would involve herself beyond the power of extraction, in all the wars of interest and intrigue, of individual avarice, envy, and ambition, which assume the colors and usurp the standard of freedom. The fundamental maxims of her policy would insensibly change from liberty to force.... She might become dictatress of the world. She would be no longer the ruler of her own spirit.[19]

Across the Atlantic, the Hessian princes continued to make profitable treaties with England during the French Revolution and the Napoleonic Wars. They built magnificent palaces and private houses for the artists of their court and laid out beautiful public squares and parks. But they also founded new agricultural colonies, with each settler receiving 30 acres and a loan to purchase livestock and three years' exemption from taxes and military service. They established a garrison hospital, a library, and a lyceum, a home for orphans and a woman's foundation.[20]

In 1848, a short-lived revolution swept across Germany. In the spring, a National Assembly was elected and met in the Hessian city of Frankfurt. For five months, the people's delegates met in St. Paul's Church and debated the draft of a Bill of Rights, modeled after the American Constitution. Their efforts were in vain—the might of the monarchy and its conservative supporters prevailed. In December 1848, the National Assembly was dissolved.

But during World War II, on the night of October 22, 1943, a massive Allied air raid shattered the center of Kassel, destroying the beautiful residence of the former sovereigns. In a few hours the glory of the past turned into dust. There were no more princes left and no more throne.

Selected Chronology of Events during the American Revolution

March 1765:	British Parliament passes the Stamp Act—the first direct tax on the American Colonies
March 1766:	British Parliament repeals the Stamp Act after boycott of British goods in the American Colonies
June 1767:	British Parliament passes Townshend Acts, taxing tea
March 5, 1770:	Boston Massacre
December 16, 1770:	Boston Tea Party
September 5, 1774:	First Continental Congress meets in Philadelphia
April 17, 1775:	Battle of Lexington and Concord
May 10, 1775:	Second Continental Congress meets in Philadelphia
June 16, 1775:	George Washington accepts command of Continental Army
June 17, 1775:	Battle of Breed's (Bunker) Hill
March 17, 1776:	British evacuate Boston
July 4, 1776:	Congress adopts Declaration of Independence
August 27, 1776:	Battle of Long Island

October 28, 1776:   Battle of White Plains

November 16, 1776:   Fort Washington in Manhattan falls to the
                          British

December 26, 1776:   Battle of Trenton

September 26, 1777:   British capture Philadelphia

October 17, 1777:   British army surrenders at Saratoga

Winter of 1777–1778: American troops endure winter at Valley Forge

February 1778:   France and America become allies

June 28, 1778:   Battle of Monmouth

December 28, 1778:   British seize Savannah

1779–1780:   British concentrate on winning in the southern
                          colonies

May 12, 1780:   Charleston falls to the British

October 7, 1780:   Battle of King's Mountain

January 17, 1781:   Battle of Cowpens

October 19, 1781:   British surrender at Yorktown

April 15, 1783:   Congress ratifies the Preliminary Articles of
                          Peace

June, 1783:   The American army disbands

September 3, 1783:   Signing of Treaty of Paris, formally ending the war

November 1783:   The loyalists and British evacuate New York

1789:   Constitution of the United States written

April 30, 1789:   Washington takes oath of office as the first
                          President of the United States of America

Notes

PROLOGUE

1. U.S. Bureau of the Census, *Historical Statistics of the United States*, 2 vols. (Washington, D.C.: U.S. Government Printing Office, 1975).

2. Elizabeth McKee Williams, "Childhood, Memory and the American Revolution," in *Children and War Reader*, ed. James Martin (New York: New York University Press, 2002); Ray Raphael, *A People's History of the American Revolution: How Common People Shaped the Fight for Independence* (New York: The New Press, 2001).

3. John C. Dann, ed., *The Revolution Remembered: Eyewitness Accounts of the War for Independence* (Chicago: University of Chicago Press, 1980).

4. Horst Dippel, "Sources in Germany for the Study of the American Revolution," *Quarterly Journal of the Library of Congress* 33 (July 1976), pp. 199–217; Rodney Atwood, *The Hessians: Mercenaries from Hessen-Kassel in the American Revolution* (New York: Cambridge University Press, 1980).

5. Ron Wertheimer, "The Incomplete Promise of Liberty." *New York Times*, 10 January 2003, p. 51.

CHAPTER ONE

1. Thomas Hutchinson, cited in Alfred F. Young, *The Shoemaker and the Tea Party: Memory and the American Revolution* (Boston: Beacon Press, 1999), p. 37.

2. Edward Gerrish (Garrick), "Testimony," in *Legal Papers of John Adams*, Vol. 3, *Cases 63 and 64: The Boston Massacre Trials*, ed. L. Kinvin Wroth and Hiller B. Zobel (Cambridge, Mass.: Belknap Press of Harvard University Press, 1965), p. 50.

3. Captain John Goldfinch, "Testimony," in Wroth and Zobel, *Legal Papers*, p. 187.

    4. Gerrish (Garrick), "Testimony," p. 50.

    5. John Greenwood, *A Young Patriot in the American Revolution: 1775–1783: The Wartime Services of John Greenwood* (Tyrone, Pa.: Westvaco, 1981), p. 40.

    6. David McCullough, *John Adams* (New York: Simon and Schuster, 2001), pp. 67–68.

    7. Wroth and Zobel, *Legal Papers,* p. 269.

    8. Francis S. Drake, *Tea Leaves: Being a Collection of Letters and Documents Relating to the Shipment of Tea to the American Colonies in the Year 1773 by the East India Tea Company* (Boston: A. O. Crane, 1884), Introduction.

    9. Peter Edes to Grandsons, Bangor, Maine, 16 February 1836, Massachusetts Historical Society, Boston.

    10. Joshua Wyeth, cited in Drake, *Tea Leaves,* Introduction.

    11. William Tudor, ibid.

    12. John Adams, ibid.

    13. Robert Leckie, *George Washington's War: The Saga of the American Revolution* (New York: Harper Collins, 1992), p. 81.

    14. Harvard College, *Records of the College Faculty* IV (1 March 1775–1781), pp. 4–5.

CHAPTER TWO

    1. Arthur B. Tourtellot, *William Diamond's Drum: The Beginning of the War of the American Revolution* (Garden City, N.Y.: Doubleday, 1959), p. 20.

    2. "The Fifer at Lexington," in *Hours with the Living Men and Women of the American Revolution,* Benson J. Lossing, ed. (New York: Funk and Wagnalls, 1889), chap. 1.

    3. Ibid., p. 11.

    4. Elizabeth Clarke to Her Niece Lucy Allen, Lexington, 19 April 1841, Massachusetts Historical Society, Boston.

    5. Lucy Hosmer, "Diary, April 19, 1775," Cary Library, Lexington, Mass. http://hastings.lexintonma.org.

    6. Tourtellot, *William Diamond's Drum,* p. 199.

    7. John L. Bell, personal communication, 10 May 2002.

    8. Robert Leckie, *George Washington's War: The Saga of the American Revolution* (New York: Harper Collins, 1992), p. 149.

    9. Dorothy Dudley, "The Diary of Dorothy Dudley: From April 18, 1775 to July 19, 1776," in *Theatrum Majorum* (Cambridge, Mass.: The Ladies Centennial Commission, 1876), p. 21.

    10. John Greenwood, *A Young Patriot in the American Revolution: 1775–1783: The Wartime Services of John Greenwood* (Tyrone, Pa.: Westvaco, 1981), p. 42. Original manuscript written in 1809, University of Michigan, Clements Library, Ann Arbor.

    11. Ibid., p. 43.

    12. Ibid., p. 44.

    13. Ibid., p. 46.

    14. Dudley, "Diary," p. 23.

15. Ibid., p. 24.

16. Greenwood, *Young Patriot,* p. 49.

17. Ibid.

18. Robert Steele to William Summer, 10 July 1825, Samuel Swett Papers on the Battle of Bunker Hill, New York Historical Society, New York.

19. Ibid.

20. Ibid.

21. Abigail Adams, "Letter to John Adams, June 17, 1775," in *Adams Family Correspondence,* Vol. 1, L. H. Butterfield, Wendall D. Garrett, and Marjorie E. Sprague, eds. (Cambridge, Mass.: Belknap Press of Harvard University Press, 1963), p. 222.

22. John Quincy Adams to Joseph Sturge, March 1846, Adams Family Papers, Massachusetts Historical Society, Boston.

23. Dudley, "Diary," p. 24.

24. Ibid., p. 26.

25. Ray Raphael, *A People's History of the American Revolution: How Common People Shaped the Fight for Independence* (New York: The New Press, 2001), p. 62.

26. Israel Trask, in John C. Dann, ed., *The Revolution Remembered: Eyewitness Accounts of the War for Independence* (Chicago: University of Chicago Press, 1980), p. 409.

27. Greenwood, *Young Patriot,* pp. 59–60.

28. Ibid., p. 61.

29. Ibid.

30. Dudley, "Diary," pp. 57–58.

31. Henry Goddard Pickering, *Nathaniel Goddard: A Boston Merchant: 1767–1853* (New York: Riverside Press, 1906), p. 60.

32. Greenwood, *Young Patriot,* p. 64.

33. Dudley, "Diary," p. 60.

34. Ibid., p. 61.

35. Abigail Adams, cited in David McCullough, *John Adams* (New York: Simon and Schuster, 2001), p. 143.

36. Trask, *Revolution Remembered,* pp. 409–410.

37. Dudley, "Diary," pp. 87–88.

CHAPTER THREE

1. Joseph P. Martin, *A Narrative of Some of the Adventures, Dangers, and Sufferings of a Revolutionary Soldier, Interspersed with Anecdotes of Incidents that Occurred within His Own Observation* (Howell, Me.: Glazier, Masters, 1830), p. 13.

2. Rodney Atwood, *The Hessians: Mercenaries from Hessen-Kassel in the American Revolution* (New York: Cambridge University Press, 1980), chap. 2.

3. Johannes Reuber, *Tagebuch des Grenadiers Johannes Reuber* (Frankfurt am Main, Germany: Stadtarchiv, 1776–1783), pp. 76–77.

4. Martin, *Narrative,* p. 21.

5. Reuber, *Tagebuch,* p. 81.

6. Will Sands to His Parents, 14 August 1776, in *The World Turned Upside Down: Children of 1776: The Story of an Annapolis Family,* Ann Jensen, ed. (Annapolis, Md.: Sands House, 1993), pp. 14–16.

7. Martin, *Narrative,* pp. 26–33.

8. Ibid., p. 36.

9. Reuber, *Tagebuch,* pp. 63–84.

10. Martin, *Narrative,* p. 41.

11. Reuber, *Tagebuch,* pp. 85–86.

12. Depositions of Elizabeth Cain and Abigail Palmer, Papers of the Continental Congress, 22 March 1777.

13. Lydia Minturn Post, cited in Mary Beth Norton, *Liberty's Daughters: The Revolutionary Experience of American Women: 1750–1800* (Ithaca, N.Y.: Cornell University Press, 1996), p. 205; Margaret Morris, Private Journal, 21 December 1776, Rutgers University Special Collections and University Archives.

14. Reuber, *Tagebuch,* p. 90.

15. Polly Wharton to Her Cousin Mary, 25 December 1776, in *Going to School in 1776,* John J. Loeper, ed. (New York: Athenum, 1973), pp. 69–70.

16. David How, *Diary of David How* (New York: Morrisania, 1865), p. 50; John Greenwood, *A Young Patriot in the American Revolution: 1775–1783: The Wartime Service of John Greenwood* (Tyrone, Pa.: Westvaco, 1981), pp. 80–81. Original manuscript written in 1809, University of Michigan, Clements Library, Ann Arbor.

17. Ibid., pp. 82–84.

18. Reuber, *Tagebuch,* p. 91.

19. Greenwood, *Young Patriot,* pp. 84–85.

20. Reuber, *Tagebuch,* pp. 92–93.

CHAPTER FOUR

1. Johannes Reuber, *Tagebuch des Grenadiers Johannes Reuber* (Frankfurt am Main, Germany: Stadtarchiv, 1776–1783), p. 94.

2. Ibid., p. 95.

3. Joseph P. Martin, *A Narrative of Some of the Adventures, Dangers, and Sufferings of a Revolutionary Soldier, Interspersed with Anecdotes of Incidents that Occurred Within His Own Observation* (Howell, Me.: Glazier, Masters, 1830), pp. 44–45.

4. Ibid., p. 50.

5. Cited in Elizabeth A. Fenn, *Pox Americana: The Great Smallpox Epidemic of 1775–1782* (New York: Hill and Wang, 2001), p. 93.

6. John Adams to Abigail Adams II, 5 July 1777, Massachusetts Historical Society, Boston.

7. Hugh McDonald, "A Teenager in the Revolution," *Historical Times* (1966), p. 37.

8. Reuber, *Tagebuch,* p. 95.

9. McDonald, "A Teenager in the Revolution," p. 39.

10. Robert Morton, "Diary," *Pennsylvania Magazine of History and Biography* 1 (1877), pp. 3–4.

11. Sally Wister, *Sally Wister's Journal: A True Narrative* (Philadelphia: Ferris and Leach, 1902), pp. 318–319.

12. Morton, "Diary," pp. 7–8.

13. Reuber, *Tagebuch,* p. 96.

14. Morton, "Diary," pp. 9–12.

15. Martin, *Narrative,* pp. 53–54.

16. Morton, "Diary," pp. 14–15.

17. Ibid., pp. 26–27.

18. McDonald, "A Teenager in the Revolution," p. 40.

19. Morton, "Diary," p. 22.

20. Martin, *Narrative,* pp. 64–65.

21. Morton, "Diary," p. 28.

22. Martin, *Narrative,* pp. 68–69.

23. Morton, "Diary," pp. 30, 34–35, 37.

24. Martin, *Narrative,* pp. 73–74.

25. Wister, *Sally Wister's Journal,* pp. 468–469, 472–473.

CHAPTER FIVE

1. Joseph P. Martin, *A Narrative of Some of the Adventures, Dangers, and Sufferings of a Revolutionary Soldier, Interspersed with Anecdotes of Incidents that Occurred within His Own Observation* (Howell, Me.: Glazier, Masters, 1830), p. 75.

2. Ibid., p. 76.

3. Ibid., p. 82.

4. Hugh McDonald, "A Teenager in the Revolution," *Historical Times,* (1966), p. 46.

5. Pierre Du Ponceau, "The Autobiography of Peter Stephen Du Ponceau," *Pennsylvania Magazine of History and Biography* 63, no. 1 (1939), pp. 189–195.

6. Martin, *Narrative,* p. 86.

7. Du Ponceau, "Autobiography," p. 208.

8. Ibid., p. 209.

9. Rebecca Franks to Nancy, 27 February 1778, in *The American Jewish Woman: A Documentary History,* compiled by Jacob R. Marcus (New York: Ktav, 1981), p. 1047.

10. Du Ponceau, "Autobiography," p. 209.

11. Sally Wister, *Sally Wister's Journal: A True Narrative* (Philadelphia: Ferris and Leach, 1902), pp. 183–185.

12. Du Ponceau, "Autobiography," p. 211.

13. Ibid., pp. 211–212.

14. Ibid., p. 212.

15. Wister, *Sally Wister's Journal,* pp. 35–36.

16. Martin, *Narrative,* p. 90.

17. Ibid., p. 95.

18. Ibid., pp. 96–97.

19. Henry D. Biddle, ed., *Extracts from the Journal of Elizabeth Drinker* (Philadelphia: J. B. Lippincott Company, 1889), p. 107.

20. Jean De Crevecouer, "Narrative of the Wyoming Massacre: July 1778," in *The American Revolution: Writings from the War of Independence* (New York: Library of America, 2001), pp. 481–482.

21. Ibid., p. 486.

22. Frances Slocum, "The Child Captive of Wyoming," in *Hours with the Living Men and Women of the Revolution,* Benson J. Lossing, ed. (New York: Funk and Wagnalls, 1889), pp. 86–94.

23. Martin, *Narrative,* pp. 97–98.

24. Ibid., p. 100.

25. Mary Gould Almy, "Mrs. Almy's Journal: Siege of Newport, R.I., August 1778," *Newport Historical Magazine* 1 (1881), pp. 17–36.

26. Mary Palmer Tyler, *Grandmother Tyler's Book* (New York: G. P. Putnam's Sons, 1925), p. 58.

27. Johannes Reuber, *Tagebuch des Grenadiers Johannes Reuber* (Frankfurt am Main, Germany: Stadtarchiv), pp. 119–120.

28. Elizabeth Lichtenstein Johnston, *Recollections of a Georgia Loyalist* (Spartanburg, S.C.: The Reprint Company, 1972), p. 48. Original published in 1901.

29. Ibid., p. 49.

30. Reuber, *Tagebuch,* p. 120.

CHAPTER SIX

1. Joseph P. Martin, *A Narrative of Some of the Adventures, Dangers, and Sufferings of a Revolutionary Soldier, Interspersed with Anecdotes of Incidents that Occurred Within His Own Observation* (Howell, Me.: Glazier, Masters, 1830), pp. 111–113.

2. Johannes Reuber, *Tagebuch des Grenadiers Johannes Reuber* (Frankfurt am Main, Germany: Stadtarchiv), pp. 111–113.

3. Elizabeth Lichtenstein Johnston, *Recollections of a Georgia Loyalist* (Spartansburg, S.C.: The Reprint Company, 1972), pp. 57–58. Original published in 1901.

4. Ibid., p. 61.

5. Ibid., p. 63.

6. Martin, *Narrative,* pp. 121, 123.

7. Valentin Asteroth, *Das Tagebuch des Sockenstrickers Valentin Asteroth aus Treysa 1778–1831* (Schwalmstadt-Treysa, Germany: Stadtgeschichtlicher Arbeitskreis, 1992), pp. 51–53.

8. Ibid., p. 55.

9. Cited in Robert Leckie, *George Washington's War: The Saga of the American Revolution* (New York: Harper Collins, 1992), p. 509.

10. Samuel Baldwin, "Charleston, S.C. during the Siege by the British: March 20–April 20, 1780," *New Jersey Historical Proceedings* 2 (1846–1847), pp. 78–79.

11. Ibid., pp. 80–82.

12. Ibid., p. 82.

13. Ibid., p. 84.

14. Asteroth, *Tagebuch,* p. 60.

15. Elizabeth Fenn, *Pox Americana: The Great Smallpox Epidemic of 1775–1782* (New York: Walker and Co., 2002), p. 122.

16. Eliza Wilkinson, *Letters of Eliza Wilkinson during the Invasion and Possession of Charleston, S.C. by the British in the Revolutionary War* (New York: S. Coleman, 1839), letter III, p. 108.

17. Ibid., letter IV, p. 108.

18. James Collins, *A Revolutionary Soldier* (Clinton, La.: Feliciana Democrat, 1859), p. 41.

19. Ibid., p. 51.

20. Thomas Young, "Memoir of Major Thomas Young: A Revolutionary Patriot of South Carolina," *The Orion* 3 (Oct 1843), p. 86.

21. Ibid., p. 87.

22. Collins, *Revolutionary Soldier,* pp. 53–54.

23. Martin, *Narrative,* p. 151.

CHAPTER SEVEN

1. Rayford W. Logan, ed., *Memoirs of a Monticello Slave: As Dictated to Charles Campbell in the 1840's by Isaac, One of Thomas Jefferson's Slaves* (Charlottesville: University of Virginia Press, 1951), pp. 17–18.

2. Ibid., p. 20.

3. Thomas Young, "Memoir of Major Thomas Young: A Revolutionary Patriot of South Carolina," *The Orion* 3 (Oct 1843), p. 88.

4. James P. Collins, *A Revolutionary Soldier* (Clinton, La.: Feliciana Democrat, printer, 1859), pp. 57–58.

5. Sam B. Smith and Harriet Chappel Owsley, eds., *The Papers of Andrew Jackson,* Vol. 1, *1770–1803* (Knoxville: University of Tennessee Press, 1980), pp. 5–7.

6. Emily Geiger, "The Fair Courier," in *Hours with the Living Men and Women of the Revolution,* Benson J. Lossing, ed. (New York: Funk and Wagnalls, 1889), chap. III.

7. Mildred Smith, letter to Elizabeth Ambler, from York(town), 1780, Elizabeth Ambler Papers, Earl Swem Library, William and Mary Colonial Williamsburg Library.

8. Elizabeth Ambler, letter to Mildred Smith, from Richmond, 1781, Elizabeth Ambler Papers, Earl Swem Library, William and Mary Colonial Williamsburg Library.

9. Joseph P. Martin, *A Narrative of Some of the Adversities, Dangers, and Sufferings of a Revolutionary Soldier, Interspersed with Anecdotes of Incidents that Occurred within His Own Observation* (Howell, Me.: Glazier, Masters, 1830), p. 162.

10. Ibid., p. 165.

11. Ebenezer Denny, "Journal: September 1–November 1, 1781," in *The American Revolution: Writings from the War of Independence* (New York: Library of America, 2001), pp. 721–722.

12. John Hudson, "Such Had Been the Flow of Blood," *American History Illustrated* 16, no. 6 (1981), pp. 20–21.

13. Martin, *Narrative,* p. 168.

14. Ibid., p. 167.

15. Denny, "Journal," p. 723.

16. Martin, *Narrative,* p. 171.

17. Denny, "Journal," p. 724.

18. Johann Conrad Döhla, *A Hessian Diary of the American Revolution* (Norman: University of Oklahoma Press, 1990), p. 172.

19. Denny, "Journal," p. 725.

20. Martin, *Narrative,* p. 174.

21. Hudson, "Such had been," pp. 22–23.

22. Denny, "Journal," p. 725.

23. Martin, *Narrative,* p. 174.

24. Logan, *Memoirs,* p. 20.

25. Döhla, *Hessian Diary,* p. 174.

26. Henry D. Biddle, ed., *Extracts from the Journal of Elizabeth Drinker* (Philadelphia: J. B. Lippincott, 1889), p. 137.

27. Anna Rawle, "Diary, October 25, 1781," in *Weathering the Storm: Women of the American Revolution,* Elizabeth Evans, ed. (New York: Charles Scribner's Sons, 1975), pp. 294–295.

28. Eliza Wilkinson, "Letter, 1782," in *Letters of Eliza Wilkinson during the Invasion and Possession of Charleston, S.C. by the British in the Revolutionary War,* Caroline Gilman, ed. (New York: S. Colman, 1839), p. 108.

29. Smith, Letter to Elizabeth Ambler. From York (town), 1782.

CHAPTER EIGHT

1. Christopher Hawkins, *The Adventures of Christopher Hawkins* (New York: Arno Press, 1968), pp. 11–12.

2. John C. Dann, ed., *The Revolution Remembered: Eyewitness Accounts of the War for Independence* (Chicago: University of Chicago Press, 1980), pp. 135–144, 158–162, 327–330, 406–415; "Prisoners and Mariners in the Revolutionary War," http://www.usmm.org/revolution.html.

3. Ebenezer Fox, "The Revolutionary Adventures of Ebenezer Fox of Roxbury, Massachusetts," in *Narratives of the American Revolution,* Hugh F. Rankin, ed. (Chicago: R. R. Donnelly and Sons, 1976), pp. 39–40. Original published by Munroe and Francis, Boston, in 1838.

4. Andrew Sherburne, *Memoirs of Andrew Sherburne: A Pensioner of the Navy of the American Revolution* (Providence, R.I.: H. H. Brown, 1831), pp. 35–36.

5. Hawkins, *Adventures,* p. 12.

6. John Blatchford, *Narrative of Remarkable Occurrences in the Life of John Blatchford* (New London, Conn.: T. Green, 1807).

7. Ibid., p. 24.

8. Ibid., p. 27.

9. Ibid., p. 45.

10. Israel Trask in Dann, *Revolution Remembered,* pp. 412–414.

11. Ibid., p. 412.

12. Ibid., p. 414.

13. Marion Kaminkow and Jack Kaminkow, *Mariners of the American Revolution* (Baltimore, Md.: Magna Carta, 1967), p. XIII.

14. Sherburne, *Memoirs,* p. 103.

15. Ibid., p. 80.

16. H. W. Brands, *The First American: The Life and Times of Benjamin Franklin* (New York: Anchor Books, 2002), pp. 584–585.

17. Sherburne, *Memoirs,* p. 103.

18. Fox, "Revolutionary Adventures," p. 72.

19. Sherburne, *Memoirs,* p. 113.

20. Hawkins, *Adventures,* pp. 66–73.

21. Sherburne, *Memoirs,* p. 113.

22. Ibid., p. 119.

23. Ashbel Green, *The Life of Ashbel Green* (New York: Robert Carter and Brothers, 1849).

24. Julie Winch, *A Gentleman of Color: The Life of James Forten* (New York: Oxford University Press, 2002).

25. James Forten to William Lloyd Garrison, 23 February 1831, Boston Public Library, Massachusetts.

26. Fox, "Revolutionary Adventures," pp. 106–107.

CHAPTER NINE

1. William L. Stone, trans., *Letters and Journals Relating to the War of the American Revolution and the Capture of the German Troops at Saratoga by Mrs. General Riedesel* (Albany, N.Y.: Joel Munsell, 1867).

2. Walter Hart Blumenthal, *Women Camp Followers of the American Revolution* (Philadelphia: George S. MacManus, 1952), p. 17.

3. Louise Hall Tharp, *The Baroness and the General* (Boston: Little, Brown and Co., 1962).

4. Stone, *Letters and Journals,* p. 41.

5. Marvin L. Brown Jr., ed., *Baroness von Riedesel and the American Revolution: Journal and Correspondence on a Tour of Duty: 1776–1783* (Chapel Hill: University of North Carolina Press, 1965), Introduction.

6. Ibid., Introduction.

7. Stone, *Letters and Journals,* p. 87.

8. Ibid., pp. 127–128.

9. Ibid., pp. 134–135.

10. Hannah Winthrop to Mercy Warren, 11 November 1777, Warren Papers, Massachusetts Historical Society, Boston.

11. Stone, *Letters and Journals,* p. 147.

12. Thomas Jefferson, cited in Brown, *Baroness von Riedesel,* Introduction.

13. Thomas Jefferson to Riedesel, 4 July 1779, in *The Papers of Thomas Jefferson,* Vol. 3, Julian P. Boyd, ed. (Princeton, N.J.: Princeton University Press, 1951), p. 24.

14. Riedesel to Thomas Jefferson, 4 December 1779, in Boyd, *Papers of Thomas Jefferson,* p. 312.

15. Stone, *Letters and Journals,* p. 177.

16. Thomas Jefferson to Riedesel, 3 May 1780, in Boyd, *Papers of Thomas Jefferson,* p. 368.

17. Paul Riedesel, "General Friedrich Adolph Riedesel," http://www.myerchin.org/BiographyGeneralRiedesel.html.

18. Stone, *Letters and Journals,* p. 207.

19. Riedesel, "General Friedrich Adolph Riedesel."

CHAPTER TEN

1. "A List of Personal Supplies to Be Taken on the Voyage of the Frigate *Boston* to France," in David McCullough, *John Adams* (New York: Simon and Schuster, 2001), photo insert 12 between pp. 144 and 145.

2. John Quincy Adams to John Adams, 13 October 1774, Adams Family Papers, reel 344, Massachusetts Historical Society, Boston.

3. John Quincy Adams to John Adams, June 1777, cited in Joseph E. Illick, "John Quincy Adams: The Maternal Influence," *Journal of Psychohistory* 4 (fall 1976), p. 186.

4. John Quincy Adams to Abigail Adams, 12 April 1778, Adams Family Papers, reel 349, Massachusetts Historical Society, Boston.

5. John Quincy Adams to Abigail Adams, 20 April 1778, Adams Family Papers, reel 349, Massachusetts Historical Society, Boston.

6. John Quincy Adams to Abigail Adams, 5 June 1778, Adams Papers, Library of Congress, Washington, D.C.

7. John Quincy Adams to Abigail Adams, 27 September 1778, Adams Family Papers, reel 349, Massachusetts Historical Society, Boston.

8. Abigail Adams to John Quincy Adams, 19 January 1780, Adams Family Papers, reel 351, Massachusetts Historical Society, Boston.

9. David Grayson Allen, Robert J. Taylor, Marc Friedlander, and Celeste Walker, eds., *Diary of John Quincy Adams,* Vol. 1 (Cambridge, Mass.: Belknap Press of Harvard University Press, 1981), pp. 1–2.

10. Ibid., p. 10.

11. Cited in Paul C. Nagel, *John Quincy Adams: A Public Life, a Private Life* (New York: Alfred A. Knopf, 1997), p. 19.

12. John Quincy Adams to Abigail Adams, 17 February 1780, Adams Family Papers, reel 351, Massachusetts Historical Society, Boston.

13. Abigail Adams to John Quincy Adams, 20 March 1780, Adams Family Papers, reel 351, Massachusetts Historical Society, Boston.

14. McCullough, *John Adams,* p. 251.

15. John Adams to John Quincy Adams, 20 December 1780, Adams Family Papers, reel 352, Massachusetts Historical Society, Boston.

16. John Quincy Adams to John Adams, 21 December 1780, Adams Family Papers, rcel 352, Massachusetts Historical Society, Boston.

17. John Adams to John Quincy Adams, 23 December 1780, Adams Family Papers, reel 352, Massachusetts Historical Society, Boston.

18. John Adams to John Quincy Adams, 28 December 1780, Adams Family Papers, reel 352, Massachusetts Historical Society, Boston.

19. Abigail Adams to John Quincy Adams, 21 January 1781, Adams Family Papers, reel 354, Massachusetts Historical Society, Boston.

20. John Adams to John Quincy Adams, 14/18 May 1781, Adams Family Papers, reel 354, Massachusetts Historical Society, Boston.

21. Abigail Adams to John Quincy Adams, 26 May 1781, Adams Family Papers, reel 354, Massachusetts Historical Society, Boston.

22. John Quincy Adams to John Adams, 18 February 1781, Adams Family Papers, reel 354, Massachusetts Historical Society, Boston.

23. Cited in Phyllis Lee Levin, *Abigail Adams: A Biography* (New York: St. Martin's Press, 2001), p. 133.

24. John Quincy Adams to John Adams, 1 September 1781, Adams Family Papers, reel 355, Massachusetts Historical Society, Boston.

25. John Quincy Adams to John Adams, 12/23 October 1781, Adams Family Papers, reel 355, Massachusetts Historical Society, Boston.

26. John Adams to John Quincy Adams, 15 December 1781, Adams Family Papers, reel 355, Massachusetts Historical Society, Boston.

27. John Adams to John Quincy Adams, 5 February 1782, Adams Family Papers, reel 356, Massachusetts Historical Society, Boston.

28. Abigail Adams to John Quincy Adams, 13 November 1782, Adams Family Papers, reel 359, Massachusetts Historical Society, Boston.

29. John Quincy Adams to Abigail Adams, 23 July 1783, Adams Family Papers, reel 361, Massachusetts Historical Society, Boston.

30. Ibid.

31. John Quincy Adams to John Adams, 1/20 February 1783, Adams Family Papers, reel 360, Massachusetts Historical Society, Boston.

32. John Quincy Adams to Abigail Adams, 23 July 1783, Adams Family Papers, reel 361, Massachusetts Historical Society, Boston.

33. Ibid.

34. John Adams to John Quincy Adams, 27 April 1783, Adams Family Papers, reel 360, Massachusetts Historical Society, Boston.

35. John Quincy Adams to John Adams, 12 May 1783, Adams Family Papers, reel 360, Massachusetts Historical Society, Boston.

36. John Adams to John Quincy Adams, 3 July 1783, Adams Family Papers, reel 361, Massachusetts Historical Society, Boston.

37. Allen, *Diary of John Quincy Adams,* p. 182.

38. John Quincy Adams to Abigail Adams, 4 September 1783, Adams Family Papers, reel 361, Massachusetts Historical Society, Boston.

39. Allen, *Diary of John Quincy Adams,* p. 283.

CHAPTER ELEVEN

1. Mary Palmer Tyler, *Grandmother Tyler's Book* (New York: G. P. Putnam's Sons, 1925), pp. 68–69.

2. Dan Huntington, *Memories, Counsels, and Reflections* (Cambridge, Mass.: Metcalf and Co., 1857), p. 6.

3. Lydia Minturn Post, *Personal Recollections of the American Revolution: A Private Journal Prepared from Authentic Domestic Records,* Sidney Barclay, ed. (New York: A. O. F. Randolph, 1866), p. 118.

4. Johannes Reuber, *Tagebuch des Grenadiers Johannes Reuber* (Frankfurt am Main, Germany: Stadtarchiv), p. 149.

5. Johann Conrad Döhla, *A Hessian Diary of the American Revolution,* Bruce Burgoyne, ed. (Norman: University of Oklahoma Press, 1990), p. 220.

6. Joseph P. Martin, cited in Jim Murphy, *A Young Patriot: The American Revolution as Experienced by One Boy* (New York: Clarion Books, 1996), pp. 85–87.

7. Ibid., p. 87.

8. Ibid., p. 87.

9. Ebenezer Fox, "The Revolutionary Adventures of Ebenezer Fox of Roxbury, Massachusetts," in *Narratives of the American Revolution,* Hugh F. Rankin, ed. (Chicago: R. R. Donnelly & Sons, 1976), p. 160.

10. Linda Grant de Pauw, *Founding Mothers: Women in America in the Revolutionary Era* (Boston: Houghton Mifflin, 1975), p. 148.

11. Ibid., p. 144.

12. Sarah Scofield Frost, "Diary of Sarah Scofield Frost, June 1783," in *Kingston and the Loyalists of the Spring Fleet 1783,* Walter Bates, ed. (St. John, Canada: Barnes and Co., 1889), p. 5.

13. De Pauw, *Founding Mothers,* pp. 146–147.

14. Ibid., pp. 147–148.

15. Elizabeth Lichtenstein Johnston, *Recollections of a Georgia Loyalist* (Spartanburg, S.C.: The Reprint Company, 1972), pp. 211, 221. Original published in 1901.

16. Ray Raphael, *A People's History of the American Revolution: How Common People Shaped the Fight for Independence* (New York: The New Press, 2001), pp. 179, 185.

17. Reuber, *Tagebuch,* p. 169.

18. Rodney Atwood, *The Hessians: Mercenaries from Hessen-Kassel in the American Revolution* (New York: Cambridge University Press, 1980), pp. 238–239.

19. Inge Auerbach, *Die Hessen in Amerika 1776–1783* (Marburg, Germany: Historische Kommission für Hessen, 1996), pp. 357–366; *Staatsarchiv Marburg, Kirchenbuch der Garnisonsgemeinde Kassel* (Marburg, Germany: Staatsarchiv, 1781–1818), pp. 42, 982, 992, 995.

20. George Fenwick Jones, "The Black Hessians: Negroes Recruited by the Hessians in South Carolina and Other Colonies," *South Carolina Historical Magazine* 83, no. 4 (1982): 287.

21. Eliza Morton Quincy, *Memoirs of the Life of Eliza S. M. Quincy* (Boston: J. Wilson and Son, 1861), pp. 41–42.

22. Ibid., pp. 50–51.

23. Ibid., pp. 51–52.

24. Howard H. Peckham, ed., *The Toll of Independence* (Chicago: University of Chicago Press, 1974), p. 130; Elizabeth A. Fenn, *Pox Americana: The Great Smallpox Epidemic of 1775–82* (New York: Hill and Wang, 2001), pp. 21, 274–275.

25. Joseph P. Martin, cited in Barnet Schecter, *The Battle for New York* (New York: Walker and Co., 2002), p. 389.

CHAPTER TWELVE

1. John Resch, *Suffering Soldiers: Revolutionary War Veterans, Moral Sentiment, and Political Culture in the Early Republic* (Amherst: University of Massachusetts Press, 1999), p. 118.

2. Jim Murphy, *A Young Patriot: The American Revolution as Experienced by One Boy* (New York: Clarion Books, 1996), p. 89.

3. John C. Dann, ed., *The Revolution Remembered: Eyewitness Accounts of the War for Independence* (Chicago: University of Chicago Press, 1980), p. XVI.

4. Theodore J. Crackel, "Revolutionary War Pension Records and Patterns of American Mobility, 1780–1830," *Journal of the National Archives* 16 (1984), p. 156.

5. C. S. McElfish, "Washington Plagued with Dental Ills," *Journal of the Colorado Dental Association, 79* (Winter, 2000), pp. 28–29.

6. Julie Winch, *A Gentleman of Color: The Life of James Forten* (New York: Oxford University Press, 2002), Introduction.

7. Rayford Logan, ed., *Memoirs of a Monticello Slave* (Charlottsville: University of Virginia Press, 1951), p. 4.

8. Pierre Du Ponceau, "The Autobiography of Peter Stephen Du Ponceau," *Pennsylvania Magazine of History and Biography* 63, no. 1 (1939), pp. 189–194.

9. Elizabeth Brent to Nancy Fischer, ca. 1810, Virginia Historical Society, Richmond.

10. Mary Beth Norton, *Liberty's Daughters: The Revolutionary Experience of American Women: 1750–1800* (Ithaca, N.Y.: Cornell University Press, 1996), p. 229.

11. Ibid., p. 230.

12. Ibid., p. 263.

13. Ibid., p. 260.

14. Ibid., p. 283.

15. John Adams to Abigail Adams II, 13 August 1783, Adams Family Papers, Massachusetts Historical Society, Boston.

16. Samuel Flagg Bemis, *John Quincy Adams and the Foundation of American Foreign Policy* (Westport, Conn.: Greenwood Press, 1981).

17. Nancy Loughridge, "Andrew Jackson," in *Reference Guide to United States Military History: 1607–1815,* Charles Reginald Shrader, ed. (New York: Facts on File, 1991), p. 170.

18. Benson J. Lossing, ed., *Hours with the Living Men and Women of the Revolution* (New York: Funk and Wagnalls, 1889), p. 94.

19. John Quincy Adams, address as Secretary of State, 4 July 1821.

20. Rodney Atwood, *The Hessians: Mercenaries from Hessen-Kassel in the American Revolution* (New York: Cambridge University Press, 1980), pp. 251–253.

Bibliography

Adams Family Papers, Massachusetts Historical Society, Boston.

Adams Papers, Library of Congress, Washington, D.C.

Allen, David Grayson, Robert J. Taylor, Marc Friedlander, and Celeste Walker, eds. *Diary of John Quincy Adams*. Vol. 1, *November 1779–March 1786*. Cambridge, Mass.: Belknap Press of Harvard University Press, 1981.

Almy, Mary Gould. "Mrs. Almy's Journal: Siege of Newport, R.I., August 1778." *Newport Historical Magazine* 1 (1881): 17–36.

Asteroth, Valentin. *Das Tagebuch des Sockenstrickers Valentin Asteroth aus Treysa 1778–1831*. Edited by Heinz Krause. Schwalmstadt-Treysa, Germany: Stadtgeschichtlicher Arbeitskreis, 1992.

Atwood, Rodney. *The Hessians: Mercenaries from Hessen-Kassel in the American Revolution*. New York: Cambridge University Press, 1980.

Auerbach, Inge. *Die Hessen in Amerika 1776–1783*. Marburg, Germany: Historische Kommission für Hessen, 1996.

Bacon, Margaret Hope. *The Quiet Rebels: The Story of the Quakers in America*. Philadelphia: New Society, 1985.

Baldwin, Samuel. "Charleston, S.C. during the Siege by the British: March 20–April 20, 1780." *New Jersey Historical Proceedings* 2 (1846–1847), 78–86.

Becker, John P. *The Sexagenary or Reminiscences of the American Revolution*. Albany, N.Y.: W. C. Little, 1866.

Bemis, Samuel F. *John Quincy Adams and the Foundation of American Foreign Policy*. Westport, Conn.: Greenwood Press, 1981.

Biddle, Henry D., ed. *Extracts from the Journal of Elizabeth Drinker*. Philadelphia: J. B. Lippincott, 1889.

Blatchford, John. *Narrative of Remarkable Occurrences in the Life of John Blatchford*. New London, Conn.: T. Green, 1807.

Blumenthal, Walter Hart. *Women Camp Followers of the American Revolution*. Philadelphia: George S. MacManus, 1952.

Boston and the American Revolution. Washington, D.C.: Division of Publications, National Park Service, U.S. Department of the Interior, 1998.

Boston Globe Special Supplement, "The Boston Tea Party," 1974. pp. 52, 60

Boyd, Julian P., ed. *The Papers of Thomas Jefferson.* Vol. 3. Princeton, N.J.: Princeton University Press, 1951.

Bragg, Arial. *Memoirs of Colonel Arial Bragg.* Milford, Conn.: George W. Stacy, 1846.

Brands, H. W. *The First American: The Life and Times of Benjamin Franklin.* New York: Anchor Books, 2002.

Breck, Samuel. "A Child of the Revolution." In *Camps and Firesides of the Revolution,* ed. Albert Hart and Mabel Hill Bushnell. Charlottesville: University of Virginia Library Electronic Text Center, 8 April 2002.

Brookhiser, Richard. *America's First Dynasty: The Adamses: 1735–1918.* New York: The Free Press, 2002.

Brown, Marvin L., Jr., ed. *Baroness von Riedesel and the American Revolution: Journal and Correspondence of a Tour of Duty: 1776–1783.* Chapel Hill: University of North Carolina Press, 1965.

Buckley, Gail. *American Patriots: The Story of Blacks in the Military from the Revolution to Desert Storm.* New York: Random House, 2001.

Burgoyne, Bruce. *Diaries of a Hessian Chaplain and the Chaplain's Assistant.* Pensauken, N.J.: Johannes Schwalm Historical Association, 1990.

———. *Enemy Views: The American Revolutionary War as Recorded by the Hessian Participants.* Bowie, Md.: Heritage Press, 1996.

Butterfield, L. H., and Marc Friedlander, eds. *Adams Family Correspondence.* Vol. 3, *April 1778–September 1780.* Cambridge, Mass.: Belknap Press of Harvard University Press, 1973.

———. *Adams Family Correspondence.* Vol. 4, *October 1780–September 1782.* Cambridge, Mass.: Belknap Press of Harvard University Press, 1973.

Butterfield, L. H., Wendell D. Garrett, and Marjorie E. Sprague, eds. *Adams Family Correspondence.* Vol. 1, *December 1761–May 1776.* Cambridge, Mass.: Belknap Press of Harvard University Press, 1963.

———. *Adams Family Correspondence.* Vol. 2, *June 1776–March 1778.* Cambridge, Mass.: Belknap Press of Harvard University Press, 1963.

Collins, James P. *A Revolutionary Soldier.* Edited by John M. Roberts. Clinton, La.: Feliciana Democrat Printers, 1859.

Crackel, Theodore J. "Revolutionary War Pension Records and Patterns of American Mobility, 1780–1830." *Journal of the National Archives* 16 (1984): 155–167.

Dann, John C., ed. *The Revolution Remembered: Eyewitness Accounts of the War for Independence.* Chicago: University of Chicago Press, 1980.

Davis, Burke. *Black Heroes of the American Revolution.* San Diego, Calif.: Harcourt, Brace, Jovanovich, 1976.

De Crevecoeur, Jean. "Narrative of the Wyoming Massacre: July 1778." Reprinted in *The American Revolution: Writings from the War of Independence.* New York: Library of America, 2001.

Denny, Ebenezer. "Journal: May 1–15, 1781; June 18–July 7, 1781; September 1–November 1, 1781; January 4–December 13, 1782." Reprinted in *The American Revolution: Writings from the War of Independence.* New York: Library of America, 2001.

De Pauw, Linda Grant. *Founding Mothers: Women in America in the Revolutionary Era.* Boston: Houghton Mifflin, 1975.

Depositions of Elizabeth Cain and Abigail Palmer, Papers of the Continental Congress, 22 March 1777.

Dippel, Horst. "Sources in Germany for the Study of the American Revolution." *Quarterly Journal of the Library of Congress* 33 (July 1976): 199–217.

Dodge, David Low. "Autobiography." In *Memorial of Mr. David L. Dodge.* Boston: S. K. Whipple, 1854.

Döhla, Johann Conrad. *A Hessian Diary of the American Revolution.* Translated and edited by Bruce Burgoyne. Norman: University of Oklahoma Press, 1990.

Drake, Francis Samuel. *Tea Leaves: Being a Collection of Letters and Documents Related to the Shipment of Tea to the American Colonies in the Year 1773 by the East India Tea Company.* Boston: A. O. Crane, 1884. (Reprinted by Singing Tree Press, Detroit, Mich., 1970.)

Drinker, Elizabeth. *Extracts from the Journal of Elizabeth Drinker.* Edited by Henry D. Biddle. Philadelphia: J. B. Lippincott, 1889.

Dudley, Dorothy. "The Diary of Dorothy Dudley: From April 18, 1775 to July 19, 1776." In *Theatrum Majorum.* Cambridge, Mass.: Ladies Centennial Commission, 1876.

Du Ponceau, Pierre. "The Autobiography of Peter Stephen Du Ponceau." *Pennsylvania Magazine of History and Biography* 62, no. 1 (1939):189–194.

Elizabeth Ambler Papers, Earl Swem Library, William and Mary Colonial Williamsburg Library. (Reprinted in "Old Virginia Correspondence." *Atlantic Monthly* 84, July–Dec 1899, 535–549.)

Elizabeth Brent to Nancy Fischer, ca. 1810, Virginia Historical Society, Richmond.

Elizabeth Clarke to Her Niece Lucy Allan, Lexington, 19 April 1841, Massachusetts Historical Society, Boston. (Reprinted in Tourtellot, Arthur Benson. *William Diamond's Drum: The Beginning of the War of the American Revolution.* Garden City, N.Y.: Doubleday, 1959.)

Evans, Elizabeth. *Weathering the Storm: Women of the American Revolution.* New York: Charles Scribner's Sons, 1975.

Fenn, Elizabeth A. *Pox Americana: The Great Smallpox Epidemic of 1775–82.* New York: Hill and Wang, 2001.

Fischer, David Hackett. *Washington's Crossing.* New York: Oxford University Press, 2004.

Fletcher, Ebenezer. "The Trials of Ebenezer Fletcher, Fifer in Colonel Nathan Hale's Regiment." In *Crumbs for Antiquarians.* Vol. 2. Edited by Charles J. Bushnell. Privately printed, 1866.

Fox, Ebenezer. "The Revolutionary Adventures of Ebenezer Fox of Roxbury, Massachusetts." In *Narratives of the American Revolution,* ed. Hugh F. Rankin. Chicago: R. R. Donnelly and Sons, 1976.

Frost, Sarah Scofield. "Diary of Sarah Scofield Frost." In *Kingston and the Loyalists of the Spring Fleet 1783,* ed. Walter Bates. St. John, Canada: Barnes and Co., 1889.

Gerrish, Edward. "Anonymous Summary of the Crown's Evidence: Rex vs. Preston." In *Legal Papers of John Adams.* Vol. 3, *The Boston Massacre Trial,* ed. L. Kinvin Wroth and Hiller B. Zobel. Cambridge, Mass.: Belknap Press of Harvard University Press, 1965.

Goldfinch, Capt. Lt. John. "Sworn Testimony: Rex vs. Wemm." In *Legal Papers of John Adams,* Vol. 3, *The Boston Massacre Trial,* ed. L. Kinvin Wroth and Hiller B. Zobel. Cambridge, Mass.: Belknap Press of Harvard University Press, 1965.

Green, Ashbel. *The Life of Ashbel Green.* New York: Robert Carter and Brothers, 1849.

Greene, Evarts Boutell. *The Revolutionary Generation 1763–1790.* New York: MacMillan, 1943.

Greenwood, John. *A Young Patriot in the American Revolution: 1775–1783: The Wartime Services of John Greenwood.* Tyrone, Pa.: Westvaco, 1981. (Original manuscript written in 1809, Clements Library, Ann Arbor, University of Michigan.)

Hahn, Harold M. *Ships of the American Revolution.* Annapolis, Md.: Naval Institute, 1988.

Harvard College. *Records of the College Faculty* IV (1 March 1775–1781): 4–5.

Hawkins, Christopher. *The Adventures of Christopher Hawkins.* New York: Arno Press, 1968.

Hibbard, Billy. *Memoirs of the Life and Travels of B. Hibbard, Minister of the Gospel.* New York: Arthur, 1843.

Hicks, Edward. *Memoirs of the Life and Religious Labors of Edward Hicks.* Philadelphia: Merrihew and Thompson, 1851.

Hosmer, Lucy. April 19, 1775 (unpublished diary). Cary Library, Lexington, Mass.

How, David. *Diary of David How.* New York: Morrisania, 1865.

Hudson, John. "Such Had Been the Flow of Blood." *American History Illustrated* 16, no. 6 (1981): 18.

Hull, Mary E. *The Boston Tea Party in American History.* Berkeley Heights, N.J.: Enslow, 1999.

Huntington, Dan. *Memories, Counsels, and Reflections. By an Octogenary. Addressed to His Children and Descendants, and Printed for Their Use.* Cambridge, Mass.: Metcalf and Co., 1857.

Hutchins, Levy. *The Autobiography of Levi Hutchins.* Cambridge, Mass.: Riverside Press, 1865.

Illick, Joseph E. "John Quincy Adams: The Maternal Influence." *Journal of Psychohistory* 4 (fall 1976): 185–195.

James Forten to William Lloyd Garrison, 23 February 1831, Boston Public Library, Massachusetts.

Jensen, Ann, ed. *The World Turned Upside Down: Children of 1776: The Story of an Annapolis Family.* Annapolis, Md.: Sands House, 1993.

Johnston, Elizabeth Lichtenstein. *Recollections of a Georgia Loyalist.* Spartanburg, S.C.: The Reprint Company, 1972. (Original published by De La More Press, 1901.)

Jones, George Fenwick. "The Black Hessians: Negroes Recruited by the Hessians in South Carolina and Other Colonies." *South Carolina Historical Magazine* 83, no. 4 (1982): 287.

Kaminkow, Marion, and Jack Kaminkow. *Mariners of the American Revolution.* Baltimore, Md.: Magna Carta, 1967.

Kipping, Ernst. *The Hessian View of America: 1776–1783.* Monmouth Beach, N.J.: Freneau, 1971.

Kirchenbuch der Garnisonsgemeinde Kassel. Marburg, Germany: Staatsarchiv, 1781–1818.

Leckie, Robert. *George Washington's War: The Saga of the American Revolution.* New York: Harper Collins, 1992.

Levin, Phyllis Lee. *Abigail Adams: A Biography.* New York: St. Martin's Press, 2001.

Loeper, John J., ed. *Going to School in 1776.* New York: Athenum, 1973.

Logan, Rayford, ed. *Memoirs of a Monticello Slave: As Dictated to Charles Campbell in the 1840's by Isaac, One of Thomas Jefferson's Slaves.* Charlottesville: University of Virginia Press, 1951.

Lossing, Benson J., ed. *Hours with the Living Men and Women of the Revolution.* New York: Funk and Wagnalls, 1889.

Loughridge, Nancy. "Andrew Jackson." In *Reference Guide to United States Military History: 1607–1815,* ed. Charles Reginald Shrader. New York: Facts on File, 1991.

Martin, Joseph Plumb. *A Narrative of Some of the Adventures, Dangers, and Sufferings of a Revolutionary Soldier, Interspersed with Anecdotes of Incidents that Occurred within His Own Observation.* Howell, Me.: Glazier, Masters, 1830.

Mason, Jeremiah. *Memoirs, Autobiography and Correspondence of James Mason.* Kansas City, Mo.: Lawyers International, 1917.

McCullough, David. *John Adams.* New York: Simon and Schuster, 2001.

McDonald, Hugh. "A Teenager in the Revolution.": *Historical Times* (special issue), 1966.

McElfish, C. S. "Washington Plagued with Dental Ills." *Journal of the Colorado Dental Association,* 79 (Winter 2000), pp.28–29.

Morris, Albert C., ed. *Sally Wister's Journal.* Philadelphia: Ferris and Leach, 1902.

Morris, Margaret. Private Journal Kept during a Portion of the Revolutionary War for the Amusement of a Sister. 21 December 1776. Rutgers University Special Collections and University Archives.

Morton, Robert. "Diary." *Pennsylvania Magazine of History and Biography* 1 (1877): pp. 1–39.

Murphy, Jim. *A Young Patriot: The American Revolution as Experienced by One Boy.* New York: Clarion Books, 1996.

Nagel, Paul C. *John Quincy Adams: A Public Life, a Private Life.* New York: Alfred A. Knopf, 1997.

Norton, Mary Beth. *Liberty's Daughters: The Revolutionary Experience of American Women: 1750–1800*. Ithaca, N.Y.: Cornell University Press, 1996.

Packard, Hezekiah. *Memoirs of Reverend Hezekiah Packard*. Brunswich, Maine: J. Griffin, 1850.

Peckham, Howard H., ed. *The Toll of Independence: Engagements and Battle Casualties of the American Revolution*. Chicago: University of Chicago Press, 1974.

Peter Edes to Grandsons, Bangor, Maine, 16 February 1836, Massachusetts Historical Society, Boston.

Pickering, Henry Goddard. *Nathaniel Goddard: A Boston Merchant: 1767–1853*. New York: Riverside Press, 1906.

Post, Lydia Minturn. *Personal Recollections of the American Revolution: A Private Journal Prepared from Authentic Domestic Records*. Edited by Sydney Barclay. New York: A. O. F. Randolph, 1866.

"Prisoners and Mariners in the Revolutionary War," http://www.usmm.org/revolution.html.

Quaife, M. M., ed. "A Boy Soldier under Washington: The Memoirs of Daniel Granger." *The Mississippi Valley Historical Review* 16, no. 4 (March 1930): 535–560.

Quincy, Eliza S. Morton. *Memoirs of the Life of Eliza S. M. Quincy*. Boston: J. Wilson and Son, 1861.

Raphael, Ray. *A People's History of the American Revolution: How Common People Shaped the Fight for Independence*. New York: The New Press, 2001.

Rawle, Anna. "Diary, October 25, 1781." in *Weathering the Storm: Women of the American Revolution*. Elizabeth Evans, ed. New York: Charles Scribner's Sons, 1975.

Rebecca Franks to Nancy, 27 February 1778. In *The American Jewish Woman: A Documentary History*. Compiled by Jacob R. Marcus. New York: Ktav, 1981.

Resch, John. *Suffering Soldiers: Revolutionary War Veterans, Moral Sentiment, and Political Culture in the Early Republic*. Amherst: University of Massachusetts Press, 1999.

Reuber, Johannes. *Tagebuch des Grenadiers Johannes Reuber*. Frankfurt am Main, Germany: Stadtarchiv, 1776–1783.

Riedesel, Frederike Charlotte L. *Letters and Journals Relating to the War of the American Revolution and the Capture of the German Troops at Saratoga*. Albany, N.Y.: Munsell, 1867.

Riedesel, Paul. "General Friedrich Adolph Riedesel." http://www.myerchin.org/BiographyGeneralRiedesel.html.

Ryerson, Richard Alan, Joanna M. Revelas, Celeste Walker, Gregg L. Lint, and Humphrey J. Costello, eds. *Adams Family Correspondence*. Vol. 5, *October 1782–November 1784*. Cambridge, Mass.: Belknap Press of Harvard University Press, 1993.

Samuel Swett Papers on the Battle of Bunker Hill, New York Historical Society, New York.

Sands, Will. "Letters from Philadelphia: July 20 and August 14, 1776." In *The World Turned Upside Down*, ed. Ann Dowsett Jensen. Annapolis, Md.: Sands House, 1993.

Scheer, George T., and Hugh Franklin, eds. *Rebels and Redcoats*. New York: World Publishing, 1957.

Sellers, John, et al. *Manuscript Sources in the Library of Congress for Research on the American Revolution*. Washington, D.C.: Library of Congress, 1975.

Shecter, Barnet. *The Battle for New York*. New York: Walker and Co., 2002.

Sherburne, Andrew. *Memoirs of Andrew Sherburne: A Pensioner of the Navy of the American Revolution*, 2nd. ed. Providence, R.I.: H. H. Brown, 1831.

Shrader, Charles R., ed. *Reference Guide to United States Military History*. New York: Facts on File, 1991.

Shy, John. *A People Numerous and Armed: Reflections on the Military Struggle for American Independence*. Ann Arbor: University of Michigan Press, 1990.

Silcox-Jarrett, Diane. *Heroines of the American Revolution: America's Founding Mothers*. Chapel Hill, N.C.: Green Angel Press, 1998.

Smith, Sam B., and Harriet Chappell Owsley, eds. *The Papers of Andrew Jackson*. Vol. 1, *1770–1803*. Knoxville: University of Tennessee Press, 1980.

Stone, Stephen, and William Stone. *The Family of John Stone*. Albany, N.Y.: Joel Munsell, 1888.

Stone, William L., trans. *Letters and Journals Relating to the War of the American Revolution and the Capture of the German Troops at Saratoga by Mrs. General Riedesel*. Albany, N.Y.: Joel Munsell, 1867.

Stubenrauch, Bob. *Where Freedom Grew*. New York: Dodd, Mead, 1970.

Taylor, Peter K. *Indentured to Liberty: Peasant Life and the Hessian Military State, 1688–1815*. Ithaca, N.Y.: Cornell University Press, 1994.

Tharp, Louise Hall. *The Baroness and the General*. Boston: Little, Brown and Co., 1962.

Tourtellot, Arthur Bernon. *William Diamond's Drum: The Beginning of the War of the American Revolution*. Garden City, N.Y.: Doubleday, 1959.

Tyler, Mary Palmer. *Grandmother Tyler's Book: The Recollections of Mary Palmer Tyler: 1775–1866*. New York: G. P. Putnam's Sons, 1925.

U.S. Bureau of the Census. *Historical Statistics of the United States*. 2 vols. Washington, D.C.: U.S. Government Printing Office, 1975.

Van Cleve, Benjamin. "Memoirs of Benjamin Van Cleve." *Quarterly Publications of the Historical and Philosophical Society of Ohio* 17 (1922): 291–292.

Warren Papers, Massachusetts Historical Society, Boston.

Warren-Adams Letters, Massachusetts Historical Society, Boston.

Wertheimer, Ron. "The Incomplete Promise of Liberty." *New York Times*, 10 January 2003, p. 51.

Wharton, Polly. "Christmas Letter to Her Cousin Mary, Trenton, N.J., Christmas Day, 1776." In *Going to School in 1776*, ed. John J. Loeper. New York: Atheneum, 1973.

Widmer, Kemble. "The Christmas Campaign: The Ten Days of Trenton and Princeton." Trenton: New Jersey Historical Commission, 1975.

Wilkinson, Eliza. *Letters of Eliza Wilkinson during the Invasion and Possession of Charleston, S.C. by the British in the Revolutionary War*. Edited by Caroline Gilman. New York: S. Colman, 1839. (Reprinted by Arno Press, 1969.)

Williams, Elizabeth McKee. "Childhood, Memory and the American Revolution."
    In *Children and War Reader*, ed. James Martin. New York: New York
    University Press, 2002.

Winch, Julie. *A Gentleman of Color: The Life of James Forten*. New York: Oxford
    University Press, 2002.

Winslow, Anne. *Diary of Anne Green Winslow: A Boston School Girl of 1771*.
    Edited by Alice Morse Earl. Boston: Houghton Mifflin, 1894.

Wister, Sally. *Sally Wister's Journal: A True Narrative: Being a Quaker Maiden's
    Account of Her Experiences with Officers of the Continental Army,
    1777–1778*. Edited by Albert Cook Myers. Philadelphia: Ferris and Leach,
    1902.

Wood, Gordon. *The American Revolution*. New York: Modern Library, 2002.

Wroth, L. Kinvin, and Hiller B. Zobel, eds. *Legal Papers of John Adams*. Vol. 3,
    Cases 63 and 64: The Boston Massacre Trials. Cambridge, Mass.: Belknap
    Press of Harvard University Press, 1965.

Young, Alfred Fabian. *The Shoemaker and the Tea Party: Memory and the American
    Revolution*. Boston: Beacon Press, 1999.

Young, Thomas. "Memoir of Major Thomas Young: A Revolutionary Patriot of
    South Carolina." *The Orion* 3 (Oct 1843): 86–88.

Index

About the Author

EMMY E. WERNER is the author of *A Conspiracy of Decency: The Rescue of Danish Jews during World War II* (2002); *Through the Eyes of Innocents: Children Witness World War II* (2000); and *Reluctant Witnesses: Children's Voices from the Civil War* (1998).